Enhancing Financial Decision-Making Through AI and Accounting Systems

Ionica Oncioiu
Titu Maiorescu University, Constanta, Romania

IGI Global
Scientific Publishing
Publishing Tomorrow's Research Today

Vice President of Editorial Melissa Wagner
Director of Acquisitions Mikaela Felty
Director of Book Development Jocelynn Hessler
Production Manager Mike Brehm
Cover Design Jose Rosado

Published in the United States of America by
IGI Global Scientific Publishing
701 East Chocolate Avenue
Hershey, PA, 17033, USA
Tel: 717-533-8845 | Fax: 717-533-7115
Website: https://www.igi-global.com E-mail: cust@igi-global.com

Library of Congress Cataloging-in-Publication Data

Names: Oncioiu, Ionica, 1972- editor
Title: Enhancing financial decision-making through AI and accounting systems / edited by Ionica Oncioiu.
Description: Hershey, PA : IGI Global Scientific Publishing, 2026. | Includes bibliographical references and index. | Summary: "This book delves into the evolving intersection of AI and accounting systems, examining how these technologies are reshaping the landscape of financial decision-making"-- Provided by publisher.
Identifiers: LCCN 2025023872 (print) | LCCN 2025023873 (ebook) | ISBN 9798337336268 hardcover | ISBN 9798337336275 paperback | ISBN 9798337336282 ebook
Subjects: LCSH: Finance--Technological innovations | Decision making | Artificial intelligence
Classification: LCC HG173 .E544 2026 (print) | LCC HG173 (ebook)
LC record available at https://lccn.loc.gov/2025023872
LC ebook record available at https://lccn.loc.gov/2025023873

British Cataloguing in Publication Data
A Cataloguing in Publication record for this book is available from the British Library.

Editorial Advisory Board

Table of Contents

Detailed Table of Contents

In an increasingly volatile financial ecosystem, static risk models are no longer enough. This chapter explores the transformative potential of machine learning algorithms in delivering real-time risk assessment to support more agile and data-driven financial decision-making. The authors examine how models such as ensemble learners, deep neural networks, and time-series forecasting architectures can dynamically interpret transactional and behavioral data to flag emerging threats, anomalies, and opportunities. The discussion extends beyond technical efficiency to confront deeper questions of algorithmic transparency, ethical safeguards, and systemic bias—areas often overlooked in the rush to automate. Drawing from real-world use cases and implementation blueprints, the chapter ultimately argues for a paradigm shift: from reactive risk reporting to proactive, adaptive risk intelligence that evolves with the financial landscape. In doing so, it offers a roadmap not just for technologists, but for financial leaders navigating uncertainty in the age of AI.

This chapter examines how entropy and uncertainty, concepts rooted in physics and information theory, can be translated into innovative approaches for risk assessment in finance. Traditional financial models often rely on assumptions of normality, equilibrium, and linearity, which limit their ability to anticipate extreme events and systemic instabilities. By contrast, entropy-based methods provide tools to capture disorder, complexity, and hidden structures in financial data. The chapter situates these methods within a broader interdisciplinary dialogue, bridging physics, complexity science, and finance. Through conceptual discussion and illustrative examples, the authors argue that entropy not only enhances the quantitative description of uncertainty but also supports more resilient strategies for decision-making under incomplete information. Ultimately, the chapter aims to show how physics-inspired

Preface

The digital transformation of the global economy has reached a scale and speed unprecedented in history. Artificial intelligence (AI), advanced accounting systems, and the growing reliance on algorithmic decision-making represent not merely technical upgrades but a fundamental reconfiguration of financial practice and corporate governance. What was once the exclusive domain of human expertise—evaluating risks, forecasting outcomes, and allocating resources—is now increasingly mediated, enhanced, or even replaced by machine learning algorithms and intelligent accounting platforms.

Artificial intelligence has moved beyond experimental prototypes to become an integral part of financial ecosystems. Predictive analytics enables companies to anticipate market fluctuations with greater precision; natural language processing accelerates the interpretation of complex regulatory frameworks; and anomaly detection strengthens fraud prevention. These applications not only enhance efficiency but also challenge long-standing assumptions about professional judgment, accountability, and the role of human intuition in financial decision-making.

Accounting systems, traditionally viewed as passive repositories of financial data, are being transformed into dynamic, AI-driven engines of insight. Modern enterprise resource planning (ERP) systems, robotic process automation (RPA), and intelligent auditing tools no longer serve merely to record past transactions but to generate real-time strategic recommendations. The integration of AI into accounting frameworks thus blurs the line between compliance and strategy, turning financial reporting into a predictive and prescriptive instrument.

The book *Enhancing Financial Decision-Making Through AI and Accounting Systems* situates itself at the nexus of these transformative forces. It explores how organizations can harness the power of AI-enhanced accounting to support evidence-based decision-making, reduce uncertainty, and respond proactively to emerging risks. Far from treating AI as an isolated innovation, this volume presents it as part of a broader reorganization of economic processes and managerial logics.

The significance of this book lies not only in its subject matter but in its timing. Across industries and jurisdictions, decision-makers confront the twin challenges of navigating digital disruption and ensuring ethical, transparent governance. Regulators and professional bodies debate how to balance innovation with accountability, while companies grapple with issues of data security, algorithmic bias, and the cultural shift required to integrate AI into financial practice.

This collection provides theoretical insights and applied research that resonate with academics, practitioners, and policymakers alike. For researchers, it advances understanding of how AI reshapes accounting theory and practice. For managers and financial professionals, it offers practical frameworks for deploying intelligent systems in ways that enhance both profitability and resilience. For policymakers, it raises questions of standardization, regulation, and trust in AI-driven financial environments.

In an era defined by uncertainty, speed, and complexity, the intersection of AI and accounting systems may well determine the future trajectory of financial decision-making. By bringing together perspectives from technology, management, and accounting, this book charts a path toward a more informed, transparent, and adaptive financial ecosystem.

The author Mustafa Kayyali of the first chapter *"Machine Learning Algorithms for Real-Time Risk Assessment"* investigates the transformative role of artificial intelligence in enhancing financial risk management, showing how machine learning models such as ensemble learners, deep neural networks, and time-series forecasting can dynamically process transactional and behavioral data to anticipate threats, anomalies, and opportunities. By combining technical perspectives with real-world use cases, the chapter highlights a paradigm shift from static and reactive models toward proactive, adaptive intelligence capable of evolving with the financial landscape, while also addressing the challenges of algorithmic transparency, ethical safeguards, and systemic bias that accompany the rapid drive toward automation. The results emphasize that AI-based approaches not only increase efficiency in decision-making but also demand frameworks that ensure interpretability and accountability, making this contribution relevant both for technologists and for financial leaders navigating uncertainty in the age of AI.

An innovative perspective on the application of physics-inspired methods in finance is revealed by Mădălina Mihăilescu, the author of the second chapter *"Entropy and Uncertainty: Physics-Inspired Approaches to Risk Assessment in Finance."* The objective of this research is to examine how entropy and uncertainty, concepts originating in physics and information theory, can be translated into innovative approaches for financial risk assessment. By contrasting traditional financial models, which often rely on restrictive assumptions such as normality, equilibrium, and linearity, with entropy-based methods, the chapter shows how new tools can capture disorder, complexity, and hidden structures in financial data. Within a broader interdisciplinary dialogue that bridges physics, complexity science, and finance, the author emphasizes that entropy enhances the quantitative description of uncertainty and supports more resilient strategies for decision-making under incomplete information. Through conceptual discussions and illustrative examples, the chapter demonstrates how physics-inspired perspectives enrich both theoretical models and practical applications, ultimately contributing to more robust financial risk management in complex and volatile environments.

The ethical implications of the evolution of accounting roles in the era of Artificial Intelligence are presented by Shefali Shefali and Manjit Kour, the authors of the third chapter *"Transforming the Profession: The Ethical Challenges in Evolution of Accounting Roles in the Era of Artificial Intelligence."* The chapter emphasizes that the development of Smart accounting has gained major importance, particularly during the COVID-19 pandemic, which created both challenges and opportunities for integrating accounting practices into more holistic and technology-driven frameworks. The authors show that technological innovations such as cloud computing, data analytics, fraud detection, and predictive tools have significantly enhanced the robustness and adaptability of accounting systems, while Artificial Intelligence has reshaped efficiency and accuracy in financial practices. At the same time, the chapter highlights the ethical challenges posed by this transformation, pointing to the need for accountability, transparency, and responsibility in the adoption of AI-driven tools. Furthermore, the analysis underscores the synergies between accounting systems and Smart accounting tools, demonstrating their essential role in enhancing operational performance and in redefining the professional responsibilities of accountants in the digital age.

The transformation of managerial practices in the context of artificial intelligence is analyzed by Diana Andreea Mândricel, the author of the fourth chapter *"Future of Management: From Traditional Models to AI-Driven Governance."* The study underlines how classical frameworks, long grounded in hierarchy and standardized procedures, are increasingly insufficient in dynamic environments that demand flexibility and rapid adaptation. In contrast, AI-supported governance provides advanced capabilities such as real-time data analysis, predictive modeling, and scenario simulation, which enable organizations to extend decision-making beyond traditional human limitations. By addressing issues of resource allocation, organizational resilience, and institutional trust, the chapter illustrates how algorithms can enhance managerial effectiveness while simultaneously raising new ethical questions related to transparency, accountability, and legitimacy. Ultimately, the contribution emphasizes the emergence of hybrid governance models, where human judgment and technological efficiency coexist, ensuring that innovation is guided by contextual awareness and long-term sustainability.

The rapid changes in the financial sector, together with the increasing complexity of auditing requirements, have accelerated the adoption of technologies that transform traditional practices. Tarun Sai Raavi and Radhika Ramanchi, the authors of the fifth chapter *"Predictive Auditing with AI and ML: A Qualitative Investigation of Emerging Tools in the Accounting Sector"*, examine how artificial intelligence and machine learning are reshaping the auditing profession by addressing long-standing limitations such as the time-consuming preparation of manual samples, the detection of complex fraud schemes, and the management of massive transaction datasets. Their analysis shows that predictive auditing, supported by AI-driven algorithms, introduces faster, more accurate, and more reliable methods for financial assurance, thereby altering not only efficiency but also the very role of auditors in safeguarding transparency. Particular emphasis is placed on the profound changes occurring within the Big Four accounting firms—Deloitte, PwC, EY, and KPMG—which are at the forefront of this technological revolution. By situating predictive auditing in the broader context of digital innovation, the chapter demonstrates how emerging tools are not simply supporting the audit process but fundamentally redefining its scope, accountability, and impact on financial markets.

The complexity of fraud in its digital forms and the pressing need for innovative detection mechanisms is addressed by Mustafa Kayyali, the author of the sixth chapter *"Enhancing Fraud Detection with AI in International Systems."* The study illustrates how artificial intelligence, particularly machine learning, is reshaping the frameworks through which fraud is identified and prevented across global financial networks. Moving beyond traditional rule-based methods, the chapter situates AI within a landscape of dynamic, data-driven approaches that enhance both speed and accuracy in recognizing anomalies. At the same time, the author draws attention to the legal and ethical dilemmas associated with intelligent systems, such as the opacity of algorithms, the governance of cross-border financial data, and the risks of overreliance on automated processes in areas as sensitive as financial integrity. The discussion provides a nuanced perspective that highlights both the promise and the perils of AI in fraud detection, advocating for the construction of a cooperative international framework that ensures transparency, regulatory alignment, and ethical safeguards, while leveraging AI's potential to fortify trust and resilience in financial systems.

The transformation of strategic management in the age of artificial intelligence is examined by Diana Andreea Mândricel, the author of the seventh chapter *"Strategic Management in the Age of AI: Redefining Financial Decision-Making."* The analysis shows that algorithmic tools are increasingly complementing, and in some cases replacing, traditional practices centered on human judgment and linear forecasting. AI introduces capacities for real-time analysis and adaptive learning, which allow managers to identify hidden regularities, simulate multiple strategic scenarios, and test decisions against uncertain conditions. These new instruments expand the horizon of managerial rationality but also bring forward pressing questions related to bias, opacity, and legitimacy. What emerges from this discussion is not a complete abandonment of classical governance, but the rise of hybrid approaches that combine computational precision with human oversight. In this sense, the chapter highlights how AI is not merely an operational aid but a structural force capable of reshaping long-term strategies, redefining the distribution of authority, and anchoring decision-making in a more experimental and forward-looking framework.

The integration of artificial intelligence into corporate governance and its implications for oversight are examined by Mustafa Kayyali, the author of the eighth chapter *"AI in Corporate Governance: Strengthening Oversight."* The chapter shows how technologies such as machine learning, predictive analytics, and intelligent auditing systems are reshaping boardroom practices, influencing disclosure mechanisms, and redefining what it means to govern responsibly. Far beyond its role as a technical instrument, AI is presented as an active participant in decision-making processes, capable of shaping strategies for risk mitigation and accountability. At the same time, the discussion emphasizes the vulnerabilities created by algorithmic opacity, systemic bias, and the possible erosion of human authority in corporate decision-making. Through a critical approach, the author highlights how governance structures can adapt AI responsibly by embedding transparency, ethical safeguards, and regulatory foresight into their operational frameworks. Ultimately, the chapter argues for a reconceptualization of oversight in the age of intelligent systems, where governance is not reduced to control and compliance, but redefined as a collective moral and strategic responsibility.

The relativity of value in financial decision-making is investigated by Mădălina Mihăilescu, the author of the ninth chapter *"Relativity of Value: Time, Space, and Context in AI-Supported Financial Decisions."* The chapter argues that, while classical finance often treats value as fixed and intrinsic, contemporary markets reveal its dynamic and situational character, shaped by temporal horizons, spatial heterogeneity, and contextual framing. Advances in artificial intelligence allow these dimensions to be integrated in real time, generating adaptive frameworks for evaluating assets and managing risks. From this perspective, the author highlights both the potential and the epistemological challenges of embedding contextual awareness into algorithmic decision-making, particularly issues related to bias, interpretability, and robustness. This line of inquiry calls for a paradigm shift in which financial theory is reframed through the lens of relativity and supported by AI, leading to more nuanced, flexible, and context-sensitive approaches to investment and risk management. By bridging theoretical debates with practical applications, the chapter emphasizes that value cannot be understood in isolation but only in relation to time, space, and the evolving digital environment that shapes financial choices.

This comprehensive volume positions itself at the intersection of financial theory, technological innovation, and institutional governance, providing an integrated account of how artificial intelligence and advanced accounting systems are reshaping decision-making in a rapidly evolving global context. The originality of the book does not reside merely in documenting technological change, but in critically examining its epistemological, methodological, and normative consequences. By moving beyond the instrumental view of AI as a tool for efficiency, the chapters collectively highlight its role as a transformative framework that reorganizes knowledge production, redistributes decision-making authority, and redefines the temporal and spatial dimensions of value in finance.

From a research perspective, the contributions dialogue with multiple strands of literature: behavioral finance and its concerns with bounded rationality, information economics and its treatment of asymmetries, computational accounting and its emphasis on automation, as well as the ethics of technology with its focus on bias, transparency, and legitimacy. The volume thereby extends existing debates, situating itself within an emerging body of scholarship that regards digital technologies not only as operational enhancements but as drivers of paradigmatic shifts.

On the policy front, the chapters resonate with ongoing international initiatives—such as the European Union's Artificial Intelligence Act, the OECD's frameworks on digital governance, and global efforts in sustainable finance—that all grapple with balancing innovation with regulatory coherence. The analyses contained here suggest that the future of financial decision-making will not be determined by technological capability alone, but by the institutional architectures and normative frameworks that govern its use.

In this sense, the volume speaks simultaneously to scholars, practitioners, and regulators: to scholars, it offers fertile ground for rethinking the conceptual apparatus of finance and accounting; to practitioners, it delivers frameworks for operationalizing AI in complex organizational environments; and to regulators, it highlights the urgency of designing adaptive, anticipatory governance systems. Ultimately, this book contributes to a broader intellectual project: the construction of a financial ecosystem that is analytically rigorous, technologically sophisticated, and socially responsive, capable of navigating uncertainty without sacrificing legitimacy or inclusiveness.

Acknowledgment

Looking back, we wish to thank all the persons who made the publishing of the present volume possible: Jan Travers, Melissa Wagner, Erin Wesser, Christina Henning, Nicole Elliott, Kristina Byrne, Lindsay Johnston, Joshua Witman, Nick Newcomer, Jaimie Watts, Josephine Dadeboe, Jordan Tepper, Sean Eckman, Elizabeth Barrantes, Katie McLoughlin and many other IGI-Global team members, reviewers, collaborators, and all the contributing authors: without your efforts and dedication this editorial project would have never been possible.

Acknowledgment

Chapter 1
Machine Learning Algorithms for Real-Time Risk Assessment

Mustafa Kayyali
https://orcid.org/0000-0003-3300-262X
Maaref University of Applied Sciences, Syria

ABSTRACT

In an increasingly volatile financial ecosystem, static risk models are no longer enough. This chapter explores the transformative potential of machine learning algorithms in delivering real-time risk assessment to support more agile and data-driven financial decision-making. The authors examine how models such as ensemble learners, deep neural networks, and time-series forecasting architectures can dynamically interpret transactional and behavioral data to flag emerging threats, anomalies, and opportunities. The discussion extends beyond technical efficiency to confront deeper questions of algorithmic transparency, ethical safeguards, and systemic bias—areas often overlooked in the rush to automate. Drawing from real-world use cases and implementation blueprints, the chapter ultimately argues for a paradigm shift: from reactive risk reporting to proactive, adaptive risk intelligence that evolves with the financial landscape. In doing so, it offers a roadmap not just for technologists, but for financial leaders navigating uncertainty in the age of AI.

DOI: 10.4018/979-8-3373-3626-8.ch001

INTRODUCTION

Risk has always been a shadow cast across the world of finance—a persistent uncertainty, a silent variable in every decision, every transaction. For centuries, the art of risk assessment has relied on human judgment, static models, and lagging indicators (Ridwan, 2025). In boardrooms and trading floors, risk was something you calculated after the fact, something you reviewed in hindsight with spreadsheets, ratios, and percentages. It was reactive, retrospective, and oftentimes too late. But the financial world doesn't operate at the pace it once did. Markets shift in milliseconds. Customer behavior mutates in real time. Fraud doesn't wait for the quarterly report. The risk landscape is no longer slow, or static—it's dynamic, hyper-connected, and data-rich.

In this new era, traditional risk models are straining under pressure. Linear assumptions no longer hold. Historical patterns fail to predict black swan events (Kjoersvik & Bate, 2022). We are in an age of information overload, where risk hides not in the absence of data, but in the inability to make sense of it all fast enough. What's needed now is not just better tools—but smarter systems. Systems that can learn, adapt, and evolve. Systems that don't just follow rules, but discover patterns. Systems that don't sleep. Enter machine learning.

This chapter begins with a simple but powerful proposition: that machine learning is not just an enhancement to risk assessment—it is a reinvention of it. Real-time risk assessment powered by machine learning algorithms marks a fundamental shift from backward-looking analysis to forward-sensing prediction. It moves us from manual reviews to automated vigilance, from statistical rigidity to cognitive flexibility. Algorithms, when trained on the right data and calibrated with ethical foresight, can detect fraud as it happens, adjust credit scoring dynamically, and signal early warnings for systemic instability (Balcıoğlu, 2021). But this is not a story of blind automation. Nor is it a celebration of machines replacing human insight. What we propose is something more measured and thoughtful—a partnership between human judgment and algorithmic intelligence. A hybrid model where financial analysts, compliance officers, and executives work alongside machine learning systems that continuously scan, analyze, and forecast potential threats and deviations.

This chapter explores the architectural, operational, and ethical dimensions of implementing machine learning for real-time risk assessment in financial environments. We begin by unpacking why traditional methods are no longer sufficient in a real-time economy, and move on to examine the strengths and limits of various machine learning models—ranging from decision trees and support vector machines to deep learning and reinforcement-based systems (Challoumis, 2024). We delve into practical implementation strategies, discussing data sourcing, model training, deployment pipelines, and performance monitoring. But equally importantly, we consider the risks that come with this new territory: algorithmic opacity, bias embedded in data, and the very real danger of overreliance on black-box models in high-stakes decision-making.

Ultimately, we argue that real-time machine learning-based risk assessment must be designed not just to be fast or accurate, but to be interpretable, adaptive, and fair. Speed without ethics is dangerous. Accuracy without context is misleading. Intelligence without governance is chaos (Liu & Zheng, 2022). The financial sector is at a crossroads. The old methods are familiar, even comfortable—but increasingly irrelevant. The new methods promise agility and foresight, but they demand humility, rigor, and reflection. This chapter is a guide for decision-makers ready to step into that future—armed not just with algorithms, but with understanding.

THE SHIFTING LANDSCAPE OF RISK: WHY REAL-TIME ASSESSMENT MATTERS

Risk—what a strange and slippery concept. We talk about it with such confidence, throw it around in strategy meetings and analyst reports as if it were a solid object. But let's be honest: risk is vapor until it materializes. It's potential energy—charged, invisible, always on the brink of becoming real. And the financial world, which once had the luxury of time to make sense of risk, now lives in a rhythm so fast, so relentlessly reactive, that by the time you've measured it, it's already changed shape. Not long ago, risk was a quarterly conversation. It belonged to auditors and risk committees, tucked inside tidy reports with color-coded matrices and hedged language. There were dashboards, yes, and data—but the culture of risk was steeped in retrospection. It was something you analyzed after it knocked. After the default. After the crash. After the loss had already found its way into the books.

Today, that model feels almost quaint. We're living in a different tempo now—a tempo defined by milliseconds, not months. Where financial decisions are automated, global, and interconnected in ways that are difficult to trace (Amiri et al, 2024). A rumor in one corner of the internet can shave billions off a company's value before lunchtime. A misstep in one algorithm's logic can cascade through trading systems like a domino run doused in lighter fluid. Cyberattacks, once rare and targeted, are now an ambient threat, lurking like background noise (Mallick & Nath, 2024). Climate instability, geopolitical tremors, viral misinformation—all of them feeding into a swirling, real-time portrait of risk that refuses to sit still.

In this environment, the old ways break down. The dashboards aren't fast enough. The models, built on historical assumptions, stumble when faced with novel threats. The neat categories—credit, market, operational—begin to blur. Risk is no longer something that arrives in a clean envelope. It erupts mid-conversation, disrupts the flow, rewrites the script. It is dynamic, shape-shifting, and increasingly unpredictable. And if we're still relying on yesterday's data to make decisions about today, we're playing a dangerous game of catch-up.

This is precisely where real-time risk assessment enters—not as a luxury, but as a necessity. And not just as a technological upgrade, but as a conceptual one. Real-time risk assessment isn't merely about speed. It's not just plugging faster processors into slower models. It's about rethinking what it means to perceive and respond to threat. It's about awareness, adaptation, and anticipation—qualities more akin to biological reflexes than spreadsheet logic. In a real-time framework, risk becomes less about statistical probability and more about situational intelligence (Sánchez-Zas et al, 2023). It's a live feed, not a static snapshot. And this shift changes everything.

Let's pause here for a second and ask: what does it really mean to assess risk in real time? It means treating data not as archival evidence, but as a living organism. It means abandoning the false comfort of fixed thresholds and embracing fluidity. It means ingesting data as it arrives—transaction logs, click patterns, sensor alerts, market sentiment, device fingerprints, satellite weather feeds—and translating that chaos into actionable signals before the window of response slams shut.

It's not easy. It never was. But machine learning has cracked open the door. Unlike traditional models that need humans to define the variables, set the boundaries, and assume linearity, machine learning models—especially those trained on real-time data streams—can learn patterns on their own (Xu & Liang, 2021). They find nuance where humans overlook it. They spot anomalies that would otherwise be buried in the noise. They adapt as new inputs come in, adjusting their priors, recalibrating their expectations, and—in the best cases—doing so without breaking. But here's the twist: this isn't just about risk mitigation. It's about opportunity as well. Because risk, fundamentally, is not just about what can go wrong. It's also about what you might miss if you hesitate.

A real-time risk system doesn't just block suspicious activity. It can greenlight promising trends. It can spot the beginnings of behavioral shifts in consumer behavior (Cho, 2024). It can recognize a liquidity crisis before it becomes a headline. It can empower decision-makers to move—not after the storm, but in the whisper before it. And yet, for all its power, real-time assessment also brings new kinds of vulnerability. When speed becomes the priority, what happens to accuracy? When systems act without pause, do they overlook the deeper context? There's a real risk here—ironically—of over-trusting the tools we build. Especially when those tools begin to outpace our capacity to explain their reasoning. Because here's the hard truth: real-time systems often operate in shades of uncertainty. They make probabilistic judgments based on incomplete information. They can surface false positives—or worse, false negatives—at scale. And when they do, the consequences are immediate and amplified. Imagine a fraud detection system that flags an entire batch of transactions as risky during a holiday shopping spree. Or a credit risk algorithm that blocks funding to a startup based on a misunderstood data point. The damage isn't just technical—it's reputational, ethical, even existential. That's why we need to hold two ideas at once: real-time risk assessment is essential, and it is dangerous.

There's beauty in that tension. It forces us to approach this technology with humility. To resist the urge for blind automation. To recognize that a system can be both brilliant and brittle. And to design for that complexity rather than trying to oversimplify it. What this moment demands is not just faster tools, but smarter stewardship. Not just automation, but augmentation—the fusion of machine perception with human oversight (Sharma et al, 2024). Financial institutions need to build cultures where data scientists and risk officers, compliance managers and engineers, all sit at the same table. Where the goal isn't just to catch bad actors, but to understand the systems that produce vulnerability in the first place.

Let's talk about the human side for a moment. Because real-time assessment doesn't just change how machines work—it changes how people work. It reconfigures workflows. It alters accountability. Risk managers, once used to quarterly cycles, are now being asked to interpret live signals, to act on dashboards that update by the second (Omoruyi, 2025). The pace can be disorienting. The stakes can feel paralyzing. And without proper training, without the right mental models, people can either freeze or defer too much to the machine.

This is why explainability matters. This is why interface design matters. This is why culture matters. A machine learning model can be technically flawless and still be a failure if the humans around it don't trust it, don't understand it, or don't know when to question it.

So, where does this leave us? Somewhere between urgency and uncertainty. Between what we can measure and what we can intuit. Between the promise of predictive precision and the messiness of real-world decision-making. And that's not a bad place to be. It's a real place. An honest one.

The landscape of risk has shifted, yes. But perhaps more importantly, our way of seeing it must shift too (Slota et al, 2023). We can no longer afford to think of risk as a static variable, something that sits obediently in rows and columns. Risk, in this new era, moves. It pulses. It reacts. It hides. And unless our systems can move with it, pulse with it, adapt to it—we're not managing risk. We're watching it unfold, powerless.

This chapter doesn't claim to offer the final word. The terrain is too unstable for that. But what it offers is a way of thinking—a lens. A call to look at risk not as a relic to be calculated, but as a living challenge to be met in motion. With care. With vision. And with the tools that allow us not just to see what's happening—but to act while it still matters. In this new era, timing isn't just important. It's everything.

ARCHITECTURES OF INTELLIGENCE: KEY MACHINE LEARNING MODELS IN RISK ANALYSIS

Risk, by nature, is elusive. It flickers in the gaps between data points, hides in outliers, mutates in response to the very tools built to detect it (Pillai, 2022). And yet—somehow—we've built machines to hunt it. Not perfectly, not infallibly, but persistently. What's fascinating about this endeavor isn't just the mathematics or the engineering. It's the imagination involved. The very idea that we can codify uncertainty, that we can sketch the contours of the unknown using algorithms—it's part logic, part art. And like all art, the medium matters. The architecture—the shape and structure of our models—determines not just what we can see, but how we see it.

Machine learning, as a discipline, isn't one thing. It's a constellation of methodologies, each with its own strengths, blind spots, assumptions, and quirks (Alpaydin, 2021). Some models are crisp and interpretable, like decision trees that lay out their reasoning like a well-lit hallway. Others are murky, dense, layered—deep neural networks that resemble tangled forests of synapses, where cause and effect get blurred into a kind of probabilistic poetry.

When it comes to risk analysis, the choice of model is never just a technical decision. It's philosophical. It says something about what we value—speed or accuracy, transparency or depth, prediction or explanation. And as the financial world careens deeper into real-time operations, the architecture we choose shapes not just our insights, but our ethics, our accountability, our very grip on reality. So, let's walk through this landscape. Not as tourists, but as curious builders, skeptical believers, people who know the cost of a flawed prediction.

Decision Trees and Ensemble Methods: Learning Through Simplicity and Consensus

There's something elegant about decision trees. They don't pretend to be smarter than they are. They ask questions, one after another—If this, then that. If not, go left. Each node a fork in the road. Each leaf a conclusion. In risk analysis, they're often the first tool pulled from the toolbox, and with good reason. They're intuitive. They mimic human reasoning. You can point to a prediction and say, "Here's why." But their simplicity is their limit, too. On their own, they're fragile—too prone to overfitting, to seeing ghosts in the noise. That's why we rarely use one tree alone anymore. Instead, we build forests.

Random forests, specifically—ensembles of decision trees, each trained on slightly different slices of data. They vote. They average. They temper one another's eccentricities (Korn, 2024). It's democracy in code. And it works. For credit scoring, loan default prediction, transaction risk—it's often more than good enough. Then there's boosting. Gradient boosting machines (GBMs), like XGBoost or LightGBM, take things a step further (Rufo et al, 2021). They don't just average the trees. They learn from their mistakes. One tree at a time, each trying to correct the last. It's iterative. Relentless. Surprisingly powerful. In structured financial data, where the signal lives in the subtle interactions, boosting models often outperform everything else. But here's the catch: interpretability fades. With each layer of ensemble logic, transparency erodes. It becomes harder to explain why a model flagged that loan as risky, or that transaction as suspicious. And in finance, opacity is a liability. Regulation demands answers. Clients demand fairness. And if the model can't speak its reasoning, someone has to answer for it.

Support Vector Machines: The Geometry of Judgment

SVMs feel almost old-school now. But they remain fascinating. Instead of learning patterns like a neural net or asking questions like a tree, they carve boundaries—hyperplanes—through multidimensional space (Petrini, 2023). It's geometry as judgment. For certain types of financial risk—especially classification problems with cleanly separable classes—SVMs are elegant and robust. They don't need massive datasets. They're less prone to overfitting in low-noise environments. And they're surprisingly precise. But they lack scalability. As dimensions and data volume grow, their performance chokes. And they struggle with streaming data, where the goal is not just to classify, but to adapt in real time. That's where other models take the lead.

Neural Networks and Deep Learning: Complexity Without Apology

Neural networks are messy. That's part of their charm. Inspired loosely by the human brain (though let's not take the metaphor too far), they consist of layers—each one transforming input into increasingly abstract representations. At first, it's numbers. Then it's edges. Then patterns. Then meaning. In risk assessment, deep learning is still controversial. It excels with unstructured data—images, text, time series, audio—but its opacity raises eyebrows. How do you justify a fraud prediction when the model has millions of parameters and no obvious explanation? How do you audit a decision that even the developer doesn't fully understand? And yet, in some contexts, the results are undeniable. Recurrent neural networks (RNNs), and their more sophisticated cousins—Long Short-Term Memory (LSTM) networks and Gated Recurrent Units (GRUs)—can model time dependencies beautifully (Tsantekidis et al, 2022). They're perfect for risk that evolves—credit risk over time, behavioral drift, fraud that unfolds in patterns across minutes or hours. Convolutional networks (CNNs), usually reserved for vision tasks, have been adapted for spatial analysis in transactional graphs (Li et al, 2021). Imagine detecting network fraud not by looking at transactions in isolation, but by analyzing their topology. That's the kind of thinking CNNs enable. Still, the cost is interpretability. These models are smart, but secretive. You can't open them up and find a simple rule. You find math. Layers. Activation maps. Not the kind of thing you bring to a compliance review. So, we're torn. Do we sacrifice clarity for accuracy? Or do we accept simpler models with slightly worse performance but clearer reasoning? There's no easy answer.

Bayesian Models: Probabilistic Humility

While deep learning often feels bold and declarative, Bayesian models whisper in probabilities. They don't tell you what is—they tell you how confident they are (Chivers, 2024). And in risk analysis, where uncertainty is the air we breathe, that humility is invaluable. Bayesian inference allows for the explicit modeling of uncertainty. In credit scoring, for instance, Bayesian models can show how confidence changes as more data comes in. In fraud detection, they help differentiate between a true anomaly and an outlier that's just... odd. What's beautiful about Bayesian models is their ability to incorporate prior knowledge—historical patterns, expert intuition, external constraints. They're not just learning machines; they're reasoning machines. But they're hard. Computationally demanding. Slow to scale. And, in many environments, too nuanced for teams trained in more conventional tools. Still, as we push toward real-time adaptive systems, the idea of models that **update their beliefs** as they receive new evidence—that feels not just appealing, but essential.

Hybrid Models and Meta-Architectures: The Best of All Worlds?

No single model will solve everything. That's become increasingly clear. The future belongs to hybrid architectures—ensembles that combine symbolic reasoning with deep learning, or tree models layered atop neural embeddings, or Bayesian wrappers around streaming predictions (Rane et al, 2024). Some systems use neural nets to extract features, decision trees to make judgments, and Bayesian filters to assess confidence—all in one pipeline. Others rely on reinforcement learning to dynamically adjust risk thresholds based on feedback loops, user behavior, or systemic stress indicators. The trend is clear: we're not building monolithic models. We're composing systems. Modular, dynamic, multi-modal. It's architectural pluralism—intelligence as bricolage. But complexity brings fragility. These systems are harder to test. Harder to debug. Harder to govern. And in high-stakes finance, where consequences ripple quickly, that fragility is a risk in itself.

Choosing the Right Architecture: More Than Just Performance Metrics

There's a temptation to reduce model selection to AUC scores and confusion matrices. But that's a mistake. The architecture we choose should reflect the environment we're in, the values we hold, the trade-offs we're willing to accept. In some settings—say, anti-money laundering—recall matters more than precision. Better a few false alarms than a missed crime. In others, like credit underwriting, fairness and interpretability are non-negotiable. A model that can't justify its decision isn't just a bad tool—it's a liability. And then there's the question of feedback (Davies, 2025). Does the model learn over time? Does it handle concept drift? Can it be retrained easily, or does it require laborious recalibration? These operational questions matter just as much as predictive power. Ultimately, the model isn't just a mathematical object. It's a participant in a larger system—legal, organizational, human. And like any participant, it must be accountable.

FROM DATA STREAMS TO DECISIONS: IMPLEMENTING REAL-TIME RISK FRAMEWORKS

There's something almost poetic about watching a data stream. It pulses like breath, never quite still, never exactly the same. Tiny packets of insight float past—transactions, clicks, keystrokes, GPS coordinates, biometric ticks—each one meaningless on its own, yet hinting at patterns if you know how to look. And if risk lives anywhere in the modern financial system, it lives here—in the stream, not the snapshot (Daníelsson, 2022). It's in the velocity, the rhythm, the aberrations. The trouble is, most institutions still treat data like sediment. They store it. Archive it. Mine it. But they don't *listen* to it. Not while it's moving. Not while it's whispering the very signs of trouble they'll discover too late.

Implementing a real-time risk framework begins, oddly enough, not with code or servers, but with a change in posture (Cohen, 2025). It demands a shift in how we relate to data—less as a static resource to be collected and more as a living signal to be interpreted. That shift is cultural before it's technical. It forces an organization to move from being reactive to becoming responsive, from being historically obsessed to being presently alert.

The technology, while impressive, is only one piece of the equation. The real challenge? Making sure the system doesn't just run—but *learns*, *adapts*, *guides*. And that the humans around it trust it enough to act on its signals, but not so blindly that they surrender discretion (Gigerenzer, 2022). Walking that tightrope—between automation and agency—is where the real intelligence lives.

Let's start with the most underappreciated part: data ingestion. Not sexy, not shiny, but absolutely foundational. You can't build a real-time risk system on stale data. You just can't. The delay between an event and its registration must shrink to near zero. That means event-driven architectures. Kafka streams. Apache Flink. Redis queues. Custom APIs. It means redesigning legacy systems that were never built for immediacy and learning to tolerate messiness, partiality, noise (Praveen, 2024). In real-time environments, perfection is the enemy. You take what you get, and you learn to think probabilistically, not definitively. But stream processing is not enough. It needs direction—filters, enrichers, interpreters. Raw data is just that—raw. A single transaction might be innocuous, but a flurry of them—split-second withdrawals, erratic locations, deviations from behavioral norms—might mean fraud. Or panic. Or a system under attack.

This is where feature engineering comes alive, not as an offline exercise in model training, but as a *live synthesis* of signal. Temporal windows. Frequency counters. Contextual overlays. Real-time risk frameworks need to build features not once, but continuously, for every entity in the system—user, account, merchant, system node (Hassan, 2024). It's like trying to paint a moving car while you're also trying to predict whether it's about to crash. And still, all of this effort would be in vain if it weren't funneled into an engine that can reason. Not just match patterns, but anticipate deviations. That's where the models come in. And yes, you can drop in the machine learning architectures—your forests, your nets, your probabilistic learners—but here's where things get personal: you can't just train them once. Not anymore. You need pipelines that retrain continuously or incrementally. Models that evolve alongside the environment. Because what's risky today might not be tomorrow. And what was normal a week ago might now be a red flag. But let's not romanticize this. Real-time modeling has its own mess. Data drifts. Concepts mutate. Class imbalance becomes a hydra. You can't rely on standard metrics. Precision, recall, accuracy—they're all warped when the ground truth is in flux. You don't always know if your flag was right. Sometimes there's no feedback loop. Sometimes the label never arrives. So what do you do?

You simulate. You stress-test. You build sandboxes with synthetic anomalies and watch how your models behave under pressure. You inject adversarial examples, let the models stumble, and retrain them on their mistakes. It's part science, part theater. But necessary. Because when your system is running live, you don't get second takes. And here's another uncomfortable truth: false positives matter. A lot. Too many alerts and people stop paying attention. Too few, and you miss the bomb under the floorboards. The art is in calibration. You build not just for detection, but for tolerance. The system must know when to speak, and when to shut up. But even that isn't enough. Because once the model has made its prediction, the question becomes—*who decides what happens next?*

This is the moment most frameworks fumble. They stop at the prediction. They score the risk. And then... silence. But in a real-time system, prediction without action is just decoration. You need orchestration. Rules engines. Automated triggers. Escalation paths. If transaction risk exceeds threshold X, freeze. If behavioral anomaly clusters Y times in Z minutes, flag and notify (Ali, 2024). If the system's own confidence drops below a certain threshold—pause the flow, ask for human review. And that human review? It has to be more than an afterthought. The system needs a UI, not just for observation, but for interaction. Risk isn't just scored—it's interpreted. Annotated. Overruled. Escalated. Suppressed. And those interactions must loop back into the system. That's where real learning happens—not just in the batch-trained model, but in the space between human override and algorithmic assertion. And what of explanation? A decision that can't be explained is a liability, especially in regulated environments. Which is why explainability isn't a feature—it's a necessity. Whether through SHAP values, LIME approximations, counterfactual simulations, or bespoke interpreters, real-time frameworks must come with interpretive layers (Bhattacharya, 2022). These don't slow the system down; they *ground* it, offer it coherence. Because if a bank executive gets an alert saying that $30 million in liquidity is at risk, you better believe they'll ask why. And let's not forget the operational chaos that lives behind the scenes. Real-time systems are hungry. They need monitoring—latency checks, throughput gauges, anomaly feedback loops, model drift alerts. Without constant tuning, the system either chokes or becomes noise. You need site reliability engineering. You need observability stacks—Grafana, Prometheus, OpenTelemetry. You need incident response plans, rollback options, shadow deployments (Chapman & Holmes, 2024). Because if you're going to make decisions on the fly, you better have the agility to recover when you get it wrong. And you will get it wrong.

That's the final truth of real-time risk frameworks: they are fallible. Just like us. They hallucinate patterns. They miss the obvious. They surprise you with their brilliance, and frustrate you with their blindness. They are mirrors of the data they consume and the logic they encode. So how do you trust them? You don't. Not blindly. You *build trust.* Iteratively. Through testing. Through transparency. Through human-in-the-loop design. Through fail-safes. Through humility. The goal isn't perfection. It's resilience. The system must bend, not break. It must alert, not panic. It must adapt, not ossify.

At the end of the day, implementing a real-time risk framework is less about technology and more about design. About creating an ecosystem where data flows, models reason, actions trigger, and humans remain involved—not as bystanders, but as stewards (McGowan & Bell, 2022). It's about bridging the gap between signals and decisions. Between detection and response. Between information and understanding. Because risk doesn't wait. It doesn't queue up politely for the next batch run. It's already moving. Already mutating. And if we want to meet it head-on, we'll need systems that can move just as fast. Systems that don't just *see* the stream—but *think* inside it. And maybe—just maybe—systems that learn not just from what went wrong, but from what *almost* went wrong. The near misses. The close calls. The flickers at the edge of the graph. Because that's where the future lives—not in certainty, but in foresight. And real-time risk intelligence? It's not about avoiding risk altogether. It's about dancing with it—eyes open, reflexes sharp, judgment intact.

CHALLENGES OF TRUST, BIAS, AND INTERPRETABILITY IN ML RISK MODELS

You can build a model that predicts loan defaults with near-perfect precision, a fraud detection system that flags anomalies before they escalate, a dynamic credit scoring engine that updates itself in milliseconds—but none of it matters if no one trusts the system. No matter how elegant the algorithm, how optimized the code, how thrilling the performance metrics, if the outputs aren't trusted—deeply, intuitively, and consistently—then what you've built is not a risk model. It's just noise dressed as intelligence.

Trust, like risk, is invisible until it fails. And when it fails in machine learning systems—especially those wired into financial infrastructures—the consequences reverberate (Youvan, 2024). You can lose clients. Damage reputations. Invite regulatory scrutiny. Worse still, you risk creating invisible harm: biased denials of service, false positives that punish the innocent, blind spots that miss emerging threats. We don't just need smart models. We need *credible* ones. Human-compatible ones. And that's where things get tricky. Because the very things that make machine learning powerful—its flexibility, its autonomy, its pattern-finding superpowers—also make it hard to understand. Hard to explain. And even harder to audit. We want models that see what we can't, but not so alien that we can't ask *why* they saw it. And as we push these systems into real-time environments, the pressure mounts. The speed of insight must not outrun the speed of accountability.

Let's start with trust. Or rather, let's start with its absence. You can feel it in the way people hesitate to act on an alert unless a human co-signs it. Or how they override model outputs that feel too aggressive, too out of step with instinct. This isn't stubbornness—it's survival. Financial professionals have spent years honing gut-level judgments. Asking them to hand the wheel to a model—especially one trained on abstract correlations, fed by partial truths, and shielded in opacity—feels like asking a pilot to fly blind on someone else's coordinates. So how do we bridge that gap?

Not with dashboards. Not with jargon. With *transparency*. But interpretability isn't just about opening the black box. It's about making the system's reasoning legible *in context*. Not just showing that a variable mattered, but explaining why, how, and to what effect. Imagine telling a loan officer that a borrower was denied funding because of "feature importance scores." It's absurd. The decision has to make narrative sense. It has to *fit* with human understanding, even if the insight came from patterns beyond human reach.

Some techniques help. SHAP values. LIME explanations. Counterfactual examples (Bhattacharya, 2022). They create bridges between model logic and human intuition. But these are approximations, not truths. They illuminate slices of the model, not the whole terrain. Worse, they can be gamed—intentionally or not. And for truly complex models, the explanations risk becoming just as opaque as the predictions they're meant to demystify. And then comes bias. Bias is the ghost in every dataset. It's not just in what data you include—it's in what you *don't*. Historical patterns are rarely neutral (Esposito et al, 2021). They carry the imprint of policy, prejudice, and power. If a region was redlined fifty years ago, the residue of that discrimination may still live in its lending data. If fraud detection systems disproportionately flag foreign-sounding names, that bias might trace back to training data that reflected enforcement disparities, not actual behavior.

Machine learning doesn't invent bias. It amplifies what's already there. And in financial contexts, that amplification can be devastating (Mehrabi et al, 2021). A model that marginally over-penalizes one demographic group can, at scale, institutionalize exclusion. It can deny loans, increase premiums, trigger false fraud alerts—quietly, systematically, without ever announcing itself as discriminatory. And here's the real kicker: sometimes bias *looks* like accuracy. If historical data shows higher default rates in certain groups—not because of actual creditworthiness, but because of structural disadvantage—the model might "correctly" learn those patterns. It's doing its job. But it's doing it without context. Without ethics. Without memory. And unless someone intervenes—adjusts the training data, revises the objective function, embeds fairness constraints—the model will keep doing what it was trained to do: reproduce the past.

Fixing this isn't as easy as removing protected attributes. Bias seeps in through proxies. Zip codes. Employment types. Browsing history. It hides behind correlation, behind signal strength (Chun, 2021). You can't fight it with superficial filters. You have to dig. Interrogate. Intervene. But even that presumes we've agreed on what fairness means. And in machine learning, that's a swamp. Equalized odds? Demographic parity? Individual fairness? Each definition comes with trade-offs. Optimizing for one may violate another. And the answers aren't mathematical—they're political, cultural, moral. So, who decides?

This is the part we often skip. The part where real people make judgment calls about trade-offs that affect lives. Should a fraud model be more aggressive, even if it means more false positives? Should a loan approval model prioritize demographic equity, even if it slightly reduces accuracy? These aren't just questions for data scientists (Sriram, 2024). They're questions for risk officers, compliance teams, ethicists, the public. And yet, too often, these decisions are buried inside model pipelines—coded once, reviewed rarely, understood by few. Interpretability, then, is about *more* than transparency. It's about *governance*. About creating systems where decisions can be traced, reviewed, contested. Where stakeholders have the tools—not just the permissions—to understand how models behave (Shevlane et al, 2023). And where accountability doesn't vanish into the code.

There's also the issue of *dynamic risk environments*. Real-time systems don't just predict—they adapt. They learn from feedback, update thresholds, adjust weights. That's good for responsiveness. But it complicates trust. A model that behaved one way last week may behave differently today. And unless those changes are tracked, explained, and documented, users will start to feel like they're dealing with a moving target. And sometimes, they are. Concept drift is real. Behavioral norms shift. Fraud patterns evolve. Economic conditions fluctuate. And models trained in one environment may falter in another. But retraining isn't just technical—it's ethical (Kaakandikar, 2025). If you retrain a model and its outputs shift significantly, you're affecting real people. Their credit scores. Their access to services. Their financial futures. Shouldn't someone be informed?

This is where we need versioning. Audit trails. Model change logs. A way to trace not just what the model predicted, but *what version of the model* made that prediction (Mayer et al, 2022). Only then can we begin to build systems where trust is earned, not assumed. And what about explainability in ensemble models? Boosted trees, bagged forests, blended architectures—they perform beautifully but defy simplification. They're not one model, they're many. And their logic is distributed across layers and trees and voting mechanisms.

Explaining such systems isn't impossible. But it's exhausting. And often unsatisfying. You can say that Feature A contributed 17% to the decision. But what does that *mean* to the person on the other side of the screen? What does it mean to the regulator? The journalist? The person who got denied a mortgage? Interpretability must be audience-specific. The same model may need different explanations for different stakeholders. A developer wants feature importance metrics. A compliance officer wants policy alignment (Karlsson et al, 2022). A customer wants plain language fairness. And the system must be able to deliver *all three*—truthfully, coherently, simultaneously.

That's not a technical feature. That's design. Design for accountability. For dignity. For intelligibility. Because trust is not a function of accuracy. It's a function of *relationship*. Between people and machines. Between organizations and their users. Between predictions and consequences. So where does this leave us? In a space of tension. Of contradiction. Of difficult trade-offs. We want models that are powerful *and* understandable. Fast *and* fair. Dynamic *and* stable. We want systems that act boldly, but explain themselves humbly. That's the real challenge of machine learning in risk: it's not just about finding the signal. It's about translating that signal into judgment, into action, into human terms. Because trust isn't a given. It's built. Over time. Through transparency, fairness, reliability, and humility. And if our models can't reflect those values, then they're not models of risk. They're risks themselves.

TOWARD ETHICAL, ADAPTIVE, AND SCALABLE RISK INTELLIGENCE

Let's be honest with ourselves: the systems we're building—these so-called intelligent frameworks for real-time risk detection—are not neutral. They're not just mathematical. They're not just code. Every decision to include one dataset and exclude another, to optimize for speed over transparency, to trust the model's signal over a human's hesitation—all of it is ethical. All of it is political. All of it matters.

We tend to think of risk intelligence as a technological pursuit. Something sleek, fast, frictionless. But that's a seductive illusion. What we're really building, when we build these systems, is a *philosophy of judgment at scale*. We're encoding priorities (Valov, 2025). Drawing invisible lines around what counts as risky and what doesn't. And if we don't step back and ask *who benefits, who's harmed, who's accountable*—then we're not just automating risk assessment. We're automating inequity, surveillance, exclusion. Just because a model can act in real time doesn't mean it should. Just because it can learn fast doesn't mean it understands. And just because it flags anomalies doesn't mean it knows what matters. That's where the ethical part starts.

Ethical risk intelligence means refusing to treat efficiency as a proxy for wisdom (Floridi, 2023). It means asking questions that don't have clear answers: What kind of risk are we willing to tolerate? Who do we build margin for? Whose data do we rely on, and whose stories does that data leave out? Take credit risk, for example. Imagine a system that scores borrowers using thousands of variables—purchase history, device data, location pings. It's accurate, maybe uncannily so. But what is it really measuring? Behavior? Income? Or just how closely someone resembles those who've defaulted in the past? And what happens when those patterns reflect structural inequalities—when zip codes double as race proxies, or job categories penalize freelancers, or behavioral anomalies are just the artifacts of poverty?

An ethical system wouldn't just optimize around that. It would confront it. It would recognize that fairness is not the absence of bias, but the *presence of attention* to who's being hurt and how. That's not something an algorithm can do alone. That requires humans—policymakers, ethicists, regulators, affected communities—at the table, designing not just the system's functions, but its purpose (Firoozi & Firoozi, 2024). But ethics, let's be clear, isn't just about fairness. It's also about *power*. Who owns the model? Who owns the data? Who gets to intervene when it behaves badly? And who gets to define what "badly" even means? This is where adaptability matters. A system that can't adapt—ethically, behaviorally, structurally—is brittle. It may work beautifully in the lab, or during the first few months of deployment. But risk isn't static. Fraudsters evolve. Markets lurch. New threats emerge that have no historical precedent. What you thought you were measuring last week morphs into something unrecognizable.

A truly adaptive system doesn't just tweak its parameters. It *rethinks its assumptions*. It questions its own confidence. It signals uncertainty (Hezavehi et al, 2021). It pauses when it should, rather than forcing predictions from the unknown. And sometimes, adaptability means knowing when to back off. When to hand the decision back to a human. When to step out of the loop. Because not everything needs a machine. Not everything should be predicted. There's wisdom in restraint. But adaptability isn't just about the model. It's about the organization. The people. The infrastructure around the intelligence. You need pipelines that can absorb feedback, not just in the form of labeled data but in the form of *lived experience*. You need governancc structures that are flexible, not bureaucratic (Jarrahi et al, 2023). You need cultures that are open to updating beliefs—not just retraining models, but rewriting policies.

That's harder than it sounds. Institutions love consistency. Models that shift over time, systems that question their own authority—these are threatening, operationally messy (Issar & Aneesh, 2022). But if we want risk intelligence that grows with the world rather than calcifying inside it, we have to build that mess into the DNA. Rigidity is comfortable. It's also dangerous. And now we arrive at scale (Ravn, 2022). Because all of this—the ethics, the adaptability—is meaningless if it can't scale. If it stays trapped in the prototype, the pilot, the whitepaper. We need systems that can operate across institutions, jurisdictions, data regimes. Systems that aren't just customized, but *configurable*. That can be deployed in a small regional bank and a sprawling multinational—with sensitivity to local context and global regulation. But scalability doesn't mean making everything uniform. It means making everything *resilient to variation*. Different regions have different risk profiles. Different communities have different definitions of harm. Scaling risk intelligence means not just deploying models everywhere, but tuning them everywhere (Fulton et al, 2024). It means building feedback loops that are sensitive to local dynamics, not just global KPIs. And let's not forget the infrastructure. Real-time risk assessment at scale requires robust data pipelines, streaming architecture, distributed storage, low-latency processing. But those are just the bones. The soul is in how those systems relate to the people they serve. Are they explainable? Accountable? Responsive to redress? Can an affected person challenge a decision? Can a regulator audit the process? Can an internal reviewer spot a shift in behavior before it becomes a scandal?

Scalability without accountability is just automation. And automation without humanity is just risk, hiding in plain sight (Lin, 2024). Here's the hard truth: there's no such thing as a neutral risk model. Every threshold, every weight, every training set is a value judgment. We need to stop pretending otherwise. And once we stop pretending, we can start designing systems that wear their values on their sleeve. Systems that declare what they optimize for, what trade-offs they're willing to make, what risks they're willing to absorb so that others don't have to (Lu et al, 2021). That's what ethical, adaptive, and scalable risk intelligence looks like. It doesn't pretend to be perfect. It doesn't erase uncertainty. It doesn't chase prediction for its own sake. It listens. It learns. It takes responsibility. And above all, it remembers that behind every data point is a life. Behind every outlier is a story. Behind every flagged transaction is a human being trying to do something—earn, save, protect, escape, survive. If our models can't hold space for that—if they reduce people to patterns, anomalies, deviations—then they're not intelligent. They're just efficient. And efficiency without care is not intelligence. It's neglect. So, let's build better. Let's build models that remember their limits, systems that adapt with grace, infrastructures that scale with empathy. Let's not settle for risk frameworks that just run fast. Let's demand that they *think deeply*. Let's refuse to call something "intelligent" unless it also understands something about justice, context, and human worth. Because the future of finance won't be measured only in margins and models. It will be measured in trust. In fairness. In foresight. And maybe—just maybe—in whether we had the courage to ask not just *what works*, but *what's right*.

CONCLUSION

We began this chapter by questioning the adequacy of traditional risk assessment models in a world that no longer moves slowly. Through every example, every framework, and every line of code, we have returned to the same essential truth: real-time risk assessment is no longer optional—it is inevitable. In a global financial system defined by uncertainty and speed, the ability to identify, assess, and respond to risk as it unfolds is not just a competitive advantage—it is a prerequisite for survival. But machine learning is not a silver bullet. It does not solve the problem of risk—it redefines how we approach it. It replaces static thresholds with dynamic baselines, rule-based alerts with adaptive models, and rigid forecasts with continuously learning predictors. Yet the introduction of these powerful tools also raises new, profound questions. How do we ensure that the models we trust to detect anomalies do not encode biases that go unseen?

How do we balance efficiency with fairness? What happens when a system flags a false positive—or worse, misses a real one?

There is no easy answer. And that is the point. The deployment of machine learning for real-time risk assessment forces financial institutions to reckon with both technical complexity and human responsibility. Risk, in this new paradigm, is no longer just a number on a dashboard. It is a fluid concept, shaped by behavioral patterns, geopolitical volatility, cyber threats, and algorithmic interpretation. In such an environment, risk management becomes less of a department and more of a living, breathing process—perpetually in motion.

We must design systems that are not just fast, but explainable. We must build infrastructures that do not just scale, but adapt. We must train models not just to detect what is statistically unusual, but what is contextually significant. And most of all, we must remember that the algorithms we build are mirrors of the data we feed them—and by extension, of the values we encode. Therein lies the real challenge—and the real opportunity. Real-time risk assessment through machine learning opens the door to a new kind of financial decision-making: one that is proactive rather than reactive, evidence-based rather than assumption-driven, and continuous rather than episodic. But it also calls for new skills, new frameworks of accountability, and a cultural shift that embraces collaboration between technologists, financial experts, and ethicists.

As we close this chapter, we do not offer a definitive roadmap—because the landscape is still unfolding. Instead, we offer a call to action: to approach this technological frontier not with naïve enthusiasm or cynical resistance, but with clarity, curiosity, and caution. Let us not merely automate risk assessment—let us reimagine it. Let us not outsource judgment to machines, but enhance our judgment through them. And let us remember, in this pursuit of intelligent systems, that the most essential intelligence may still be our own: the wisdom to ask not just what machine learning *can* do, but what it *should* do. In that spirit, the future of financial risk management isn't just fast or smart. It's human.

REFERENCES

Ali, T. (2024). Next-generation intrusion detection systems with LLMs: real-time anomaly detection, explainable AI, and adaptive data generation (Master's thesis, T. Ali).

Alpaydin, E. (2021). *Machine learning*. MIT Press. DOI: 10.7551/mitpress/13811.001.0001

Amiri, Z., Heidari, A., Jafari, N., & Hosseinzadeh, M. (2024). Deep study on autonomous learning techniques for complex pattern recognition in interconnected information systems. *Computer Science Review*, *54*, 100666. DOI: 10.1016/j.cosrev.2024.100666

Balcıoğlu, Y. S. (2024). Revolutionizing Risk Management AI and ML Innovations in Financial Stability and Fraud Detection. In Navigating the Future of Finance in the Age of AI (pp. 109-138). IGI Global.

Bhattacharya, A. (2022). *Applied Machine Learning Explainability Techniques: Make ML models explainable and trustworthy for practical applications using LIME, SHAP, and more*. Packt Publishing Ltd.

Challoumis, C. (2024, October). The economics of AI-How machine learning is driving value creation. In *XVI International Scientific Conference* (pp. 94-125).

Chapman, R., & Holmes, P. (2024). *Observability with Grafana: Monitor, control, and visualize your Kubernetes and cloud platforms using the LGTM stack*. Packt Publishing Ltd.

Chivers, T. (2024). *Everything is Predictable: How Bayesian Statistics Explain Our World.* Simon and Schuster.

Cho, M. (2024). *Protecting Financial Consumers in the Era of BD• ML Innovations: What Behavioral Patterns to be Tamed?* And How.

Chun, W. H. K. (2021). *Discriminating data: Correlation, neighborhoods, and the new politics of recognition.* MIT Press. DOI: 10.7551/mitpress/14050.001.0001

Cohen, A. (2025). Browser Security Posture Analysis: A Client-Side Security Assessment Framework. arXiv preprint arXiv:2505.08050.

Daníelsson, J. (2022). *The illusion of control: why financial crises happen, and what we can (and can't) do about it.* Yale University Press.

Davies, D. (2025). *The Unaccountability Machine: Why Big Systems Make Terrible Decisions—and How the World Lost Its Mind.* University of Chicago Press.

Esposito, C., Landrum, G. A., Schneider, N., Stiefl, N., & Riniker, S. (2021). GHOST: Adjusting the decision threshold to handle imbalanced data in machine learning. *Journal of Chemical Information and Modeling, 61*(6), 2623–2640. DOI: 10.1021/acs.jcim.1c00160 PMID: 34100609

Firoozi, A. A., & Firoozi, A. A. (2024). Ethical Design and Development Guidelines. In *Revolutionizing Civil Engineering with Neuromorphic Computing: Pathways to Smart and Sustainable Infrastructure* (pp. 81–97). Springer Nature Switzerland. DOI: 10.1007/978-3-031-71097-1_10

Floridi, L. (2023). The ethics of artificial intelligence: Principles, challenges, and opportunities.

Fulton, R., Fulton, D., Hayes, N., & Kaplan, S. (2024). The Transformation Risk-Benefit Model of Artificial Intelligence: Balancing Risks and Benefits Through Practical Solutions and Use Cases. arXiv preprint arXiv:2406.11863.

Gigerenzer, G. (2022). *How to stay smart in a smart world: Why human intelligence still beats algorithms.* MIT Press.

Hassan, M. (2024). Real-Time Risk Assessment in SaaS Payment Infrastructures: Examining Deep Learning Models and Deployment Strategies. *Transactions on Artificial Intelligence, Machine Learning, and Cognitive Systems, 9*(3), 1–10.

Hezavehi, S. M., Weyns, D., Avgeriou, P., Calinescu, R., Mirandola, R., & Perez-Palacin, D. (2021). Uncertainty in self-adaptive systems: A research community perspective. [TAAS]. *ACM Transactions on Autonomous and Adaptive Systems, 15*(4), 1–36. DOI: 10.1145/3487921

Issar, S., & Aneesh, A. (2022). What is algorithmic governance? *Sociology Compass, 16*(1), e12955. DOI: 10.1111/soc4.12955

Jarrahi, M. H., Askay, D., Eshraghi, A., & Smith, P. (2023). Artificial intelligence and knowledge management: A partnership between human and AI. *Business Horizons, 66*(1), 87–99. DOI: 10.1016/j.bushor.2022.03.002

Kaakandikar, R. (2025). Ethical and Inclusive Upskilling for the AI Revolution. Available at *SSRN* 5169844. DOI: 10.2139/ssrn.5169844

Karlsson, F., Kolkowska, E., & Petersson, J. (2022). Information security policy compliance-eliciting requirements for a computerized software to support value-based compliance analysis. *Computers & Security, 114*, 102578. DOI: 10.1016/j.cose.2021.102578

Kjoersvik, O., & Bate, A. (2022). Black swan events and intelligent automation for routine safety surveillance. *Drug Safety, 45*(5), 419–427. DOI: 10.1007/s40264-022-01169-0 PMID: 35579807

Korn, J. (2024). Ensemble Classification: An Analysis of the Random Forest Model.

Li, Z., Liu, F., Yang, W., Peng, S., & Zhou, J. (2021). A survey of convolutional neural networks: Analysis, applications, and prospects. *IEEE Transactions on Neural Networks and Learning Systems, 33*(12), 6999–7019. DOI: 10.1109/TNNLS.2021.3084827 PMID: 34111009

Lin, H. (2024). Ethical and Scalable Automation: A Governance and Compliance Framework for Business Applications. arXiv preprint arXiv:2409.16872.

Liu, Z., & Zheng, Y. (2022). *AI ethics and governance*. Springer Singapore. DOI: 10.1007/978-981-19-2531-3

Lu, N., Liu, L., Yu, D., & Fu, B. (2021). Navigating trade-offs in the social-ecological systems. *Current Opinion in Environmental Sustainability, 48*, 77–84. DOI: 10.1016/j.cosust.2020.10.014

Mallick, M. A. I., & Nath, R. (2024). Navigating the cyber security landscape: A comprehensive review of cyber-attacks, emerging trends, and recent developments. *World Scientific News, 190*(1), 1–69.

Mayer, C., Danelljan, M., Bhat, G., Paul, M., Paudel, D. P., Yu, F., & Van Gool, L. (2022). Transforming model prediction for tracking. In *Proceedings of the IEEE/CVF conference on computer vision and pattern recognition* (pp. 8731-8740).

McGowan, V. C., & Bell, P. (2022). "I now deeply care about the effects humans are having on the world": Cultivating ecological care and responsibility through complex systems modelling and investigations. *Educational and Developmental Psychologist, 39*(1), 116–131. DOI: 10.1080/20590776.2022.2027212

Mehrabi, N., Morstatter, F., Saxena, N., Lerman, K., & Galstyan, A. (2021). A survey on bias and fairness in machine learning. *ACM Computing Surveys, 54*(6), 1–35. DOI: 10.1145/3457607

Omoruyi, N. (2025). Advanced Computational Methods for Financial Planning and Analysis Risk Assessment using Data Science-Driven Model Validation Techniques. International Journal of Research Publication and Reviews. doi: https://www. semanticscholar. org/paper/4d27d96c40e-20c0bd7df2d9220bd4b355a381c82

Petrini, L. (2023). Breaking the Curse of Dimensionality in Deep Neural Networks by Learning Invariant Representations. arXiv preprint arXiv:2310.16154.

Pillai, V. (2022). *Anomaly Detection for Innovators: Transforming Data into Breakthroughs*. Libertatem Media Private Limited.

Praveen, R. V. S. (2024). *Data Engineering Concepts: From Basics To Advance Techniques*. Addition Publishing House.

Rane, N., Choudhary, S. P., & Rane, J. (2024). Ensemble deep learning and machine learning: Applications, opportunities, challenges, and future directions. *Studies in Medical and Health Sciences, 1*(2), 18–41. DOI: 10.48185/smhs.v1i2.1225

Ravn, I. (2022). Beyond chaos and rigidity, flexstability. *New Ideas in Psychology, 66*, 100948. DOI: 10.1016/j.newideapsych.2022.100948

Ridwan, I. B. (2025). Dynamic strategic foresight using predictive business analytics: Strategic modeling of competitive advantage in unstable market and innovation ecosystems.

Rufo, D. D., Debelee, T. G., Ibenthal, A., & Negera, W. G. (2021). Diagnosis of diabetes mellitus using gradient boosting machine (LightGBM). *Diagnostics (Basel)*, *11*(9), 1714. DOI: 10.3390/diagnostics11091714 PMID: 34574055

Sánchez-Zas, C., Villagrá, V. A., Vega-Barbas, M., Larriva-Novo, X., Moreno, J. I., & Berrocal, J. (2023). Ontology-based approach to real-time risk management and cyber-situational awareness. *Future Generation Computer Systems*, *141*, 462–472. DOI: 10.1016/j.future.2022.12.006

Sharma, M., Paliwal, T., & Baniwal, P. (2024). Challenges in Digital Transformation and Automation for Industry 4.0. In AI-Driven IoT Systems for Industry 4.0 (pp. 143-163). CRC Press.

Shevlane, T., Farquhar, S., Garfinkel, B., Phuong, M., Whittlestone, J., Leung, J., . . . Dafoe, A. (2023). Model evaluation for extreme risks. arXiv preprint arXiv:2305.15324.

Slota, S. C., Fleischmann, K. R., Greenberg, S., Verma, N., Cummings, B., Li, L., & Shenefiel, C. (2023). Many hands make many fingers to point: Challenges in creating accountable AI. *AI & Society*, *38*(4), 1–13. DOI: 10.1007/s00146-021-01302-0

Sriram, H. K. (2024). Leveraging AI and Machine Learning for Enhancing Secure Payment Processing: A Study on Generative AI Applications in Real-Time Fraud Detection and Prevention. Available at *SSRN* 5203586.

Tsantekidis, A., Passalis, N., & Tefas, A. (2022). Recurrent neural networks. In *Deep learning for robot perception and cognition* (pp. 101–115). Academic Press. DOI: 10.1016/B978-0-32-385787-1.00010-5

Valov, D. (2025). The fracture that learns: Belief as a recursive system.

Xu, T., & Liang, F. (2021). Machine learning for hydrologic sciences: An introductory overview. *WIREs. Water*, *8*(5), e1533. DOI: 10.1002/wat2.1533

Youvan, D. C. (2024). Anatomy of a Financial Collapse: The Role of Technical Glitches in Modern Financial Systems.

Chapter 2
Entropy and Uncertainty:
Physics-Inspired Approaches to Risk Assessment in Finance

Mădălina Mihăilescu
https://orcid.org/0009-0003-0736-8588
Hyperion University of Bucharest, Romania

ABSTRACT

This chapter examines how entropy and uncertainty, concepts rooted in physics and information theory, can be translated into innovative approaches for risk assessment in finance. Traditional financial models often rely on assumptions of normality, equilibrium, and linearity, which limit their ability to anticipate extreme events and systemic instabilities. By contrast, entropy-based methods provide tools to capture disorder, complexity, and hidden structures in financial data. The chapter situates these methods within a broader interdisciplinary dialogue, bridging physics, complexity science, and finance. Through conceptual discussion and illustrative examples, the authors argue that entropy not only enhances the quantitative description of uncertainty but also supports more resilient strategies for decision-making under incomplete information. Ultimately, the chapter aims to show how physics-inspired perspectives can enrich both theoretical models and practical applications in financial risk management.

DOI: 10.4018/979-8-3373-3626-8.ch002

INTRODUCTION

The study of risk in finance has long been grounded in probabilistic reasoning, statistical inference, and econometric modeling. From the pioneering works of Markowitz (1952) on portfolio theory to the development of the Capital Asset Pricing Model (Sharpe, 1964) and Value-at-Risk frameworks (Jorion, 2007), risk assessment has largely been approached through tools that assume rational agents, normally distributed returns, and relatively stable market dynamics. However, the crises of the past decades—including the Asian financial crisis, the dot-com bubble, the 2008 global financial meltdown, and the COVID-19 pandemic—have exposed the fragility of such assumptions. Extreme events, nonlinear correlations, and systemic feedback loops have proven to be the rule rather than the exception in financial markets (Taleb, 2010). Against this backdrop, scholars and practitioners have increasingly turned toward alternative approaches capable of capturing the complexity, uncertainty, and emergent dynamics inherent to financial systems.

One particularly promising avenue of inquiry draws inspiration from physics, and more specifically from the concept of entropy. Originating in thermodynamics and later generalized in information theory, entropy provides a measure of disorder, uncertainty, or the lack of information in a system (Shannon, 1948; Jaynes, 1957). While physicists have used entropy to describe the dispersal of energy and the irreversibility of processes, economists and financial theorists have borrowed this notion to quantify unpredictability in markets, to evaluate portfolio diversification, and to identify hidden structures in financial data (Philippatos & Wilson, 1972; Maasoumi, 1993; Ustaoglu, 2018). Entropy-based metrics, unlike variance-based measures, are not constrained by assumptions of normality and can capture the richness of distributions, tail events, and systemic dependencies.

The concept of entropy was first introduced by Clausius in the mid-19th century as a measure of energy dispersal in thermodynamic systems. Boltzmann and Gibbs later extended this notion to statistical mechanics, framing entropy as a measure of the multiplicity of microstates compatible with a given macrostate. Shannon (1948) abstracted entropy into the domain of communication, where it quantified the uncertainty of information transmission. Jaynes (1957) further unified these perspectives through the principle of maximum entropy, which prescribes selecting the probability distribution that maximizes entropy subject to known constraints.

The migration of entropy into finance began in the 1970s, with Philippatos and Wilson (1972) proposing entropy as an alternative to variance for portfolio diversification. Their argument was that variance captures only second-order moments, whereas entropy accounts for the entire distribution of returns. Subsequent studies have applied entropy to topics ranging from stock market efficiency (Darbellay & Wuertz, 2000) to credit risk assessment (Ustaoglu, 2018) and systemic stability (Zhao et al., 2018). Entropy has thus emerged as a versatile tool for quantifying uncertainty beyond the limitations of traditional metrics.

The uncertainty dimension is equally central. Traditional finance differentiates between measurable risk and unmeasurable uncertainty, following the seminal distinction made by Knight (1921). Risk is associated with known probability distributions, while uncertainty reflects the unknown, the unforeseeable, and the structurally ambiguous. Contemporary markets, however, often blur this distinction: not only are probability distributions shifting and heavy-tailed, but the very structures generating financial data evolve in time. Entropy, as a flexible and dynamic measure, can bridge the gap between risk and uncertainty by quantifying disorder in both stable and turbulent conditions (Prokopenko et al., 2009).

Risk assessment in finance often relies on models that assume stationarity, independence, and Gaussian distributions. However, empirical evidence consistently demonstrates that financial returns are heavy-tailed, exhibit volatility clustering, and display complex correlations (Mandelbrot, 1963; Cont, 2001). These features undermine the reliability of conventional models, particularly during crises when extreme events dominate dynamics.

Knight's (1921) distinction between risk and uncertainty remains foundational, but financial practice often collapses uncertainty into risk by imposing probability distributions where none are stable. This epistemological reduction has practical consequences: risk management strategies become brittle, blind to structural changes and emergent shocks. Entropy-based approaches, by contrast, embrace uncertainty as an intrinsic property of complex systems. They provide measures that adapt to distributional changes, capture informational inefficiencies, and identify structural fragility.

Financial markets can be conceptualized as complex adaptive systems, where heterogeneous agents interact, learn, and adapt, leading to emergent collective behaviors (Arthur, 2021). Such systems resemble physical systems in their capacity for phase transitions, self-organization, and nonlinear dynamics. For example, liquidity crises resemble critical phenomena, where small perturbations can trigger cascading effects across the system.

Entropy, as a measure of disorder and uncertainty, becomes particularly relevant in this context. High entropy may reflect market unpredictability or diversification, while low entropy may indicate concentration, rigidity, or systemic fragility. Entropy can thus serve as an indicator of resilience, capturing both the diversity of market states and the adaptability of the system to shocks (Prokopenko et al., 2009).

This chapter argues that a physics-inspired framework for risk assessment, grounded in entropy and uncertainty, offers a richer lens for understanding financial systems. While mainstream risk measures such as volatility or Value-at-Risk remain valuable, they fail to capture the deeper informational and systemic dimensions of financial instability. Entropy-based approaches, by contrast, provide tools for detecting early-warning signals, identifying hidden correlations, and evaluating systemic robustness. Moreover, they align with the growing literature on complexity economics, which views markets not as equilibria but as adaptive, evolving systems characterized by feedback loops, phase transitions, and emergent patterns (Arthur, 2021).

ENTROPY-BASED METRICS IN FINANCE

The study of entropy-based metrics in finance reflects one of the most fruitful interdisciplinary transfers between physics, information theory, and economics. Traditional financial analysis has long relied on tools such as variance, covariance, and correlation to measure uncertainty and risk. While powerful, these metrics are often limited by restrictive assumptions, such as the normal distribution of returns, independence of observations, or linearity of relationships. In practice, financial markets exhibit heavy tails, volatility clustering, structural breaks, and nonlinear dependencies that undermine the effectiveness of standard models (Cont, 2001; Mandelbrot, 1963).

Entropy-based metrics offer an alternative that is less dependent on rigid assumptions and better suited to capturing complexity. Entropy, originally developed in thermodynamics and later generalized by Shannon (1948) in the field of information theory, measures the degree of disorder, unpredictability, or informational richness in a system. When applied to finance, entropy captures the degree of uncertainty in price movements, the diversity of portfolio allocations, or the informational efficiency of markets (Maasoumi, 1993; Philippatos & Wilson, 1972).

Shannon's definition of entropy has been central to the migration of the concept into finance. Shannon entropy quantifies the amount of uncertainty or information content in a system. In finance, it can be used to describe how unpredictable asset returns are, or how diversified a portfolio is.

Research has shown that markets with high entropy are generally less predictable, reflecting greater efficiency. Conversely, markets with lower entropy often exhibit exploitable patterns, concentration of trading activity, or structural rigidities (Darbellay & Wuertz, 2000). For portfolio management, entropy has been proposed as an alternative to variance. Rather than focusing solely on volatility, entropy considers the entire distribution of outcomes, which allows it to capture not only the spread of returns but also their asymmetry and potential concentration.

Shannon entropy is appealing because it is intuitive and broadly applicable. However, it also faces challenges. Estimating entropy requires reliable probability distributions, which in financial contexts are often unstable, particularly during crises. Despite this limitation, it remains one of the most widely used entropy-based measures in financial research (Cover & Thomas, 2006).

While Shannon entropy measures uncertainty in a single system, relative entropy—also known as Kullback–Leibler divergence—measures the difference between two systems or two states. In finance, this allows analysts to assess how far actual market behavior deviates from expected behavior.

For example, relative entropy can be used to compare the observed distribution of returns to a benchmark distribution, such as the normal distribution. When the divergence is large, it signals that conventional models underestimate risks, especially in the tails. This has implications for Value-at-Risk calculations, stress testing, and capital allocation.

Relative entropy is also useful for anomaly detection. Large deviations between expected and observed behavior can signal structural market changes, bubbles, or crises (Huang et al., 2015). Portfolio managers have also used relative entropy to design strategies that minimize deviation from benchmarks while retaining flexibility (Fang et al., 2017). In this way, relative entropy functions as both a diagnostic tool and a practical guide for portfolio management.

Shannon entropy is only one member of a broader family of entropy measures. Rényi entropy introduces a parameter that adjusts the sensitivity of the measure to different parts of a distribution (Rényi, 1961). This flexibility makes Rényi entropy particularly useful in finance, where analysts are often interested in tail risks and extreme events.

By adjusting the parameter, researchers can place greater emphasis on rare but impactful outcomes, such as market crashes. This aligns with the growing recognition that extreme events drive much of the risk in financial systems (Taleb, 2010). Rényi entropy has been applied in portfolio management, stress testing, and systemic risk analysis, offering a more nuanced view of uncertainty than Shannon entropy alone (Zhao et al., 2018).

Entropy has also been applied to financial time series to capture the degree of regularity or unpredictability in data. Approximate entropy (ApEn) and sample entropy (SampEn), originally developed for physiological signals, have been used to evaluate the complexity of financial markets (Pincus, 1991; Richman & Moorman, 2000).

In finance, these measures assess how predictable or irregular market returns are. High entropy values indicate randomness and inefficiency, while low values suggest deterministic patterns or predictability. Applications include detecting shifts in market regimes, evaluating the efficiency of emerging markets versus developed ones, and testing whether trading strategies actually reduce uncertainty relative to benchmarks (Zunino et al., 2007). Such measures are particularly valuable in contexts where volatility is clustered and traditional linear models fail. They offer traders and risk managers a tool to detect when markets are entering turbulent phases.

One of the limitations of correlation-based analysis in finance is that it only captures linear dependencies and cannot detect directionality. Transfer entropy, introduced by Schreiber (2000), overcomes this limitation by quantifying the direction of information flow between two time series.

In financial systems, transfer entropy has been applied to detect contagion between markets, spillovers between asset classes, and the propagation of shocks through networks of institutions (Sandoval & Franca, 2012). For example, during the global financial crisis, transfer entropy provided insights into how stress in U.S. mortgage-backed securities spread to European banking systems.

Financial markets operate across multiple time horizons. Day traders, institutional investors, and pension funds interact in the same system, but with very different temporal perspectives. Multiscale entropy (MSE) was developed to measure the complexity of time series across different scales (Costa et al., 2005). In finance, MSE has been applied to distinguish between developed and emerging markets. Developed markets often exhibit higher entropy across scales, reflecting their greater complexity and resilience. Emerging markets, by contrast, may display lower entropy at some scales, making them more vulnerable to shocks (Cai et al., 2018). Multiscale entropy also provides early-warning indicators. For example, declining entropy across multiple scales has been linked to the build-up of bubbles and impending crashes. This ability to detect systemic fragility makes MSE an important tool for both investors and regulators.

Entropy has also been applied directly to portfolio optimization. Traditional mean-variance optimization, introduced by Markowitz (1952), assumes that risk can be fully captured by the variance of returns. However, this ignores higher-order distributional features, such as skewness and kurtosis, and it can lead to concentrated portfolios that are vulnerable to shocks.

Entropy-based portfolio optimization seeks to maximize diversification by distributing weights in a way that maximizes informational richness. The result is portfolios that are more balanced and less concentrated, providing greater resilience to market turbulence (Philippatos & Wilson,

1972). Empirical studies have shown that entropy-optimized portfolios often outperform mean-variance portfolios in terms of stability and downside protection, particularly during crises (Zhou et al., 2013). For practitioners, entropy offers a way to construct portfolios that are robust to uncertainty, even when statistical assumptions about returns fail.

Modern finance is characterized by deep interconnections between institutions, markets, and instruments. Network theory has been increasingly applied to study systemic risk, and entropy provides a natural tool to quantify uncertainty and diversity in networks. For example, entropy-based centrality measures can identify institutions whose failure would cause the greatest systemic disruption (Zhao et al., 2018). Similarly, the entropy of interbank exposures can reveal whether risks are evenly distributed or concentrated in a few institutions (Markose et al., 2012).

Entropy-based systemic risk measures align with the shift in regulatory focus after the 2008 crisis, from the solvency of individual institutions to the resilience of the financial system as a whole. By capturing the informational structure of networks, entropy helps regulators anticipate cascading failures and design more effective stress tests.

ENTROPY AND SYSTEMIC RISK: INFORMATION-THEORETIC APPROACHES TO FINANCIAL STABILITY

The global financial system is an interconnected network of institutions, instruments, and markets that constantly exchange capital, information, and risk. While these linkages facilitate growth and liquidity, they also create vulnerabilities: a shock originating in one segment can propagate across borders and asset classes, triggering widespread instability. This phenomenon, often termed systemic risk, gained particular prominence during the global financial crisis of 2007–2008, when the collapse of mortgage-backed securities markets cascaded through the banking sector, froze interbank lending, and led to one of the deepest recessions in modern history (Acharya et al., 2017).

Traditional financial risk models—focused on individual institutions' solvency or asset volatility—have often underestimated systemic interdependencies. Entropy-based approaches, rooted in information theory and complexity science, provide novel tools to quantify uncertainty, capture hidden dependencies, and identify fragile structures in financial networks (Zhao et al., 2018). This section explores the application of entropy metrics to systemic risk, highlighting their role in analyzing financial networks, contagion, early-warning indicators, and macroprudential regulation.

Systemic risk refers to the possibility that distress in one part of the financial system spreads widely, impairing its core functions such as credit provision, payment processing, and capital allocation (Bisias et al., 2012). Unlike idiosyncratic risk, which affects individual institutions, systemic risk emerges from interconnectedness, common exposures, and behavioral feedback loops. It is characterized by nonlinearity: small shocks can trigger disproportionate effects, as when the failure of a medium-sized bank sets off liquidity hoarding across the system.

Entropy provides a conceptual match for systemic risk because it captures disorder and unpredictability within systems composed of interacting agents. While volatility measures local fluctuations, entropy reflects global uncertainty, accounting for dependencies and structures invisible to traditional models (Maasoumi, 1993).

Financial institutions form dense webs of bilateral exposures through interbank loans, derivative contracts, and payment systems. Network theory has emerged as a powerful framework for studying systemic risk, and entropy enriches this analysis by quantifying the diversity and concentration of connections.

An interbank network with evenly distributed exposures has high entropy, indicating diversification and resilience. Conversely, when exposures concentrate on a few institutions, entropy declines, signaling fragility. This perspective aligns with the idea of "too interconnected to fail" institutions whose distress would ripple across the network (Markose et al., 2012).

Empirical studies show that entropy-based measures can identify systemic hubs and monitor how risk concentration evolves over time. For example, during the European sovereign debt crisis, entropy analyses of interbank exposures revealed increasing reliance on a small number of counterparties, foreshadowing liquidity freezes (Battiston et al., 2016).

Such insights complement stress tests by focusing not only on capital buffers but also on the structure of connections.

One of the most alarming aspects of systemic risk is contagion: the spread of distress from one market or institution to another. Traditional correlation-based measures often fail to capture contagion because they focus on linear co-movements and cannot detect directional influences. Entropy-based measures, such as transfer entropy, offer a way to identify causal information flows.

During the global financial crisis, entropy analyses revealed how shocks in U.S. mortgage-backed securities markets transmitted to European banking systems, not simply through asset correlations but through directional spillovers in funding and derivatives markets (Sandoval & Franca, 2012). Similar methods have been applied to detect contagion between stock and bond markets, foreign exchange and commodities, and even between financial markets and real economic indicators such as unemployment or industrial production (Bekiros et al., 2017).

Liquidity risk—the possibility that assets cannot be traded quickly without substantial price concessions—plays a critical role in systemic crises. Entropy-based measures have been applied to market microstructure to capture liquidity conditions.

High entropy in order books indicates diverse participation and resilience, while declining entropy may reveal concentration of liquidity provision among a few market makers. During the 2010 "Flash Crash," entropy analyses of trading patterns highlighted sudden collapses in informational diversity, offering post-event explanations for the extreme volatility (Johnson et al., 2013).

Such approaches are valuable for regulators overseeing high-frequency trading, where microsecond imbalances can amplify systemic shocks. By monitoring entropy in trading activity, authorities can identify vulnerabilities in market infrastructure that might otherwise remain hidden.

Stress testing has become a cornerstone of macroprudential policy since the 2008 crisis. However, traditional stress tests often rely on a limited set of scenarios based on historical events or expert judgment. Entropy-based methods can enrich stress testing by generating scenarios that reflect the full distribution of possible outcomes.

For example, entropy optimization can identify scenarios that maximize uncertainty within plausible constraints, ensuring that stress tests explore extreme but possible futures (Tarashev et al., 2016). This approach reduces the risk of "fighting the last war," where regulators prepare for past crises but overlook new vulnerabilities.

Entropy-based stress testing can also evaluate the robustness of financial institutions to systemic shocks, not just idiosyncratic ones. By simulating contagion pathways and network fragility, entropy scenarios highlight how capital and liquidity buffers interact with systemic structures.

Entropy-based measures align closely with the objectives of macroprudential regulation, which seeks to safeguard the financial system as a whole rather than individual institutions. Regulators such as the Bank for International Settlements and the International Monetary Fund have emphasized the importance of monitoring systemic interconnectedness, concentration risks, and market complexity (IMF, 2016).

Entropy provides a quantitative language for these concerns. By measuring diversity, unpredictability, and information flows, entropy captures dimensions of systemic risk that complement capital ratios or leverage indicators. Policymakers can use entropy-based metrics to calibrate countercyclical tools, such as dynamic capital buffers, sectoral risk weights, or liquidity requirements.

Systemic risk is evolving beyond traditional banking and market domains. Climate change, cyber threats, and technological disruptions represent new systemic challenges. Entropy-based approaches have begun to be applied in these contexts as well.

For climate risk, entropy can measure uncertainty in scenarios related to physical shocks, such as extreme weather, and transition risks, such as sudden policy changes affecting carbon-intensive sectors (Battiston et al., 2017). Cyber risk, meanwhile, is inherently systemic: a coordinated attack on payment infrastructure could disrupt global finance. Entropy measures of network redundancy and diversity provide insights into resilience against such shocks (Kopp et al., 2017).

ENTROPY, RISK, AND FINANCIAL CRISES: GLOBAL LESSONS AND EPISTEMOLOGICAL SHIFTS

The recent history of global finance can be read as a sequence of crises that repeatedly revealed the limits of traditional risk models. Volatility and correlation have long been the preferred tools for measuring uncertainty, yet time and again they have proven insufficient to capture the complexity and fragility of financial systems. Entropy, understood as a measure of diversity and unpredictability, offers a different interpretive key. It does not limit itself to local price fluctuations but examines the global structure of the system, the way information is distributed, the concentration of risks, and the pathways through which shocks propagate. Looking back at three major moments—the Asian financial crisis of 1997, the global financial crisis of 2008, and the COVID-19 pandemic—we can see how an entropic lens could have provided early warning signals and a deeper understanding of contagion mechanisms.

The Asian financial crisis of 1997–1998 was triggered by the collapse of the Thai baht, but its true significance lay in the speed with which the problems of a relatively small economy cascaded across the region. Classical economic explanations focused on current account imbalances, overextended credit growth, and rigid exchange rate regimes. Yet from an entropic perspective the crisis reflected a steady decline in the diversity of capital flows and monetary structures. Many Southeast Asian economies had come to depend on similar patterns of short-term foreign-denominated borrowing and pegged exchange rates. This homogeneity reduced systemic entropy, leaving them exposed to common shocks. Once investors began withdrawing capital from Thailand, the lack of diversity in funding channels transformed a local imbalance into a regional meltdown. Investor behavior amplified the dynamics: expectations of depreciation in one country quickly became signals for speculative attacks in others. In informational terms, the transfer of signals across markets resembled directed flows of uncertainty. An entropic reading would have highlighted how negative expectations generated in Thailand rapidly spread to Indonesia, Korea, and Malaysia, turning a localized issue into a systemic crisis.

The global financial crisis of 2008 demonstrated even more starkly the inadequacy of volatility-based risk tools. In the years leading up to the collapse, complex derivatives such as collateralized debt obligations appeared to diversify risk by repackaging and redistributing it. In reality, exposures became concentrated in highly correlated mortgage assets. From the standpoint of entropy, this meant a reduction in the true diversity of portfolios, even as models suggested otherwise. In interbank and wholesale funding markets, reliance on a few key liquidity providers likewise eroded entropy, creating vulnerability to sudden freezes. When Lehman Brothers failed, the absence of alternatives and the extreme interdependence of institutions transformed what might have been a sectoral shock into a global catastrophe. Supervisors employing entropic measures could have observed the erosion of portfolio diversity, the homogenization of funding sources, and the declining informational richness of banking structures. These signals, invisible to Value-at-Risk models, might have offered earlier warnings of impending collapse.

The COVID-19 pandemic introduced a qualitatively different type of shock: an exogenous health crisis that simultaneously disrupted real economies and financial markets. Stock markets suffered dramatic losses in March 2020, followed by unprecedented recoveries fueled by massive fiscal and monetary interventions. In entropic terms, the pandemic showed how systemic diversity can suddenly collapse when all asset classes respond to the same uncertainty. Correlations between equities, bonds, and commodities spiked, reducing portfolio entropy and undermining diversification. At the same time, global supply chains—highly dependent on a few key nodes—illustrated how declining entropy in the real economy feeds into financial fragility. But perhaps the most striking feature was epistemic: the entropy of forecasts themselves. Epidemiological and economic models offered radically divergent projections, reflecting an extraordinary level of structural uncertainty. Entropy here expressed not just financial unpredictability but collective ignorance in the face of an unprecedented event.

Taken together, these three crises point to a common lesson: when diversity erodes and systems become more homogeneous and interconnected, entropy declines and systemic risk rises. This dynamic is not visible through standard indicators but is captured by information-theoretic tools. Moreover, crises show that entropy should not be viewed only retrospectively. It can serve prospectively as an indicator of structural fragility, a barometer of resilience.

Looking across jurisdictions, differences emerge in how entropic measures could be integrated into institutional frameworks. The European Union, with its strong tradition of preventive regulation and macroprudential oversight, offers mechanisms—such as ECB stress tests—where entropy could be readily embedded. Publishing entropy-based systemic risk indicators would add transparency and strengthen the European Systemic Risk Board's toolkit. In the United States, regulatory authority is fragmented among multiple agencies, with a continued emphasis on institution-specific solvency and market discipline. Incorporating entropy would require greater coordination, yet the innovative and complex nature of U.S. markets makes entropy especially relevant for detecting hidden concentrations. China, by contrast, combines state-dominated banking with fast-growing fintech giants and shadow credit networks. Entropy could help map risks in these opaque sectors, where vulnerabilities accumulate quickly. Moreover, China's centralized governance may enable rapid implementation of entropy-based tools, though possibly at the expense of transparency and accountability.

Beyond institutional comparisons, entropy raises epistemological questions. In the classical tradition, Frank Knight distinguished between risk, which can be measured with probabilities, and uncertainty, which cannot. Entropy blurs this boundary by quantifying uncertainty itself. It suggests that unpredictability is not merely a lack of knowledge but an intrinsic property of complex systems. In this sense, entropy does not eliminate uncertainty but transforms it into an analyzable dimension of disorder.

Entropy also shifts the conceptual focus from equilibrium to disorder and self-organization. Traditional financial models often treat equilibrium as the natural state, deviations as anomalies. Entropy instead treats fluctuations, shocks, and heterogeneity as fundamental. Markets appear less as systems converging toward stability and more as adaptive organisms whose structure evolves under the influence of information and shocks. This perspective aligns finance with complexity science, where feedback loops, nonlinearities, and emergent behaviors are central.

On a deeper level, entropy serves as a reminder of the limits of knowledge itself. Financial models aspire to predict, yet entropy quantifies the extent of unpredictability embedded in the system. It functions as a mirror, reflecting not only market properties but also the epistemic boundaries of our models. Each crisis revealed not only financial fragility but also the fragility of the analytical frameworks used to interpret it. Entropy encourages humility in risk management: uncertainty cannot be eradicated, only managed, and resilience must be built on diversity and adaptability rather than the illusion of perfect predictability.

FUTURE RESEARCH DIRECTIONS

The application of entropy and uncertainty to finance is still in its formative stages. While considerable progress has been made in developing entropy-based measures of portfolio diversification, systemic risk, and market efficiency, the potential of this framework remains only partially explored. The complexity of global financial systems, the acceleration of technological change, and the emergence of new categories of systemic risk suggest that much remains to be done. Future research must expand in several directions, ranging from methodological refinement and empirical validation to interdisciplinary integration and normative reflection.

One of the most urgent research avenues concerns the refinement of entropy estimation techniques. Financial data are notoriously noisy, non-stationary, and prone to structural breaks. Traditional approaches to entropy estimation often rely on assumptions of ergodicity or stationarity that do not hold in turbulent markets. Scholars will need to develop adaptive methods that can handle incomplete data, high-frequency trading dynamics, and sudden regime shifts. Bayesian approaches, machine learning estimators, and non-parametric density techniques may provide fruitful pathways. The challenge is not only technical but also interpretive: researchers must ensure that entropy measures are robust and transparent enough to be used by practitioners and regulators, avoiding the perception that they are black-box tools.

Another area of promising development is the integration of entropy into machine learning and artificial intelligence models. The rise of deep learning, reinforcement learning, and agent-based modeling has transformed financial forecasting and risk assessment. Yet many of these methods risk overfitting or generating opaque predictions. Entropy could play a dual role: first, as a regularization principle that prevents overfitting by maximizing informational diversity, and second, as an interpretive metric that quantifies uncertainty in model outputs. For example, entropy could help assess the confidence of neural networks in predicting asset price movements, or it could guide the design of reinforcement learning agents to balance exploration and exploitation. In this sense, entropy may become a bridge between explainability and performance in financial AI.

Research should also expand the use of entropy in cross-market and cross-border contagion analysis. Globalization has intensified the connections between financial systems, making crises increasingly international in scope. Traditional correlation-based methods have struggled to capture the nonlinear and directional flows of information across markets. Transfer entropy and related measures hold promise, but more work is needed to apply them systematically to foreign exchange, commodity, equity, and bond markets simultaneously. Comparative studies across jurisdictions could reveal whether emerging markets exhibit different entropic dynamics compared to developed economies, and how shocks in one part of the world alter informational structures elsewhere. Such analyses would be invaluable for international organizations such as the IMF, BIS, or OECD in designing cooperative frameworks for crisis prevention.

The intersection between climate risk and entropy represents another frontier. Climate change introduces profound uncertainty into financial systems, both through physical risks like extreme weather and through transition risks associated with decarbonization policies. Unlike cyclical or credit-related shocks, climate risks are structural, long-term, and characterized by deep uncertainty. Entropy could help quantify the unpredictability of climate-related scenarios and measure the resilience of financial portfolios under multiple futures. Research might explore how entropy evolves when portfolios are exposed to carbon-intensive industries versus renewable sectors, or how entropic indicators could inform green finance standards. By linking entropy to sustainability, scholars could contribute to the growing agenda of climate finance and environmental, social, and governance (ESG) investing.

Cyber risk and digital transformation also invite entropic exploration. The increasing reliance on digital infrastructures, from payment systems to blockchain platforms, creates systemic vulnerabilities that traditional financial risk models cannot capture. Future research could examine how entropy applies to network redundancy and cybersecurity resilience, quantifying the diversity of protective measures and the potential propagation of cyber shocks. Similarly, the convergence of blockchain and artificial intelligence raises questions about how entropy might serve as a tool for monitoring automated decision-making in decentralized finance. These lines of inquiry are particularly relevant as regulators grapple with fintech innovation and the systemic risks of algorithm-driven markets.

At the institutional level, entropy may reshape how scholars and practitioners think about governance and risk culture. Boards of directors, risk committees, and supervisors often operate under pressures to maximize efficiency, sometimes at the expense of resilience. Entropy-based indicators could serve as a counterbalance, reminding decision-makers that diversity and unpredictability are not inefficiencies to be eliminated but essential features of robust systems. Future research could explore how organizational structures, incentive schemes, and cultural norms respond to entropy-based metrics. Could entropic dashboards reduce herd behavior among financial institutions? Could they help align executive incentives with systemic resilience rather than short-term profitability? These questions remain open and demand interdisciplinary investigation.

There is also an epistemological dimension to future research. Entropy challenges the classical separation between risk, which is measurable, and uncertainty, which is not. By quantifying disorder and unpredictability, entropy reframes the very concept of uncertainty. Future scholarship should explore the philosophical and methodological implications of this shift. How does entropy alter the epistemology of finance? To what extent can uncertainty be domesticated through information theory, and where do the limits of quantification remain? Addressing these questions requires dialogue not only between economists and physicists but also with philosophers of science, legal scholars, and sociologists. Entropy thus invites a broader reflection on the boundaries of knowledge in financial systems.

Another promising direction involves policy applications. Regulators are increasingly interested in developing forward-looking indicators that complement stress tests and capital requirements. Entropy-based systemic risk measures could inform macroprudential policies, providing early-warning signals of concentration and fragility. Future research should focus on integrating entropy into the regulatory toolkit, assessing how it interacts with Basel standards, liquidity coverage ratios, and systemic capital buffers. Comparative studies of regulatory adoption in different jurisdictions would shed light on the feasibility and effectiveness of such integration. Researchers might also explore how public disclosure of entropy-based indicators influences market discipline, trust, and investor behavior.

Empirical validation remains an essential task. While case studies of past crises have shown the potential of entropy, large-scale empirical work is needed to confirm its predictive power. Scholars should test entropy-based models against extensive datasets, comparing their performance with established measures such as volatility, Value-at-Risk, or Expected Shortfall. Longitudinal studies could examine whether entropy provides leading indicators of crises across multiple decades and regions. Without rigorous empirical validation, entropy risks remaining an elegant concept with limited practical adoption.

Finally, future research must be interdisciplinary and comparative. Finance does not exist in isolation; it interacts with political systems, cultural practices, and technological infrastructures. Entropy provides a common language that can connect economics with physics, computer science, ecology, and sociology. Lessons from ecological resilience, for instance, where entropy has been used to measure biodiversity and adaptability, could inform financial regulation. Comparative work across disciplines could generate hybrid models that better capture the realities of global finance.

In sum, the future of entropy in finance lies not in replacing existing models but in broadening the conceptual and methodological horizons of risk assessment. By refining estimation methods, integrating with artificial intelligence, applying to climate and cyber risks, reshaping governance practices, and exploring epistemological implications, researchers can push the frontier of financial knowledge. Entropy invites us to accept uncertainty as intrinsic, to value diversity as a source of resilience, and to rethink the role of information in shaping markets. The path forward is challenging, but it is precisely in embracing complexity that finance can evolve into a discipline capable of grappling with the unpredictable realities of the twenty-first century.

CONCLUSION

The exploration of entropy and uncertainty as foundations for risk assessment in finance has highlighted both the limitations of traditional approaches and the promise of physics-inspired alternatives. Throughout this chapter, the argument has been made that volatility, Value-at-Risk, and correlation-based measures, while useful in certain contexts, fail to capture the systemic complexity, hidden interdependencies, and epistemic uncertainty that characterize modern financial systems. Entropy, in contrast, provides a multidimensional perspective that treats markets not as static equilibria but as dynamic, adaptive systems. As such, it offers both diagnostic tools for practitioners and conceptual resources for scholars and regulators.

The first contribution of entropy-based approaches is their ability to rethink the measurement of uncertainty. Classical finance, following Knight's (1921) distinction, separated risk from uncertainty: the former was seen as measurable and quantifiable, the latter as irreducible and unpredictable. Entropy complicates this dichotomy by quantifying disorder itself, turning uncertainty into a measurable dimension of systemic behavior. This move does not eliminate unpredictability but acknowledges it as intrinsic to complex systems. The consequence is a profound epistemological shift: rather than striving to reduce uncertainty to risk, entropy encourages financial theory and practice to accept uncertainty as a constitutive element of markets. This shift is not merely technical but philosophical, altering how scholars and practitioners conceptualize knowledge and ignorance in finance.

Another key insight of this chapter is the recognition that entropy captures structural features invisible to variance-based measures. Shannon entropy, Rényi entropy, and transfer entropy reveal not only the distribution of returns but also the diversity of portfolios, the degree of concentration in networks, and the directionality of information flows (Shannon, 1948;

Rényi, 1961; Schreiber, 2000). These dimensions are essential for understanding crises. In the Asian financial crisis of 1997–1998, the decline of informational diversity in capital inflows left economies vulnerable to contagion. In the 2008 global financial crisis, the homogenization of portfolios and the reliance on a narrow set of funding channels eroded systemic entropy, making the entire system brittle (Acharya et al., 2017). During the COVID-19 pandemic, the collapse of diversification across asset classes and supply chains illustrated how entropy falls during global shocks, undermining resilience (Baker et al., 2020). In each case, entropy provides a perspective that is both retrospective and potentially prospective: it explains why crises occurred but also suggests how early-warning indicators might have been constructed.

The comparative discussion of regulatory regimes reinforces this point. In the European Union, where macroprudential oversight is already institutionalized through bodies such as the European Systemic Risk Board, entropy could be integrated into stress testing and risk dashboards, complementing capital ratios and leverage indicators (European Central Bank, 2021). In the United States, where regulatory fragmentation prevails, entropy could unify diverse datasets and provide early signals of systemic fragility for the Financial Stability Oversight Council. In China, with its centralized financial governance and rapid technological transformation, entropy offers a way to map risks in opaque shadow banking and fintech sectors (Hachem & Song, 2016). These comparisons suggest that entropy is adaptable to different institutional contexts, though the pathways of implementation vary. The EU may adopt entropy as part of its culture of precautionary regulation, the U.S. as a supplement to market-based supervision, and China as a tool of centralized control.

The normative implications of entropy are equally significant. By emphasizing diversity and unpredictability as sources of resilience, entropy challenges efficiency-oriented paradigms that often reward concentration and homogeneity. From a governance perspective, entropy suggests that risk culture should shift away from short-term optimization toward long-term adaptability. For practitioners, this means constructing portfolios that maximize informational richness rather than simply minimizing variance. For regulators, it means designing policies that preserve systemic diversity, whether through countercyclical capital buffers, limits on leverage, or incentives for heterogeneous investment strategies. Entropy thus connects with broader debates about financial stability, resilience, and sustainability.

The epistemological reflections developed here are perhaps the most far-reaching. Entropy is not merely a metric; it is a paradigm that redefines how we think about risk and uncertainty. It aligns finance with complexity science, where systems are adaptive, nonlinear, and prone to emergent phenomena (Arthur, 2021). It invites humility by reminding us of the limits of prediction and the inevitability of disorder. It also offers a new language for interdisciplinary dialogue, connecting finance with physics, ecology, and information theory. In ecology, entropy measures biodiversity; in physics, it measures disorder; in finance, it measures uncertainty and systemic fragility. The commonality suggests that entropy can serve as a bridge between disciplines, fostering new insights into resilience and adaptation.

Yet challenges remain. The adoption of entropy in regulation and practice is hindered by issues of data availability, methodological standardization, and interpretability. Estimating entropy in real time requires granular, high-quality data that are not always accessible, especially in opaque markets such as over-the-counter derivatives. Differences in estimation techniques can yield inconsistent results, raising questions of comparability. Moreover, entropy's abstract nature may make it difficult to translate into concrete policy actions. Regulators accustomed to volatility and capital ratios may resist integrating entropy unless it is presented in accessible and actionable terms. Overcoming these barriers will require collaboration among academics, practitioners, and policymakers, as well as the development of standardized protocols for entropy estimation and interpretation.

Despite these obstacles, entropy represents a valuable addition to the financial risk toolkit. Its unique contribution lies in its capacity to capture dimensions of uncertainty and systemic fragility that traditional measures overlook. By quantifying diversity, concentration, and information flows, entropy enriches our understanding of financial systems and provides early-warning indicators of instability. It does not replace established measures but complements them, offering a multidimensional perspective that is particularly relevant in times of crisis.

Looking forward, the entropic paradigm suggests a shift in financial thought and practice. Rather than seeking to eliminate uncertainty, we must learn to live with it, manage it, and even embrace it as a source of adaptability. Rather than pursuing efficiency at the expense of resilience, we must value diversity and redundancy as bulwarks against systemic collapse. Rather than assuming that models can predict the future with certainty, we must accept that unpredictability is a structural feature of markets. Entropy, as both a concept and a metric, embodies this reorientation.

The crises of the past three decades—Asia, 2008, and COVID-19—demonstrate the costs of ignoring systemic entropy. They also show the potential of entropy to illuminate patterns of fragility and contagion. Comparative perspectives across jurisdictions reveal that entropy can be adapted to different regulatory cultures, while epistemological reflections highlight its role in reshaping the very concept of risk. Future research promises to extend entropy into new domains, from climate finance to artificial intelligence, underscoring its relevance for the challenges of the twenty-first century.

In conclusion, entropy and uncertainty are not peripheral considerations but central to understanding finance in an interconnected, volatile, and unpredictable world. They demand that we move beyond the comfort of variance-based models and embrace a more complex, adaptive framework. The task ahead is both scientific and normative: to refine entropy-based tools, validate them empirically, integrate them into regulation, and rethink our philosophical assumptions about risk and uncertainty. If finance is to navigate the turbulent decades ahead—marked by climate change, digital transformation, geopolitical instability, and recurring crises—it will need the language of entropy. This chapter has aimed to show that entropy is not only a technical innovation but also a conceptual revolution, one that redefines how we understand, measure, and govern risk in the global financial system.

REFERENCES

Acharya, V. V., Pedersen, L. H., Philippon, T., & Richardson, M. (2017). Measuring systemic risk. *Review of Financial Studies, 30*(1), 2–47. DOI: 10.1093/rfs/hhw088

Arthur, W. B. (2021). Foundations of complexity economics. *Nature Reviews. Physics, 3*(2), 136–145. DOI: 10.1038/s42254-020-00273-3 PMID: 33728407

Baker, S. R., Bloom, N., Davis, S. J., Kost, K. J., Sammon, M. C., & Viratyosin, T. (2020). The unprecedented stock market reaction to COVID-19. *Review of Asset Pricing Studies, 10*(4), 742–758. DOI: 10.1093/rapstu/raaa008

Battiston, S., Mandel, A., Monasterolo, I., Schütze, F., & Visentin, G. (2017). A climate stress-test of the financial system. *Nature Climate Change, 7*(4), 283–288. DOI: 10.1038/nclimate3255

Battiston, S., Puliga, M., Kaushik, R., Tasca, P., & Caldarelli, G. (2016). Debtrank: Too central to fail? Financial networks, the FED and systemic risk. *Scientific Reports, 2*(1), 541–550. DOI: 10.1038/srep00541 PMID: 22870377

Bekiros, S., Nguyen, D. K., Sandoval, L., & Uddin, G. S. (2017). Information diffusion, cluster formation and entropy-based network dynamics in financial crises. *European Journal of Operational Research, 256*(2), 473–486. DOI: 10.1016/j.ejor.2016.06.024

Bisias, D., Flood, M., Lo, A. W., & Valavanis, S. (2012). A survey of systemic risk analytics. *Annual Review of Financial Economics, 4*(1), 255–296. DOI: 10.1146/annurev-financial-110311-101754

Cai, S., Tian, L., & Zhou, W. (2018). Multiscale entropy analysis of stock markets: Evidence from developed and emerging economies. *Physica A, 503*, 454–463. DOI: 10.1016/j.physa.2018.02.181

Cont, R. (2001). Empirical properties of asset returns: Stylized facts and statistical issues. *Quantitative Finance, 1*(2), 223–236. DOI: 10.1080/713665670

Costa, M., Goldberger, A. L., & Peng, C. K. (2005). Multiscale entropy analysis of complex physiologic time series. *Physical Review Letters, 95*(19), 198102. DOI: 10.1103/PhysRevLett.95.198102 PMID: 16384029

Cover, T. M., & Thomas, J. A. (2006). *Elements of information theory* (2nd ed.). Wiley.

Darbellay, G. A., & Wuertz, D. (2000). The entropy as a tool for analysing statistical dependences in financial time series. *Physica A, 287*(3–4), 429–439. DOI: 10.1016/S0378-4371(00)00382-4

European Central Bank. (2021). *Financial Stability Review*. https://www.ecb.europa.eu/pub/financial-stability/fsr/html/index.en.html

Fang, Y., Lai, K. K., & Wang, S. (2017). Portfolio optimization using relative entropy. *European Journal of Operational Research, 259*(1), 355–365. DOI: 10.1016/j.ejor.2016.10.039

Hachem, K., & Song, Z. (2016). Liquidity regulation and unintended financial transformation in China. *NBER Working Paper No. 21880*. DOI: 10.3386/w21880

Huang, X., Zhou, H., & Zhu, H. (2015). A framework for assessing the systemic risk of major financial institutions. *Journal of Banking & Finance, 79*, 283–296. DOI: 10.1016/j.jbankfin.2015.06.014

IMF. (2016). *Macroprudential policy: Experiences and lessons for Asia and the Pacific*. International Monetary Fund.

Jaynes, E. T. (1957). Information theory and statistical mechanics. *Physical Review, 106*(4), 620–630. DOI: 10.1103/PhysRev.106.620

Johnson, N. F., Zhao, G., Hunsader, E., Meng, J., Ravindar, A., Carran, S., & Tivnan, B. (2013). Abrupt rise of new machine ecology beyond human response time. *Scientific Reports, 3*(1), 2627. DOI: 10.1038/srep02627 PMID: 24022120

Jorion, P. (2007). *Value at risk: The new benchmark for managing financial risk* (3rd ed.). McGraw-Hill.

Knight, F. H. (1921). *Risk, uncertainty, and profit*. Houghton Mifflin.

Kopp, E., Kaffenberger, L., & Wilson, C. (2017). Cyber risk, market failures, and financial stability. *IMF Working Paper WP/17/185.*

Maasoumi, E. (1993). A compendium to information theory in economics and econometrics. *Econometric Reviews*, *12*(2), 137–181. DOI: 10.1080/07474939308800260

Mandelbrot, B. (1963). The variation of certain speculative prices. *The Journal of Business*, *36*(4), 394–419. DOI: 10.1086/294632

Markose, S., Giansante, S., & Shaghaghi, A. R. (2012). 'Too interconnected to fail' financial network of US CDS market: Topological fragility and systemic risk. *Journal of Economic Behavior & Organization*, *83*(3), 627–646. DOI: 10.1016/j.jebo.2012.05.016

Markowitz, H. (1952). Portfolio selection. *The Journal of Finance*, *7*(1), 77–91. DOI: 10.1111/j.1540-6261.1952.tb01525.x

Philippatos, G. C., & Wilson, C. J. (1972). Entropy, market risk, and the selection of efficient portfolios. *Applied Economics*, *4*(3), 209–220. DOI: 10.1080/00036847200000017

Pincus, S. M. (1991). Approximate entropy as a measure of system complexity. *Proceedings of the National Academy of Sciences of the United States of America*, *88*(6), 2297–2301. DOI: 10.1073/pnas.88.6.2297 PMID: 11607165

Prokopenko, M., Boschetti, F., & Ryan, A. J. (2009). An information-theoretic primer on complexity, self-organization, and emergence. *Complexity*, *15*(1), 11–28. DOI: 10.1002/cplx.20249

Rényi, A. (1961). On measures of entropy and information. *Proceedings of the Fourth Berkeley Symposium on Mathematics, Statistics and Probability*, *1*, 547–561.

Richman, J. S., & Moorman, J. R. (2000). Physiological time-series analysis using approximate entropy and sample entropy. *American Journal of Physiology. Heart and Circulatory Physiology*, *278*(6), H2039–H2049. DOI: 10.1152/ajpheart.2000.278.6.H2039 PMID: 10843903

Sandoval, L., & Franca, I. D. P. (2012). Correlation of financial markets in times of crisis. *Physica A, 391*(1–2), 187–208. DOI: 10.1016/j.physa.2011.07.023

Schreiber, T. (2000). Measuring information transfer. *Physical Review Letters, 85*(2), 461–464. DOI: 10.1103/PhysRevLett.85.461 PMID: 10991308

Shannon, C. E. (1948). A mathematical theory of communication. *The Bell System Technical Journal, 27*(3), 379–423. DOI: 10.1002/j.1538-7305.1948.tb01338.x

Sharpe, W. F. (1964). Capital asset prices: A theory of market equilibrium under conditions of risk. *The Journal of Finance, 19*(3), 425–442. DOI: 10.2307/2977928

Taleb, N. N. (2010). *The black swan: The impact of the highly improbable* (2nd ed.). Random House.

Tarashev, N., Borio, C., & Tsatsaronis, K. (2016). Risk attribution using the Shapley value: Methodology and policy applications. *Review of Finance, 20*(3), 1189–1213. DOI: 10.1093/rof/rfv028

Ustaoglu, M. (2018). Entropy as a measure of credit risk: An application to credit default swaps. *Physica A, 503*, 380–388. DOI: 10.1016/j.physa.2018.02.163

Zhao, L., Li, W., & Cai, X. (2018). Entropy-based systemic risk measure of complex financial networks. *Physica A, 503*, 318–329. DOI: 10.1016/j.physa.2018.02.156

Zhou, R., Cai, R., Tong, G., & Wang, Y. (2013). Portfolio selection model based on entropy. *Entropy (Basel, Switzerland), 15*(12), 5338–5351. DOI: 10.3390/e15125338

Zunino, L., Tabak, B. M., Figliola, A., Pérez, D. G., Garavaglia, M., & Rosso, O. A. (2007). A multifractal approach for stock market inefficiency. *Physica A, 376*(1–2), 429–438. DOI: 10.1016/j.physa.2006.10.034

Chapter 3
Transforming the Profession:
The Ethical Challenges in Evolution of Accounting Roles in the Era of Artificial Intelligence

Shefali
Chandigarh University, India

Manjit Kour
https://orcid.org/0000-0003-1043-3187
Chandigarh University, India & North-West University, South Africa

ABSTRACT

The evolution of smart accounting is paramount, given its direct implications for accounting outcomes. Smart accounting complexity has been further accentuated during the COVID-19 pandemic. This crisis presented a prime opportunity to reconfigure the previous accounting systems into integrated frameworks that cater holistically to community needs. As the world shifts, the emphasis is now on achieving improved accounting practices through integrated models, facilitated by technological advancements such as accounting software and artificial intelligence. This chapter

DOI: 10.4018/979-8-3373-3626-8.ch003

delves deep into the robustness and adaptability of artificial intelligence. Technological integrations such as cloud computing, data analytics, fraud detection, and predictive analytics have significantly elevated the efficiency of the accounting system. Furthermore, this chapter explores the synergies between accounting systems and smart accounting tools, underscoring their role in enhancing operational performance.

INTRODUCTION

Nowadays, people are using AI in accounting, also called "smart accounting," which has completely changed the way that financial data is handled, examined, and presented. Because artificial intelligence (AI) accounting systems can process large volumes of data at rates and precisions that far outperform human capabilities. This capacity is raising the accuracy of financial forecasts, risk management, and regulatory compliance as well as increasing the efficiency of financial operations. Many regular processes and works that previously required a lot of manual labour, like data entry, error detection, and compliance checks, have been automated with the introduction of AI accounting technologies. As a result of which, accountant's work is not limited to the technical facets rather, they are now assuming more strategic responsibilities, contributing to high-level decision-making processes and offering deeper financial analysis through the use of AI-driven insights.

As the digital landscape continues to grow, there is a general concern that artificial intelligence (AI) will render traditional jobs obsolete (Rawashdeh, 2023; Sherif & Mohsin, 2021). This worry is especially common among individuals who aspire to become accountants, as they think their field will be eclipsed by the quick advancements in software and technology (Boritz & Stratopoulos, 2023). This is a mistaken belief, though, as the demand for knowledgeable and skilled accountants is rising even in spite of the revolutionary changes brought about by advanced technology (Zhang et al., 2023; Handoko et al., 2019). Many professional accountants are employed by foreign firms, particularly those who were trained by the big corporations. Accountants continue to play an important role in society because they are expected to look at the "bigger picture" while providing financial advice, assessing the financial circumstances of their clients, and emphasizing analytics and other related areas.

The work habits of accountants are changing in cycle with the advancement of technology (Moll & Yigitbasioglu, 2019). Globally, this increase will have a significant influence, particularly on people's personal and professional lives. The increasing number of new technical advances makes it more noticeable (Sherif & Mohsin, 2021). Artificial intelligence (AI) is one of the areas of technology that is growing the fastest (Battina, 2018; Kour & Kaur, 2024). AI is ready to play a significant role in the future since it can mimic human thought processes including communication and decision-making (Zhang et al., 2023). AI can effectively replace individuals in the accounting profession who perform repetitive everyday tasks (Moll & Yigitbasioglu, 2019). Accounting specialists are currently responsible for more than only keeping records and verifying numbers (Han et al., 2023). More subtly, they are about assisting current businesses in making the most of their financial resources. With the advancement of technology, professionals will face new problems, such as focusing solely on adding value to their firms (Bose et al., 2023). The emotional intelligence that people contribute to the workplace cannot be replaced, and here is where accounting professionals play a crucial role (Boritz & Stratopoulos, 2023). Superior information findings can be translated into more effective accounting methods and management by accountants by leveraging their personality qualities.

Technology will also continue to support the profession's reputation as a reliable source of guidance (Allioui & Mourdi, 2023). In response to an international request from the International Federation of Accountants, the Malaysian Institute of Accountants (MIA) in that country has begun preparing for the fourth industrial revolution. Accountants are guided in developing digital technology action plans that are customized for their unique settings. Even though AI cannot completely replace the accounting process, accountants should actively address its implications. The traditional accounting profession involves a number of operations that involve multiple technical sub-tasks, such as manual bookkeeping and accounting. AI is currently being used to take the place of monotonous tasks that accountants frequently complete (Bose et al., 2023). Software is automating routine jobs and manual accounting, which is disappearing

(Larioui & Himran, 2023). Nonetheless, accessing and operating the system remains necessary for the accountant (Kamau & Ilamoya, 2023). However, the accounting industry is also troubled by the high rate of unemployment among entry-level accountants, the growing issue of data breaches, and the growing need for accountants and financial professionals (Kroon & do Céu Alves, 2023).

Understanding the role of accountant in the era of AI is crucial for accounting professionals (Boritz & Stratopoulos, 2023). As a result, accountants must keep up with the latest developments in AI technology in order to remain competitive. Thus, the purpose of this research is to investigate how AI is affecting the accounting industry. The use of traditional accounting has significantly decreased due to the impact of AI technology on the accounting process, which has led to changes in the duties of accountants. And while adopting the AI in Accounting practices, what are the ethical concerns that accountants has to face.

BACKGROUND OF THE STUDY

Figure 1.

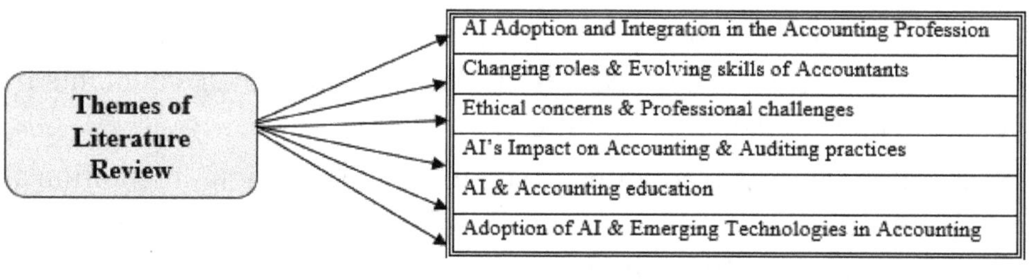

1. AI Adoption and Integration in the Accounting Profession:

Various authors presented their views and have done studies on the integration of Artificial intelligence in the accounting profession. Accountants have accepted the use of Artificial intelligence in their professional work and now accountants need to upgrade their skills and capabilities for their advancements (Salazar-Rebaza et al., 2024). Although the organizational environment, governmental backing, and positive attitude about the adoption of Artificial intelligence in organizations have a favourable effect on adopting AI in accounting (Wael Al et al., 2024) as being prepared for AI adoption can help in embracing AI in accounting (Anh et al., 2024) as training and development becomes more effective with a positive view among employees.

AI can do repetitive task better but to build judgement and to make decision using intellectual and skills, humans are needed. People skills are needed to identify any fraud and predict future challenges as it requires human brain. (Rosário, 2024) which also means that there will be job losses as well which is risky for humans and reduce the human contribution (Abdulhay, 2024; Maffei et al., 2021) still AI can help in doing data analysis in less time and making reports based on the results. That's why through AI auditors can do their work more smartly with for efficiency as well hence its better for auditors to get habitual with AI and ICT (Thottoli, 2024). Using the Technology-Organization-Environment (TOE) framework, cloud computing is found to be leading tool used for accounting instead of Blockchain and Robotic process automation (Baiod et al., 2024). Although AI is beneficial within ERP system still the adoption is lagging behind due to difficulties faced by financial managers (Khamis et al., 2023) while experienced accountants are better at accommodating AI systems than less experienced accountants but training can help freshers and less experienced to adapt with AI in accounting practices (Qatawneh et al., 2023; Grosu et al., 2023). Because of high cost, loss of jobs and lack of trust there is resistance in adopting the AI for Accounting (Vărzaru, 2022). but employees still believe that AI is transforming the accounting world and in upcoming 5 years, accountants has be open with these changes (Bakarich et. al., 2021) as benefits offered by AI adoption such as improved quality of financial statements, accuracy and reliability etc. are far greater than these insecurities faced by accountants (Al-Sammarraee et al., 2021). This all scenario, on one hand shows that how wonderful opportunities are offered by AI adoption in Accounting and Auditing practices but on other hand, it also shows the automation concerns and future role of accounting and auditing professionals (Abukhader, 2020) but to stay relevant, professionals in this field has embrace technology and shift focus on upskilling in decision making areas instead of routine work as today or tomorrow routine work will be overtaken by AI (Mohammad et. Al., 2020).

2. Changing Roles and Evolving Skills of Accountants:

With changes and benefits of AI such as fast tasks competition with better efficiency and better data analysis in less time, AI brought many challenges as well such as cybersecurity risks, high cost of implementing AI in accounting and job losses which results in fear of AI adoption and resistance to change for AI adoption (da Silva et al., 2023) and even if these concerns are ignored. Then also, although AI is changing accounting jobs and better at performing repetitive tasks but understanding the algorithms of AI and Machine learning is very difficult for accountants which makes its adaption hard for them and resist the change of using AI (Faulconbridge et. Al., 2024) still accountants can adopt AI by assuming the role of newer roles like IT specialists or business advisors along with traditional roles as done by Finnish bank's management accountant's (Rautiainen et al., 2024) along with young accountants in Indonesia (Chang et al., 2023) and sometimes accountants has to handle non-financial data as well as part of their job in the non-financial sector such as healthcare hence regular upskilling of Accountants is essential in today's world (Vesty et al., 2024). Modern accountants now expected to assume the roles of business advisors, data scientists, strategic decision-makers, and collaborators of team across departments in an organisation along with traditional roles of number- crunchers (Samanthi et al., 2023). Although (Osei-Assibey et al., 2023) tried to solve the problems accountants face while adopting the AI in accounting practices using Ghana and Nigeria's accountants as samples still the transformation of the Accounting world due to digitalization is uncertain and it's difficult to predict that how this world will look in future is still uncertain (Igou et al., 2023). But the rise of technologies is forcing the accounting profession to adapt quickly to technologies like big data, AI, blockchain, and cloud computing even after all the challenges which is shaping the external business environment as well including the political environment, ecological environment demands and COVID-19 also influenced the needed skills of accountants (Zainuddin et al., 2023). The progress of adopting AI in accounting profession in even more slower in small and medium-sized accounting firms as they can't even afford highly skilled accountants and training also requires funds which are even more limited for them (Gonçalves et al., 2022). Apart from all of these challenges, AI adoption is impacting the accountants on personal level as well. Such as AI adoption is bringing positive change in intellectual and spiritual intelligence of accountant but on other hand it is leaving negative effects on emotional intelligence of accountants (Prianthara et al., 2021). But even in the digitalised world one cannot undermine the importance of human as digital world is here to open new opportunities for human not to eradicate their role but to transform the role and for that accountants need to be upskilled (Korhonen et al., 2021) and for that universities also needs to update their curriculum as it is essential for students not an option anymore (Aldredge et al., 2021) as millennial accountants are already facing the heat of this rapid changes and now they have to learn more about these technical changes to stay relevant and advancing their careers (Handoko et al., 2019).

3. Ethical Concerns and Professional Challenges:

AI brought innovative opportunities for people in accounting firms such as helping small and medium businesses to grow by offering recommendations based on more accurate and efficient data analysis using AI tools (Massaro et al., 2024; Brivot & Cho, 2023) while toning AI with the accounting profession and opening new opportunities such as digital forensic accounting, green accounting (which focus on environmental and social aspects), and system-based auditing (Jaya & Ilahiyah, 2024). In today's highly digitalised world where Robots and Humans are working together, humans face many ethical issues such as privacy, autonomy, security, fairness, and maintaining human dignity, which are all interconnected and create social and ethical risks (Tiron-Tudor et al., 2024) along with that although most accountants have a basic understanding of AI, few fully grasp its complexities. However, ethical considerations are crucial and that regulatory bodies must create guidelines for AI use (Fülöp et al., 2023). In managerial accounting, ethical risks such as data security, privacy, misuse, accessibility, and lack of transparency arises which impacts mainly four main groups i.e., AI developers, managers adopting

AI, accountants, and regulators (Zhang et al., 2023). While solving some pre-existing problems, AI adoption brings some new challenges as well that are shown in ethical concerns like security and trust which strongly influence how users see these technologies but quality factors, particularly reliability, are key to ensuring satisfaction. (Bocean et al., 2022) similarly in small and medium firms on one hand AI offers improved accounting practices with more efficiency but on other hand, AI beings challenges with technological advancements, creating a risk for businesses if their staff is not properly trained (Abdi et al., 2021). Overall, AI adoption can improve transparency, accountability, and accuracy in accounting processes, helping reduce unethical behaviour but while adopting AI, firms may face many ethical risks, and some of these issues requires legal regulations and social interventions (Sherif & Mohsin, 2021).

4. AI's Impact on Accounting and Auditing Practices:

Auditors with an educational background in Artificial Intelligence (AI) impact the speed of producing audit reports as these auditors use their expertise in programming, technology, and logical thinking to improve efficiency and speed (Liao et al., 2024; Smith, 2024) and both accountants and auditors from small firms believes that using AI improves audit quality no major difference is witnessed about how accountants and auditors assess AI's contribution to audit quality (Musa & Lefkir, 2024). Big four accounting frims staff also believe the same i.e., that with AI, audit quality can be improved and accounting firms should adopt AI to improve the accuracy, reliability, and timeliness of financial reporting, making audits more effective (Adeoye et al., 2023). Besides accounting firms, AI adoption impacting many other streams as well like health, education and business. As AI can help in boosting sales, cutting the costs, and improving performance which is automating many workload (Khaled AlKoheji & Al-Sartawi, 2023). Due to automation of the work, accounting processes are becoming self- operating but these processes needs to be verified carefully which has shifted accountants work towards managing instead of manual tasks (Łada, 2023). AI adoption is beneficial for the firms as it causes many advantages such as Cost and time saving, Competitive advantage, Improved Audit quality, better planning and supervision, and Higher efficiency (Aljaaidi et al., 2023). With changing technological environment, Blockchain and AI is transforming the Accounting and Book keeping, and enabling globalization and digitalisation that improve efficiency and make information more flexible (Stafie & Grosu, 2023) still many accountants are not willing to accept the change due to uncertainty that digitalisation possess for future (Silva et al., 2022). But some accountants are optimist as well for the adoption of AI for accounting and believes that AI will improve their work and office condition by doing repetitive tasks in less time and more efficiently which may enable better education and skilled development among accountants and this will help upcoming accountants to thrive in tech driven phase (Holmes & Douglass, 2022). Alongside, AI also improved the accounting quality by reducing mistakes and preventing fraud (Oberoi et al., 2022). Along with these changes, AI also influencing the accounting theories and value creation by integrating AI mechanisms with latest analytical tools. And for that, accountants need to be stay updates with the skills and innovations (Li. et al.., 2020). Now accountants needs to participate in management of the company and undertake management accounting to ignore the problem of job loss and insecurities about adopting AI (Shi, 2020). Instructors needs to include more training on empathic listening in accounting programs to better prepare students for the demands of the profession. Accounting programs should focus more on teaching "soft skills," especially as AI reduces the need for accountants to be the sole source of technical knowledge. (Reddrop & Mapunda, 2019). Bhaskar (1982) made a proposal about inclusion of computers in accounting courses through 26 topics. But this proposal has many short comings (Er & Ng, 1989) like more time is allocated to not-so-important and impractical subjects so a new list was suggested that includes short supervised lab sessions along with PG diploma for accounting graduates to learn AI, computers and information systems in more details.

5. AI and Accounting Education:

With Swift development of AI, many industries are also changing and Technology acceptance model gives foundation about the factors that shows why AI is adopted and these factors includes ease of use, attitude about AI, usefulness, advantages of AI adoption and other external factors (Kayser & Telukdarie, 2024). With advent in accounting like AI, Big data, Blockchain, Cloud and Robotic automation; instead of perceiving these changes as some challenges, accountants can see these changes as opportunity as well to advance and grow their career (Ferreira & Pedrosa, 2024). And accounting educators have understood this now that's why technologies are now transforming the accounting education and courses curriculum as well. Accountants needs to adapt these changes quickly to stay relevant, competitive and financially well otherwise if they won't adapt then they will struggle in maintaining the position and keeping their jobs will be too difficult for them (Aljazeeri & Al-Sartawi, 2023). With AI adoption, the key roles of accountants needs to be redefine so that accountant remain relevant even if AI replace accountants in traditional accounting functions (Ibrahim et al., 2023; Ferreira & Pedrosa, 2023; Meiryani et al., 2022). In healthcare organizations, technologies like artificial intelligence, blockchain, big data, and cloud computing can vividly improve how accounting is done (Vărzaru, 2022). Digitization is not just about the latest technology adoption rather it requires change in mindsets and organizational culture also as accountant's role expanding from maintaining accounts to doing analysts and consultancies job as well (Coman et al., 2022). All accessible technologies should be connected with each process of accounting that will result in cloud platform creating a powerful integrated system solving many challenges about taxation, data storage, errors in accounting etc (Faccia A., 2019).

6. Adoption of AI and Emerging Technologies in Accounting:

Artificial intelligence is here to facilitate the accounting profession and not to replace it. So Accountants needs to accept and adopt the technological advancements (Jaya & Bhuana, 2024). Already adoption of 4IR technologies has enhanced the living standard, easiness in physical work, boosting agricultural productivity, health services, knowledge sharing and reduced the social problems like inequality, environment pollution to achieve Sustainable development goals (Makurumidze et al., 2024). Adoption of AI brings industrial evolution that will ensures that individuals, firms and all other stakeholders will stay competitive and relevant in fast- changing world (Singh et al., 2023) as by AI, the accounting profession is transformed from technical and task oriented work to more skills based and managerial profession (Holmes & Douglass, 2022) hence transforming the required education as well (Moore & Felo, 2022). With AI's application in the Healthcare sector, healthcare supply chain management has already advanced (Thai et al., 2024). So key AI technologies such as cloud computing, big data & blockchain, the accounting field also needs to be transformed (Moll & Yigitbasioglu, 2019). Now investors don't make investment decision solely on the basis of financial statements result, they also see that how companies are adopting the change and flexible to changing environment (Zhao et al., 2004).

MULTILEVEL STUDY ON ARTIFICIAL INTELLIGENCE (AI) ADOPTION IN ACCOUNTING PROFESSION

From the above literature analysis, various ethical and other issues are brought to light. Adopting AI in the Accounting profession, may help and make the accounting profession faster and do the technical work more easily. However various Ethical challenges are faced by different stakeholders while adopting AI in accounting and these ethical issues need to be studied by stakeholders at different levels. On each level, stakeholders faced different challenges than others. The following are the main ethical challenges faced by different stakeholders based on literature review:

1. Individual Level

At individuals upfront, various ethical issues are faced by the accountants, and these issues are discussed as follows:

Biasness: As AI systems are trained on data, and if this data contains biases (e.g., gender, race, or age biases), the AI may make unfair or discriminatory decisions. Hence, Accountants need to detect these discriminations ad biases before making decisions.

Technical knowledge: The AI-based decisions work like a "Black Box" as it use algorithms that are difficult for Accountants to understand

and beyond Accountant skills. Accountants will remain accountable for the decisions made based on AI tools.

Job Displacement: As AI can automate many routine accounting tasks, there is the potential for job losses in the profession, leading to accountants' fears about their future and career.

Over-reliance: With reliance on technology, many tasks and works that used to be performed by professionals easily in earlier times are difficult for technology savage professionals nowadays. Technology is there to make work easy for humans, but it also leads to fear of overreliance on technology.

Dehumanization of the Profession: With AI and technology adoption, the accountancy profession, and every other profession in which AI is adopted, there is a lack of human touch, which is dehumanizing the profession.

Lack of Professional Judgment: Computers and devices are not humans that may make professional judgments; they are just technological machines that may help in making judgments, but judgments need to be made by accountants based on the data analysis and results thereof.

2. Organizational Level

Companies adopting AI in the accounting profession also face various ethical issues and challenges. Some of these issues are recognized from the literature review above as follows:

Data Privacy and Security: AI relies on enormous volumes of sensitive financial and personal data to function effectively which may result in a breach of privacy and security if the data is leaked by someone. And this is happening in the real world nowadays.

Transparency: As AI uses algorithms and AI tools that require programming that is not transparent to everyone, the working of AI cannot be trusted fully. The chances of infringements and violations of organizational rules about usage of the data.

Accountability: If there is any fraud or mishappening or some kind of breach of confidential information, then no one can be held responsible if the work is done by AI as AI is not human. Hence, there is a lack of accountability after the adoption of AI in the Accounting Profession.

Workforce impact: The workforce in the firm which has adopted AI for accountancy, will feel demotivated because of the shift from human to AI. They can perceive it in any way, which can be positive i.e. AI will help them in performing tasks easily and efficiently, or negative, i.e., by adopting AI, an organization might not need all of them in the upcoming future.

Impact on organizational culture: The AI adoption will impact the organizational culture as a whole. As an organization might not need some of the staff who lack technological knowledge, employees might get afraid about their future, which may push them towards easy ways and unethical practices out of insecurity about their future and career.

Misuse of AI for manipulations: AI functions are not standardized worldwide, which may lead to manipulation and interpretation of AI according to user interest and capability. Hence, users and developers can interpret and manipulate AI's work according to their interests, which may not be in line with organizational interests.

Long-Term Sustainability: As AI is a new and ever-changing technology, its future cannot be forecasted or predicted. Hence, it becomes difficult for companies and organizations to predict the sustainability of AI and its outcomes after its adoption.

3. Industry Level

Industry consists of firms working in the same or similar field. When a change comes in the business environment, it will also impact the industry. With the advent of AI, the following are the challenges that the accounting industry has to face:

Regulatory Gaps and Compliance: Accounting standards represent a standardized form of practice that accountants need to follow while preparing and maintaining accounts. There is no such standard practice now regarding AI work. Without regulation and compliance, AI cannot be trusted with the function of accounting.

Risk of Widespread Bias: As AI is trained based on available data, the biases in the information from various authors may come into the AI database as well which is difficult to recognize as well. With authors and some recognized party of information, the business can be recognized with that person only. But in the case of AI which is based on widespread information, the biasness cannot be detected.

Global Inequality and Access to AI: AI adoption requires vast resources and skilled manpower which is not possible for small and medium-level firms. Hence, where many big firms and MNCs have adopted AI in their accountancy, medium and small firms struggle to do the same. But with the adoption of AI, big firms who are already more efficient than their developing and smaller counterparts can increase their efficiency which increases the already existing inequality and division among firms' operations.

Job Shift Across the Industry: AI adoption requires a different set of skills than traditional accounting skills. This means either the industry has to replace the existing workforce with a new tech-savvy workforce or train the existing workforce with new technologies to perform the new-age operations efficiently.

Cybersecurity Risks and Data Breaches: With the new technology adoption, although the functions and repetitive tasks are becoming easier to perform this adoption is posing a new set of risks and threats as well. These threats can have severe consequences that include cybersecurity risks and data breaches, especially for not-so-tech-savvy audiences and customers.

Monopoly by AI Vendors: With the adoption of AI in Accountancy, accounting firms will become more dependent on AI vendors. Where there are three main components of accounting firms i.e. employees, owners, and customers. There is a new cluster of stakeholders i.e. AI vendors. With these AI vendors, accounting firms can become overly dependent on them resulting in the monopoly of AI vendors over others' satisfaction and role.

4. Societal Level

Many people are working in the accounting industry making it an indispensable part of society. And with AI emerging as the new lead in the accounting industry, this is also having some impact on society as a whole. It's important to analyze how the emerging AI technology and adoption of AI in accounting practices are impacting society. Following are some of the societal impacts of AI adoption in accounting that have been recognized from the literature:

Erosion of Public Trust in Institutions: Accounting systems driven by AI can result in declining public trust in financial institutions and regulatory bodies if they are not regulated properly. Because decisions made by AI don't have human judgment and ethical reflections. The cases of AI-driven accounting errors and scams in financial audits may create doubt among the public and weaken confidence in corporate governance and regulatory institutions.

Accessibility and Digital Divide: With the increasing adoption of AI in accounting, the existing divide and difference between the technological environment of a small firm and a big firm will be deepened rather than reduced. It will be difficult for small and emerging economies to adopt AI easily, as it requires a skilled and well-trained workforce, which is not affordable for small firms. This divide exacerbates economic inequality, as only those with technological resources can fully benefit from AI-enhanced financial tools.

Impact on Financial Literacy: Due to increasing dependence on AI, individuals no longer manually do complex tasks and use AI, as AI is much more efficient in doing complex tasks and financial processes. This results in over-reliance on AI and ultimately decreases people's ability to critically assess financial information. This poses a risk, particularly if individuals make actual financial decisions based on the output of AI without understanding the financial concepts and affecting their financial literacy abilities.

Manipulation of Financial Data: AI's abilities can be both used and misused. On one side, it offers efficiency and time-saving in doing repeated tasks; on the other hand, people can misuse it for malicious and fraudulent activities, such as insider trading AI-generated financial statements to mislead investors, corporate scandals, etc. AI could be used to destabilize transparency and fairness in financial markets.

Global Inequalities: Developed and big multinational corporations can integrate AI-powered accounting and auditing in their corporate culture as they have enough resources available for it. But the same can't be said for Small or developing corporations. As the resources are limited for them, it becomes very difficult for these small enterprises to accommodate AI-powered accounting in their system. It's all leading to further increasing global inequalities.

Dependence on Big Tech: As AI-driven accounting will be dominated by Big tech companies because of more availability of funds, it will lead to dependence of small firms on Big companies. And if any change in regulations or policies is made, it will lead to disruption in the financial system all over the world. Hence, these dependencies will make small and medium firms more vulnerable in the face of Big Tech companies.

Public Awareness and Education: When public bestows financial information for accounting services, they also bestows confidence in the accountant or service provider that their information will be kept confidential as it should be. With AI-driven accounting services, this confidence in service providers and the confidentiality needs public awareness & education about this issue, otherwise the public may be susceptible to misinformation, financial scams, or unethical financial practices.

5. Regulatory Level

The integration of Artificial Intelligence (AI) in accounting presents significant challenges and opportunities for regulatory bodies. Regulators must adapt to the rapid pace of AI-driven transformations while ensuring ethical, legal, and financial stability. The following key areas highlight the impact of AI adoption in accounting at the regulatory level:

Regulatory Lag: Traditional accounting and financial regulations were made for human decision-making processes, whereas AI introduces new complications that create ambiguities leading to unethical financial practices to flourish before some regulations may be established to tackle it. So, regulators must take proactive actions and make policies flexible enough to evolve along with and in sync of AI spreads.

Accountability and Liability: Accountability is necessary to foster trust, improve performance, rectify mistakes, and encourage responsibility. Like humans, AI can't be held accountable for errors or misstatements. Regulatory bodies must establish clear accountability frameworks that outline the legal responsibility for AI-driven financial outcomes, ensuring that it does not become a tool for avoiding responsibility.

Standardization Across Jurisdictions: Accounting practices, standards, financial regulations, and laws vary across countries and regions. But as AI adoption in accounting is global, regulators must collaborate to develop harmonized AI governance standards that may ensure consistent standards, fraud detection, taxation and financial practices while respecting jurisdictional differences.

Balancing Innovation and Oversight: Regulators face new challenges in designing laws and regulations that provide a business environment for companies to grow further and make more technological advances, but they should also be stringent enough to maintain accountability and prevent financial misconduct.

Resource Constraints: With adoption, AI poses some serious threats that must be checked. Regulators must invest in AI-driven auditing tools, upskill their workforce, and collaborate with AI experts to effectively monitor and enforce compliance in AI-driven accounting systems.

THEORIES ABOUT TECHNOLOGY ADOPTION

Over the period, various theories have been developed about how technology is adopted. While adopting technology, stakeholders go through various stages and these stages and ideas need to be discussed. Following are the theories about the adoption of technology. They explored how and why individuals, organizations, or societies adopt and integrate new technologies into their routines and processes. Based on the literature review, we have the following findings regarding theses adoption theories:

1. **Technology Acceptance Model (TAM)** developed by Davis (1989)
   - **Perceived Usefulness (PU):** Although the accountants know that adopting AI will benefit them a lot and will reduce their work, particularly the repetitive nature of work and tasks. Still, Accountants are reluctant the adopt of AI in their jobs as they think that by AI, they might lose job opportunities and budding accountants have to face adversities in finding jobs and building their career in the accounting field.
   - **Perceived Ease of Use (PEOU):** With the adoption of AI in the day-to-day work, the accountant's work will reduce enormously and this will benefit them a lot. Hence, to ease their job, accountants need to adopt AI in their jobs.
2. **Unified Theory of Acceptance and Use of Technology (UTAUT)** developed by Venkatesh et al. (2003)
   - **Performance Expectancy:** Accountants and firms expect that AI will perform repetitive tasks better and faster with much more accuracy than the manual performance of the same tasks but by performing these tasks through technology, the accountants may lose their basic understanding which will impact their decisions adversely.
   - **Effort Expectancy:** The effort required in accountancy after AI adoption is much less than the effort required for doing everything manually but for adopting AI, accountants need to have technical knowledge and should learn programming, algorithms, and various tools used in AI. This makes the adoption difficult for non-tech-savvy accountants.
   - **Social Influence:** Society trusts tasks performed by machines and technology more than tasks performed by a person. But as Machines and technology cannot be held responsible and accountable for any breach of privacy, it pushes society away from AI technology adoption. With AI performing tasks, it requires data and information as well, which may be confidential for people. But AI is not accountable for privacy.
   - **Facilitating Conditions:** For large firms and MNCs, organizational and technical infrastructure supports the adoption of AI and these business organizations can adopt the AI effective-

ly because of the prevalent infrastructure required for the AI adoption. But in the case of small and medium firms, neither they need infrastructure nor they can afford the required technical staff for AI adoption. Hence, AI has been adopted by many big firms and MNCs already, but medium and small firms lag behind in adopting the AI in Accounting field.

CONCLUSION

While AI enhances efficiency, accuracy, and decision-making capabilities, it simultaneously raises significant ethical challenges, such as data privacy concerns, algorithmic biases, accountability dilemmas, and the potential erosion of professional judgment. The evolution of accounting roles necessitates a recalibration of ethical frameworks to address these challenges effectively.

As accountants increasingly rely on AI-driven systems, the profession must uphold ethical principles by fostering transparency, ensuring algorithmic fairness, and maintaining a balance between automation and human oversight. Regulatory bodies and professional organizations have a pivotal role in setting guidelines that integrate technological advancements with ethical integrity. Furthermore, continuous education and training in AI-related ethics are essential to prepare accounting professionals for the dynamic and complex environments they now operate in.

In conclusion, the integration of AI in accounting is not merely a technological shift but a profound ethical evolution. By proactively addressing these challenges, the profession can not only adapt to the era of AI but also enhance its relevance and trustworthiness in the digital age.

REFERENCES

Abdi M.D., & Bayu K.B. (2021). Exploring current opportunity and threats of Artificial intelligence on small and medium enterprises accounting function: Evidence from South West part of Ethiopia, Oromiya, Jimma and SNNPR, Bonga. Academy of Accounting and Financial Studies Journal, 25(2), 1-11.

Abukhader S.M. (2020). Extent of artificial intelligence into accounting and auditing work - An analytical attempt of job and duties. International Journal of Business Process Integration and Management, 10(2), 125-136. .DOI: 10.1504/IJBPIM.2020.117165

Adeoye, I. O., Akintoye, R. I., Theophilus, A. A., & Olagunju, O. A. (2023). Artificial intelligence and audit quality: Implications for practicing accountants. *Asian Economic and Financial Review*, *13*(11), 756–772, 23052147. DOI: 10.55493/5002.v13i11.4861

Al-Sammarraee A., & Alshareeda N. (2021). The role of artificial intelligence by using automatic accounting information system in supporting the quality of financial statement. Information Sciences Letters, 10(2), 223-254. .DOI: 10.18576/isl/100208

Al Wael, H., Abdallah, W., Ghura, H., & Buallay, A. (2024). Factors influencing artificial intelligence adoption in the accounting profession: The case of public sector in Kuwait. *Competitiveness Review*, *34*(1), 3–27, 10595422. DOI: 10.1108/CR-09-2022-0137

Aldredge, M., Rogers, C., & Smith, J. (2021). The strategic transformation of accounting into a learned profession. *Industry and Higher Education*, *35*(2), 83–88, 9504222. DOI: 10.1177/0950422220954319

Aljaaidi K.S., Alwadani N.F., & Adow A.H. (2023). The impact of artificial intelligence applications on the performance of accountants and audit firms in Saudi Arabia. International Journal of Data and Network Science, 7(3), 1165-1178. .DOI: 10.5267/j.ijdns.2023.5.007

Baiod, W., & Hussain, M. M. (2024). The impact and adoption of emerging technologies on accounting: Perceptions of Canadian companies. *International Journal of Accounting and Information Management, 18347649*(4), 557–592. Advance online publication. DOI: 10.1108/IJAIM-05-2023-0123

Battina, D. S. (2018). The future of artificial intelligence at work: A review on effects of decision automation and augmentation on workers targeted by algorithms and third-party observers. *International Journal of Innovations in Engineering Research and Technology*, *5*(7).

Boritz, J. E., & Stratopoulos, T. C. (2023). AI and the Accounting Profession: Views from Industry and Academia. *Journal of Information Systems*, *37*(3), 1–9. DOI: 10.2308/ISYS-2023-054

Bose, S., Dey, S. K., & Bhattacharjee, S. (2023). Big data, data analytics and artificial intelligence in accounting: An overview. Handbook of Big Data Research Methods. DOI: 10.4337/9781800888555.00007

Coman, D. M., Ionescu, C. A., Duică, A., Coman, M. D., Uzlau, M. C., Stanescu, S. G., & State, V. (2022). Digitization of Accounting: The Premise of the Paradigm Shift of Role of the Professional Accountant. *Applied Sciences (Basel, Switzerland)*, *12*(7), 20763417. DOI: 10.3390/app12073359

Faulconbridge, J. R., Sarwar, A., & Spring, M. (2024). Accommodating Machine Learning Algorithms in Professional Service Firms. *Organization Studies*, *1708406*(7), 1009–1037. Advance online publication. DOI: 10.1177/01708406241252930

Fülöp, M. T., Topor, D. I., Ionescu, C. A., Cifuentes-Faura, J., & Măgda , N. (2023). Ethical concerns associated with Artificial Intelligence in the Accounting profession: A curse or a blessing? *Journal of Business Economics and Management*, *24*(2), 387–404. DOI: 10.3846/jbem.2023.19251

Gonçalves, M. J. A., da Silva, A. C. F., & Ferreira, C. G. (2022). The Future of Accounting: How Will Digital Transformation Impact the Sector? *Informatics (MDPI)*, *9*(1), 22279709. DOI: 10.3390/informatics9010019

Grosu, V., Cosmulese, C. G., Socoliuc, M., Ciubotariu, M. S., & Mihaila, S. (2023). Testing accountants' perceptions of the digitization of the profession and profiling the future professional. *Technological Forecasting and Social Change*, *193*, 122630. DOI: 10.1016/j.techfore.2023.122630

Han, H., Shiwakoti, R. K., Jarvis, R., Mordi, C., & Botchie, D. (2023). Accounting and auditing blockchain review. International technology and artificial Intelligence: A literature review. *Journal of Accounting Information Systems*, *48*, 100598. DOI: 10.1016/j.accinf.2022.100598

Handoko, B. L., Mulyawan, A. N., Samuel, J., Rianty, K. K., & Gunawa, S. (2019). Facing Industry Revolution 4.0 for Millennial Accountants. *International Journal of Innovative Technology and Exploring Engineering*, *9*(1), 1037–1042. DOI: 10.35940/ijitee.A4681.119119

Holmes, A. F., & Douglass, A. (2022). Artificial Intelligence: Reshaping the Accounting Profession and the Disruption to Accounting Education. *Journal of Emerging Technologies in Accounting*, *19*(1), 53–68, 15541908. DOI: 10.2308/JETA-2020-054

Jaya, I.M.L.M., & Ilahiyah, M.E. (2024). Harmonizing accounting and artificial intelligence for the sustainability of the accounting profession. Artificial Intelligence Approaches to Sustainable Accounting, 214-228. .DOI: 10.4018/979-8-3693-0847-9.ch012

Kamau, C. G., & Ilamoya, S. L. (2023). Accounting profession: African perspective review of steps into the future. *Multidisciplinary Journal of TUM*, *2*(1), 19–26. DOI: 10.48039/mjtum.v2i1.43

Korhonen, T., Selos, E., Laine, T., & Suomala, P. (2021). Exploring the programmability of management accounting work for increasing automation: An interventionist case study. *Accounting, Auditing & Accountability Journal*, *34*(2), 253–280, 9513574. DOI: 10.1108/AAAJ-12-2016-2809

Kour, M., & Kour, R. (2024). AI and Influencer Marketing: Redefining the Future of Social Media Marketing in Industry 6.0. In Advanced Businesses in Industry 6.0 (pp. 87-103). IGI Global DOI: 10.4018/979-8-3693-3108-8.ch007

Kroon, N., & do Céu Alves, M. (2023). Examining the fit between supply and demand of the accounting professional's competencies: A systematic literature review. *International Journal of Management Education*, *21*(3), 100872. DOI: 10.1016/j.ijme.2023.100872

Larioui, A., & Himran, M. (2023). Impact of Artificial Intelligence on Operational Management and Accounting. *La Revue des Sciences Commerciales*, *22*(1), 22–44.

Liao, F.-N., Zhang, C., Zhang, J.-J., Yan, X., & Chen, T.-X. (2024). Hyperbole or reality? The effect of auditors' AI education on audit report timeliness. *International Review of Financial Analysis*, *91*, 10575219. DOI: 10.1016/j.irfa.2023.103050

Makurumidze, S., Sifile, O., Twesige, D., Gasheja, F., Gwangwava, E., Matowanyika, K., Chinofunga, S., Mbizi, R., & Sunday, K. (2024). Leveraging on the fourth industrial revolution by African accountants in the sustenance of SDGs and AU Agenda 2063. *Sustainable Development*, *9680802*. Advance online publication. DOI: 10.1002/sd.3110

Moll J., & Yigitbasioglu O. (2019). The role of internet-related technologies in shaping the work of accountants: New directions for accounting research. The British Accounting Review, 51(6), 8908389. DOI: 10.1016/j.bar.2019.04.002

Moore, W. B., & Felo, A. (2022). The evolution of accounting technology education: Analytics to STEM. *Journal of Education for Business*, *97*(2), 105–111, 8832323. DOI: 10.1080/08832323.2021.1895045

Musa, A.M.H., & Lefkir, H. (2024). The role of artificial intelligence in achieving auditing quality for small and medium enterprises in the Kingdom of Saudi Arabia. International Journal of Data and Network Science, 8(2), 835-844. .DOI: 10.5267/j.ijdns.2023.12.021

OECD. (2021). Artificial Intelligence, Machine Learning and Big Data in Finance: Opportunities, Challenges, and Implications for Policy Makers. https://www.oecd.org/finance/financial-markets/Artificial-intelligence-machine-learning-big- data-in-finance.pdf

Osei-Assibey Bonsu, M., Wang, Y., & Guo, Y. (2023). Does fintech lead to better accounting practices? Empirical evidence. *Accounting Research Journal*, *36*(2/3), 129–147, 10309616. DOI: 10.1108/ARJ-07-2022-0178

Pauceanu, A. M., Rabie, N., & Moustafa, A. (2020). Employability under the Fourth Industrial Revolution. *Economics & Sociology (Ternopil)*, *13*(3), 269–283. DOI: 10.14254/2071-789X.2020/13-3/17

Prianthara, I. B. T., Darmawan, N., Adriati, I. G. A. W., & Munidewi, I. A. B. (2021). Emotional Intelligence, Intellectual Intelligence, And Spiritual Intelligence Towards Professional Quality Of Accountant Development Artificial Intelligence As A Moderating Variable In The Era Of Industrial Revolution 4.0. *Academy of Strategic Management Journal*, *20*, 1–15.

Rautiainen, A., Scapens, R. W., Järvenpää, M., Auvinen, T., & Sajasalo, P. (2024). Towards fluid role identity of management accountants: A case study of a Finnish bank. *The British Accounting Review*, *56*(4), 8908389. DOI: 10.1016/j.bar.2024.101341

Rawashdeh A. (2023). The consequences of artificial intelligence: an investigation into the impact of AI on job displacement in accounting. Journal of Science and Technology Policy Management. DOI: 10.1108/JSTPM-02-2023-0030

Salazar-Rebaza C., Chujutalli J.F., Ríos-Sánchez N., Salazar-Quispe A., & Cordova-Buiza F. (2024). Artificial intelligence in accounting as seen by accountants. RISTI - Revista Iberica de Sistemas e Tecnologias de Informacao, E69, 676-686.

Samanthi D., & Gooneratne T. (2023). Bean counter to value-adding business partner: the changing role of the accountant and situated rationality in a multinational firm. Journal of Accounting and Organizational Change, 19(3), 513-535. .DOI: 10.1108/JAOC-04-2022-0063

Sherif, K., & Mohsin, H. (2021). The effect of emergent technologies on accountant's ethical blindness. *The International Journal of Digital Accounting Research*, *21*, 61–94, 15778517. DOI: 10.4192/1577-8517-v21_3

Thottoli, M. M. (2024). Leveraging information communication technology (ICT) and artificial intelligence (AI) to enhance auditing practices. *Accounting Research Journal*, *37*(2), 134–150, 10309616. DOI: 10.1108/ARJ-09-2023-0269

Tiron-Tudor, A., Rodgers, W., & Deliu, D. (2024). The accounting profession in the Twilight Zone: Navigating digitalisation's sided challenges through ethical pathways for decision-making. *Accounting, Auditing & Accountability Journal*, *9513574*. Advance online publication. DOI: 10.1108/AAAJ-12-2022-6173

Vărzaru, A. A. (2022). Assessing Digital Transformation of Cost Accounting Tools in Healthcare. *International Journal of Environmental Research and Public Health*, *19*(23), 16617827. DOI: 10.3390/ijerph192315572 PMID: 36497649

Zhang C., Zhu W., Dai J., Wu Y., & Chen X. (2023). Ethical impact of artificial intelligence in managerial accounting. International Journal of Accounting Information Systems, 49, 100619. DOI: 10.1016/j.accinf.2023.100619

Chapter 4
Future of Management: From Traditional Models to AI-Driven Governance

Diana Andreea Mândricel
https://orcid.org/0009-0009-0179-7887
Titu Maiorescu University, Romania

ABSTRACT

The future of management is shaped by the convergence of traditional governance models with artificial intelligence (AI). Classical approaches relied on hierarchy, standardized procedures, and human judgment, yet they often prove inadequate in volatile and complex environments. AI-driven governance introduces real-time analytics, adaptive decision-making, and predictive capabilities that extend managerial rationality beyond human limits. Algorithms can optimize resource allocation, monitor performance, and simulate strategic scenarios, offering new forms of organizational efficiency. However, these innovations raise concerns of accountability, transparency, and ethical legitimacy. This chapter explores the transition toward AI-supported governance and argues that the future of management lies in hybrid models, where technological efficiency is balanced with human oversight, contextual awareness, and long-term institutional trust.

DOI: 10.4018/979-8-3373-3626-8.ch004

INTRODUCTION

Management as a discipline and practice has always evolved in response to technological, social, and economic change. The rise of industrial capitalism in the late nineteenth and early twentieth centuries gave birth to scientific management, bureaucracy, and the administrative theories that defined the modern firm. These models emphasized stability, predictability, and control, relying on standardized procedures and hierarchical authority to ensure efficiency (Taylor, 1911; Weber, 1978). They were well suited to environments in which demand was stable, competition was relatively contained, and production processes could be optimized through routinization. Over the course of the twentieth century, variations on these models—management by objectives, total quality management, and lean production—emerged, each adjusting to new industrial challenges but maintaining the underlying logic of human-led coordination and rational planning (Drucker, 1954; Womack & Jones, 2003).

By the turn of the twenty-first century, however, it was increasingly clear that these traditional frameworks faced significant limitations. Organizations operated in environments characterized by volatility, uncertainty, complexity, and ambiguity—what scholars and practitioners often describe as *VUCA conditions* (Bennett & Lemoine, 2014). Globalization created interdependencies that amplified systemic risks, while digitalization introduced unprecedented volumes of data and accelerated communication. Crises such as the 2008 global financial meltdown, the COVID-19 pandemic, and escalating climate disruptions underscored the fragility of governance systems built for stability rather than adaptability (Tooze, 2021). Within this context, scholars began to ask whether management, as traditionally conceived, could still serve as a reliable foundation for decision-making.

Artificial intelligence (AI) has emerged as the most recent and arguably most transformative force in this debate. No longer confined to laboratories or niche applications, AI is now integral to organizational life. Firms deploy predictive analytics in supply chains, algorithmic trading systems in financial markets, natural language processing tools in customer relations, and machine learning models in credit assessment and human resource management. These technologies are not simply auxiliary tools: they fundamentally reshape decision-making by processing massive datasets, uncovering patterns invisible to humans, and in some cases acting autonomously in real time (Brynjolfsson & McAfee, 2017; Raisch & Krakowski, 2021). This diffusion of algorithmic agency into governance challenges the basic assumptions of traditional management theory.

The promise of AI-driven governance lies in its ability to extend rationality beyond human cognitive limits. Traditional models relied on bounded rationality, constrained by the limits of human attention and the quality of available information (Simon, 1947). AI expands these boundaries by integrating real-time data from diverse sources, simulating alternative futures, and continuously updating its outputs as conditions change (Chen et al., 2023). From this perspective, AI augments managerial capacity by enabling more accurate forecasting, more efficient resource allocation, and more adaptive responses to uncertainty. Organizations can, at least in principle, become more resilient by embedding AI into their governance systems.

Yet alongside these promises come significant challenges. Algorithms are not neutral instruments but socio-technical systems shaped by the data on which they are trained, the objectives defined by their designers, and the institutional contexts in which they are deployed (Crawford, 2021). As a result, AI systems can reproduce historical biases, obscure accountability, and create new vulnerabilities. Black-box models, in particular, undermine transparency by making it difficult for managers, employees, and regulators to understand why specific decisions are made (Burrell, 2016; Rudin, 2022). The diffusion of algorithmic decision-making therefore raises fundamental questions of legitimacy: who is responsible when an AI-supported decision causes harm, and how can organizations ensure that technological efficiency does not come at the expense of ethical oversight and human dignity?

The contrast between traditional and AI-driven governance reflects a deeper epistemological transformation. Traditional management theories were grounded in assumptions of linear causality, stable environments, and rational actors. They emphasized planning, control, and incremental improvement. AI-driven governance, by contrast, operates on probabilistic reasoning, dynamic adaptation, and continuous recalibration. It thrives in environments where uncertainty and complexity are pervasive, not by eliminating them but by exploiting patterns within them. For example, while traditional forecasting relies on historical data and stable trends, machine learning models can process vast, heterogeneous datasets to identify correlations that evolve in real time (Jordan & Mitchell, 2015). This shift from deterministic to probabilistic rationality changes not only how decisions are made but also how value, risk, and opportunity are defined within organizations.

The implications for authority and accountability are profound. In traditional governance, authority was hierarchically located, with managers accountable to boards and boards accountable to shareholders or other stakeholders. AI redistributes authority across socio-technical networks in which algorithms, developers, regulators, and managers all play a role. This diffusion complicates accountability. If an algorithm recommends discriminatory hiring practices because of biased training data, is the fault with the designer, the dataset, the manager who approved the recommendation, or the organization that deployed the system (Bartlett et al., 2022; Mehrabi et al., 2021)? Such questions highlight the need for governance frameworks that can account for distributed and hybrid forms of agency.

Organizational culture also requires reconsideration. Traditional models of management assumed that culture could be shaped by leadership through norms, incentives, and rituals. But when AI systems monitor performance, evaluate behavior, and provide feedback in real time, they influence culture directly. Employee experiences of algorithmic monitoring have been shown to produce both efficiency gains and heightened feelings of surveillance (Mateescu & Nguyen, 2019). Trust in organizations may be undermined if workers feel reduced to data points or if decision-making appears opaque. Conversely, when AI is deployed transparently and with clear boundaries, it can support cultures of adaptability and continuous learning. The challenge is to embed AI in ways that respect employee dignity while enhancing organizational performance.

The integration of AI into governance also reconfigures the global geography of management. Traditional models were largely national or regional in scope, shaped by specific institutional contexts. AI, however, operates on transnational infrastructures, integrating data and decision-making across borders. This produces new tensions between global efficiency and local accountability. For example, a credit scoring algorithm developed in the

U.S. may be deployed in emerging markets without adequate sensitivity to cultural and institutional differences, leading to distorted valuations or unintended discrimination (Narayanan, 2023). At the same time, jurisdictions are pursuing divergent approaches to AI governance: the EU emphasizes precaution and human rights, the U.S. prioritizes innovation and flexibility, and China integrates AI into state-led industrial policy (Huang & Pierri, 2022). These differences shape not only regulatory compliance but also organizational legitimacy in different markets.

Strategically, AI shifts the basis of competitive advantage. Traditional theories emphasized tangible resources, capabilities, and market positioning (Barney, 1991). Today, data, algorithms, and digital infrastructures increasingly determine competitiveness. Firms that control large, high-quality datasets and possess advanced AI capabilities can leverage predictive insights, optimize operations, and innovate at scale. This raises concerns about concentration of power, as a small number of technology firms dominate AI development and data infrastructures (Zuboff, 2019). For management, the challenge is to harness AI while avoiding dependency on monopolistic platforms and ensuring that competitive strategies remain adaptable to changing technological and regulatory landscapes.

Finally, the ethical dimension of AI-driven governance must be foregrounded. Bias, fairness, and inclusivity are not peripheral concerns but central to legitimacy. Traditional management relied on human judgment, which was biased but open to contestation. Algorithmic bias, by contrast, may be hidden within code and data, making it more difficult to detect and challenge (Mehrabi et al., 2021). Future governance models must therefore institutionalize mechanisms for algorithmic auditing, participatory oversight, and accountability. Ethical AI in management is not only a technical challenge but also a governance imperative, requiring new institutional arrangements that integrate technical expertise with democratic values.

This chapter situates the transition from traditional to AI-driven governance within this broader context of epistemic, institutional, and cultural transformation. It argues that the future of management lies not in replacing human judgment with algorithms but in developing hybrid governance systems that combine the computational power of AI with the contextual awareness, ethical responsibility, and legitimacy of human oversight. The following sections will analyze the trajectory from hierarchies to algorithms, the opportunities and risks of AI-driven governance, and the emerging hybrid models that balance technological efficiency with human accountability.

FROM TRADITIONAL MANAGEMENT TO AI-DRIVEN HYBRID GOVERNANCE

The history of management is often narrated as a steady evolution of organizational forms, from early hierarchical structures to increasingly flexible and networked models. Traditional management relied on clear hierarchies, vertical authority, and standardized processes to achieve efficiency and predictability. These systems were deeply embedded in industrial economies, where mass production and economies of scale required centralized coordination. However, the rise of digitalization and, more recently, artificial intelligence (AI) is fundamentally reconfiguring how organizations govern themselves. The transition from hierarchies to algorithms marks not only a technological change but also an epistemological and cultural shift in the very foundations of management.

Hierarchical management emerged in the late nineteenth and early twentieth centuries as industrial firms sought to coordinate increasingly complex production processes. Max Weber's analysis of bureaucracy captured the logic of this system: authority was legitimized by formal rules, tasks were divided into specialized functions, and decisions were made by those occupying superior positions in a clear chain of command (Weber, 1947). Hierarchy promised efficiency, impartiality, and stability. In practice, it allowed firms to mobilize large workforces and standardize output. Yet scholars have long noted that bureaucratic rigidity hampers innovation and responsiveness, particularly in volatile environments (Gouldner, 1954). The limits of hierarchy became increasingly visible as firms confronted globalization, digitization, and rapid technological change.

The advent of algorithmic governance represents a profound departure from these earlier models. Algorithms are not simply tools; they are systems of classification, prioritization, and action that can operate autonomously across organizational processes. In logistics, AI systems optimize routes and inventory in real time. In finance, algorithmic trading executes orders faster than any human could. In human resources, machine learning models rank applicants and predict turnover risks. These applications do more than augment human decision-making—they redistribute authority from managers to socio-technical systems (Kellogg et al., 2020). As algorithms take on roles previously reserved for middle managers, the vertical layers of hierarchy begin to flatten, while decision-making becomes more distributed and data-driven.

This transition has sparked debates about the future of managerial authority. On one hand, algorithms promise to eliminate inefficiencies associated with hierarchical bottlenecks. By processing information at scale and speed, they allow organizations to bypass lengthy chains of approval and empower local actors with real-time insights (Davenport & Ronanki, 2018). On the other hand, algorithms raise new questions of accountability. In hierarchical models, responsibility was clearly assigned to managers at each level. In algorithmic systems, responsibility is more diffuse: when a model produces a biased decision, who is accountable—the data scientist, the executive who approved its use, or the system itself (Kroll et al., 2017)? The clarity of hierarchy is replaced by the opacity of code, complicating traditional notions of managerial responsibility.

One of the most striking consequences of algorithmic governance is the transformation of coordination. In hierarchical systems, coordination depended on managerial oversight, reporting lines, and standardized procedures. In algorithmic systems, coordination emerges from data flows and predictive analytics. For example, ride-sharing platforms coordinate thousands of drivers and riders not through supervisors but through algorithmic matching and surge pricing mechanisms (Rosenblat, 2018). This illustrates a new form of "algorithmic Taylorism," where tasks are broken down, optimized, and monitored not by foremen but by software. Critics argue that such systems may intensify control, limit worker autonomy while obscuring managerial power behind the neutrality of code (Zuboff, 2015). The rhetoric of decentralization often masks new forms of algorithmic centralization, where platform owners hold unprecedented power over participants.

At the same time, algorithms introduce forms of flexibility that hierarchies struggled to provide. Traditional management models often lagged in responding to shifts in demand or disruptions in supply chains. Algorithmic governance, by contrast, enables rapid recalibration. During the COVID-19 pandemic, firms with AI-enabled supply chains were better able to anticipate disruptions and reallocate resources dynamically (Choi et al., 2021). Algorithms' capacity for continuous adaptation represents a major advantage in environments characterized by uncertainty. Yet this adaptability depends on the quality and scope of data. Where data is biased, incomplete, or manipulated, algorithmic systems can reproduce and amplify errors, leading to systemic fragility rather than resilience (O'Neil, 2016).

The epistemological shift from hierarchies to algorithms also transforms the role of managers. In hierarchical systems, managers were decision-makers and supervisors, interpreting information and directing subordinates. In algorithmic systems, managers increasingly become curators of data and overseers of models. Their role shifts from deciding directly to shaping the conditions under which algorithms decide (Möhlmann & Zalmanson, 2017). This redefinition requires new skills: statistical literacy, ethical awareness, and the ability to question algorithmic outputs. It also requires humility, as managers must accept that algorithms may detect patterns they cannot. Yet managerial oversight remains essential, particularly to ensure fairness, transparency, and legitimacy.

Scholars have described this transformation as a move from "management by hierarchy" to "management by algorithm" (Lee et al., 2015). The latter relies not on authority and rules but on continuous feedback, predictive analytics, and real-time adjustments. While this shift enhances efficiency, it also raises risks of dehumanization. Workers subject to algorithmic scheduling or performance tracking often report loss of autonomy, heightened stress, and reduced trust (Mateescu & Nguyen, 2019). Thus, algorithmic management must be carefully designed to balance efficiency with employee well-being. Organizations that fail to do so risk undermining motivation and loyalty, leading to long-term inefficiencies despite short-term gains.

A further implication of algorithmic governance is its impact on organizational structure. Traditional hierarchies relied on vertical integration, with layers of middle management ensuring control and communication. As algorithms take over monitoring and coordination functions, organizations may flatten, reducing the need for intermediate layers. This can increase agility and reduce costs but also erode career pathways and opportunities for employee development. Research suggests that middle managers often serve as cultural mediators and innovators, roles that algorithms cannot easily replace (Balogun & Johnson, 2004). Eliminating them entirely may weaken organizational learning and adaptability. The challenge lies in rethinking rather than removing management roles in the algorithmic era.

Critically, algorithms also alter the dynamics of power and surveillance. In hierarchical systems, surveillance was conducted by supervisors through observation and reporting. In algorithmic systems, surveillance is embedded in data collection and analysis. Employees may be tracked continuously through sensors, apps, and performance metrics. While this enhances efficiency, it also risks creating cultures of mistrust and resistance. Scholars warn of "digital panopticons" where workers internalize constant monitoring, leading to stress and disengagement (Moore et al., 2018). For organizations, the key is to design algorithmic governance systems that are transparent, participatory, and respectful of privacy. Otherwise, the promise of efficiency may be undermined by the costs of alienation.

The broader social and ethical implications of algorithmic governance also merit attention. Hierarchical systems were criticized for bureaucratic rigidity and inequity, but they at least operated within visible structures of accountability. Algorithms, by contrast, may create invisible forms of discrimination, particularly when trained on biased data. In hiring, lending, and insurance, algorithmic models have been shown to disadvantage minority groups even when protected categories are excluded (Raghavan et al., 2020). This raises ethical questions about fairness, equity, and justice in algorithmic management. Scholars argue for algorithmic audits, fairness-aware design, and regulatory oversight to ensure that algorithmic governance does not reproduce systemic inequalities under the guise of neutrality (Binns, 2018).

From a strategic perspective, the move from hierarchies to algorithms reshapes the sources of competitive advantage. Hierarchical organizations competed through scale, efficiency, and control of resources. Algorithmic organizations compete through data, connectivity, and learning speed. The firms that dominate today's digital economy—such as Amazon, Google, and Alibaba—leverage algorithmic governance to orchestrate complex ecosystems, coordinating millions of actors without relying on traditional hierarchies (Kenney & Zysman, 2016). This suggests that algorithmic management is not a marginal phenomenon but central to contemporary capitalism. Yet concentration of data and power also raises concerns about monopolization, dependency, and fragility. The long-term resilience of algorithmic governance remains uncertain.

Looking forward, rethinking management requires recognizing both the potential and the perils of algorithmic governance. Organizations must move beyond simplistic narratives of replacement—algorithms versus managers—to explore hybrid models that combine algorithmic efficiency with human oversight, ethical judgment, and cultural sensitivity. Scholars increasingly argue for "augmented management," where algorithms handle routine optimization while humans provide context, empathy, and normative guidance (Shrestha et al., 2019). Such hybrid systems may preserve the strengths of traditional management while embracing the advantages of AI.

On the other hand, AI-driven governance rests on a diverse set of technologies, including machine learning, natural language processing, computer vision, and reinforcement learning. Each of these technologies enables specific governance practices. Machine learning, for instance, allows organizations to identify patterns in large datasets, supporting functions such as fraud detection, credit risk assessment, and market forecasting (Domingos, 2015). Natural language processing enhances communication and monitoring, enabling sentiment analysis of employee feedback or real-time scanning of regulatory updates (Chowdhury, 2020). Reinforcement learning supports adaptive decision-making in complex environments such as supply chain optimization or dynamic pricing (Silver et al., 2017). Together, these tools form the technical infrastructure of algorithmic governance, providing continuous streams of insights that reshape how managers allocate resources, monitor performance, and evaluate risks.

In practice, AI-driven governance manifests in diverse organizational domains. In finance, algorithmic systems dominate trading, executing the majority of orders in major markets within microseconds (MacKenzie, 2021). In human resources, AI-driven platforms are used to screen applicants, predict employee attrition, and recommend promotions (Bogen & Rieke, 2018). In operations, predictive maintenance systems use sensor data and machine learning to anticipate equipment failures before they occur, reducing downtime and costs (Lee et al., 2019). In customer service, chatbots and recommendation engines personalize interactions, shifting governance of consumer relationships from human agents to algorithmic systems (Grewal et al., 2020). These practices illustrate how AI-driven governance extends beyond decision support to decision execution, embedding algorithms into the very fabric of organizational processes.

One defining feature of AI-driven governance is real-time monitoring. Traditional governance systems relied on periodic reports and ex-post evaluations, often creating lags between events and managerial responses. AI changes this dynamic by enabling continuous tracking of activities and immediate feedback loops. For example, in logistics, AI systems track shipments in real time and reroute them in response to disruptions such as weather events or strikes (Ivanov & Dolgui, 2020). In workplace management, wearable sensors and monitoring apps generate constant streams of data on employee productivity and well-being, allowing organizations to respond dynamically (Moore, 2018). Real-time monitoring enhances adaptability but also blurs boundaries between work and surveillance, raising ethical questions about autonomy and privacy.

Another important aspect is predictive governance. AI systems do not merely describe the present; they anticipate the future. Predictive analytics enables firms to forecast demand fluctuations, credit defaults, or equipment breakdowns with increasing accuracy (Shmueli & Koppius, 2011). These predictive capabilities support proactive governance: rather than reacting to problems, organizations can intervene in advance. However, prediction is probabilistic, not deterministic. Overreliance on predictive models risks creating false confidence and neglecting low-probability but high-impact events. Moreover, predictive governance shifts responsibility: when decisions are made based on algorithmic forecasts, accountability for errors becomes diffuse. If a model underestimates demand and leads to losses, is the blame on the model, the manager, or the data scientist?

AI-driven governance also introduces challenges of explainability. Many machine learning models, particularly deep learning systems, operate as "black boxes" whose inner workings are opaque even to their designers (Goodfellow et al., 2016). This opacity undermines trust among employees, managers, and regulators. For governance to be legitimate, stakeholders must understand and contest decisions. Explainable AI (XAI) has emerged as a field seeking to make algorithmic outputs interpretable, using methods such as feature attribution or model simplification (Gunning & Aha, 2019). Yet explainability often comes at the cost of accuracy, and simplified explanations may mislead more than they clarify. Balancing performance with transparency remains one of the most pressing challenges of AI-driven governance.

Bias and fairness represent another major area of concern. Algorithms trained on historical data reproduce the patterns and inequities embedded in those datasets. In hiring, AI systems have been shown to disadvantage women and minority applicants if trained on past recruitment data skewed toward male candidates (Raghavan et al., 2020). In lending, models may discriminate indirectly by using proxies for race or socioeconomic status. Bias in AI-driven governance is particularly pernicious because it is often hidden behind the veneer of objectivity. Ensuring fairness requires careful dataset curation, continuous auditing, and the inclusion of ethical considerations in model design (Barocas et al., 2019). Yet organizations often face tensions between fairness and efficiency, especially when biased models appear more profitable in the short term.

Accountability is further complicated by the distributed nature of AI systems. In hierarchical governance, responsibility followed clear reporting lines. In algorithmic governance, responsibility is shared across developers, data providers, managers, and regulatory authorities. Kroll et al. (2017) argue that accountability frameworks must be reimagined for the algorithmic age, incorporating legal, technical, and organizational mechanisms to ensure that responsibility does not evaporate. This may include algorithmic auditing, documentation of design choices, and clear chains of approval for deployment. Without such mechanisms, organizations risk "responsibility gaps" where no actor is clearly answerable for harmful outcomes.

AI-driven governance also reshapes organizational culture. Traditional governance relied on leadership, incentives, and norms to align behavior. Algorithms, by contrast, govern through metrics and feedback loops. Workers subject to algorithmic scheduling or performance tracking often feel that they are managed by data rather than by people, leading to alienation and stress (Wood et al., 2019). At the same time, algorithmic governance can foster cultures of continuous learning, where feedback is immediate and adaptation is rewarded. The cultural impact depends on how AI is integrated: whether as a tool that empowers workers with insights or as a mechanism of surveillance and control. Designing algorithmic systems that respect dignity and autonomy is essential for sustainable governance.

At the strategic level, AI-driven governance alters how organizations pursue competitive advantage. Firms with superior AI capabilities can process data faster, make more accurate predictions, and adapt more quickly to environmental changes. This shifts competition from resources and scale toward data and algorithms (Cockburn et al., 2018). However, the advantages of AI are unevenly distributed. Large technology firms with vast datasets and computational resources enjoy disproportionate power, raising concerns about concentration and dependency. Organizations must therefore consider not only how to integrate AI internally but also how to navigate ecosystems dominated by powerful platform firms.

Regulatory responses to AI-driven governance are also evolving. Governments recognize that algorithmic systems pose risks to fairness, transparency, and systemic stability. The European Union has taken the lead with its AI Act, which imposes strict obligations on high-risk applications, including many financial and managerial systems (European Commission, 2021). Other jurisdictions, such as Canada and Singapore, are experimenting with regulatory sandboxes and voluntary guidelines (Government of Canada, 2020; Monetary Authority of Singapore, 2018). The diversity of approaches reflects broader debates about how to balance innovation with protection. For organizations, regulatory uncertainty adds another layer of complexity to AI-driven governance.

Hybrid models arise from the recognition that AI and human cognition excel in different domains. Algorithms are unmatched in processing large-scale quantitative data, identifying statistical correlations, and optimizing specific functions. Humans, by contrast, bring interpretive flexibility, ethical awareness, and the ability to navigate ambiguity. Research in decision science suggests that complex environments require both forms of intelligence: computational models to process information and human actors to contextualize and legitimize decisions (Kleinberg et al., 2018). A purely algorithmic system risks becoming brittle in the face of unexpected shocks, while a purely human system may be overwhelmed by complexity. Hybrid models offer a way to combine the strengths of both.

In practice, hybrid governance often takes the form of human-in-the-loop systems. These systems rely on algorithms to generate recommendations or predictions, but they require human approval before decisions are executed. In healthcare, for example, diagnostic algorithms assist physicians by flagging anomalies in medical images, but doctors make the final call (Topol, 2019). In finance, algorithmic trading systems operate within boundaries set by human managers, who intervene when markets exhibit unusual volatility. This arrangement preserves accountability and ensures that algorithmic outputs are subject to interpretive scrutiny. However, hybrid models must avoid the risk of automation bias, where humans defer too readily to algorithmic judgments without critical evaluation (Skitka et al., 2000).

Hybrid models also raise questions about organizational structure. Traditional hierarchies were built around clear chains of command and responsibility. In hybrid systems, authority is distributed across humans and machines, requiring new governance frameworks. One proposal is the creation of algorithmic accountability boards, where interdisciplinary teams review the design, deployment, and outcomes of AI systems (Wagner, 2018). These boards can serve as institutional mechanisms for ensuring that algorithms are aligned with organizational values and societal norms. They also provide a forum for contestation, allowing stakeholders to question and refine algorithmic practices. Such innovations illustrate how hybrid governance reshapes not only decision-making processes but also organizational design.

Trust is central to the viability of hybrid models. Employees and stakeholders must trust both the algorithms and the humans who oversee them. Research shows that trust in AI depends on perceptions of transparency, reliability, and fairness (Dietvorst et al., 2015). If algorithms are perceived as black boxes, users may resist their recommendations; if they are too opaque, managers may be reluctant to rely on them. Conversely, if algorithms are overly trusted, human oversight may become perfunctory. Building trust requires careful calibration: algorithms must be explainable enough to justify decisions, but not so simplified that explanations mislead. Hybrid models thrive when trust is distributed appropriately between human and machine actors.

Hybrid governance also intersects with ethics. Algorithms often reproduce historical biases embedded in data, while humans are subject to conscious and unconscious prejudices. Combining the two does not automatically cancel out these risks; it may even exacerbate them. For example, studies of predictive policing have shown that biased algorithms reinforced existing prejudices among human officers, creating feedback loops of discrimination (Lum & Isaac, 2016). Designing hybrid systems requires explicit attention to fairness, diversity, and inclusivity. Ethical oversight committees, bias audits, and participatory design processes can help mitigate these risks. The challenge is to ensure that human oversight enhances rather than legitimizes algorithmic bias.

At the strategic level, hybrid models enable organizations to pursue ambidexterity—the ability to exploit existing efficiencies while exploring new opportunities (O'Reilly & Tushman, 2013). Algorithms excel at exploitation, optimizing current processes for efficiency. Humans excel at exploration, imagining new possibilities and questioning established routines. Hybrid governance allows organizations to balance both imperatives. In supply chain management, for instance, algorithms optimize logistics, while managers strategize about alternative suppliers and long-term risks. In marketing, algorithms personalize recommendations, while human leaders craft brand narratives that resonate culturally. The synergy of human exploration and algorithmic exploitation creates resilience in uncertain environments.

Hybrid governance is not without challenges. One issue is the distribution of responsibility. When decisions are made jointly by humans and algorithms, responsibility becomes blurred. If a human approves an algorithmic recommendation, are they fully responsible for the outcome, or does responsibility also rest with the designers and trainers of the model? Scholars call this the "responsibility gap" of AI (Matthias, 2004). Addressing it requires clear allocation of accountability, documentation of decision processes, and legal frameworks that recognize distributed agency. Without such mechanisms, hybrid governance risks creating accountability vacuums.

Another challenge concerns skills and competencies. Managers in hybrid systems must be able to interpret algorithmic outputs, question their assumptions, and integrate them with contextual knowledge. This requires new forms of literacy, including statistical reasoning, ethical awareness, and critical thinking about AI (Long & Magerko, 2020). Organizations must invest in training to ensure that employees can engage meaningfully with algorithmic systems. Hybrid models succeed only when humans are empowered to exercise informed oversight, rather than acting as passive approvers.

Hybrid governance also has implications for employee experience. Workers monitored by AI systems often report feelings of surveillance and stress, particularly when algorithms evaluate performance continuously (Parent-Rocheleau & Parker, 2021). Hybrid systems can mitigate these effects if they incorporate human managers who contextualize data, provide empathetic feedback, and support worker autonomy. By contrast, if human oversight is minimal or perfunctory, workers may perceive algorithms as oppressive, undermining trust and morale. Designing hybrid governance therefore requires balancing efficiency with human dignity.

At the societal level, hybrid models raise questions of legitimacy. Organizations operate within broader ecosystems of stakeholders, regulators, and publics. If governance is perceived as overly algorithmic, legitimacy may be undermined. Hybrid models provide opportunities for enhancing legitimacy by combining algorithmic efficiency with human accountability. Yet this requires transparent communication with stakeholders about how decisions are made, who is responsible, and how fairness is ensured (Bryson & Winfield, 2017). Hybrid governance must be publicly defensible, not only technically effective.

Future directions for hybrid governance are emerging. Some scholars propose collaborative intelligence systems, where humans and AI continuously learn from each other, creating feedback loops of mutual adaptation (Wilson & Daugherty, 2018). Others advocate for value-sensitive design, embedding ethical principles into algorithms from the outset while ensuring human oversight throughout (Friedman & Hendry, 2019). Still others call for polycentric governance, where multiple actors—managers, regulators, civil society—share responsibility for algorithmic oversight (Polyakova & Meserole, 2019). These approaches highlight the diversity of pathways for developing hybrid models, underscoring that no single template fits all contexts.

CONCLUSION

The study of management has always been about more than efficiency. It has reflected deeper questions about how humans organize collective effort, how authority is legitimized, and how societies imagine the future of work and governance. As the twenty-first century advances, the arrival of artificial intelligence (AI) brings a profound disruption to these long-standing questions. To conclude the exploration of management's transition from traditional models to AI-driven governance, it is necessary to move beyond the descriptive and focus on what these transformations mean for leadership, organizations, and societies in the decades ahead.

One of the clearest insights is that the discipline of management must now contend with the erosion of its most stable categories. Concepts such as hierarchy, decision-making, and accountability were once taken for granted. They provided a shared grammar through which scholars and practitioners could discuss organizational design. Yet in a world where algorithms act as agents—classifying, predicting, and sometimes deciding—these categories are destabilized. Hierarchy does not disappear, but it ceases to be the primary locus of coordination. Decision-making is no longer the exclusive privilege of human managers but is shared with algorithmic processes. Accountability is diffused across networks of humans and machines. For management research, this is not merely a technical adjustment but a paradigmatic shift that requires rethinking its very foundations.

Equally significant is the cultural and philosophical redefinition of authority. Traditional management models often equated authority with position: one's place in a hierarchy determined one's right to decide. AI disrupts this logic by introducing authority without position. Algorithms command attention and shape behavior not because of formal rank but because of their perceived accuracy, speed, or indispensability. This raises difficult questions: on what basis should authority be recognized in algorithmic systems? How can organizations ensure that this authority remains legitimate and contestable? Addressing these questions requires a renewed philosophy of governance—one that is attuned to both human dignity and technological capability.

The implications for leadership are profound. Leadership will no longer be measured primarily by one's ability to direct subordinates but by one's capacity to integrate diverse forms of intelligence—human and artificial—into coherent strategies. Leaders must become interpreters of algorithmic outputs, mediators between machine recommendations and human values, and stewards of ethical standards in environments where efficiency often tempts organizations to cut corners. This requires new competencies: digital literacy, ethical imagination, and cross-disciplinary fluency. Future managers must be as comfortable reading algorithmic dashboards as they are leading human teams, as capable of questioning data correlations as they are of inspiring collective purpose.

Another area that emerges strongly in conclusion is education and the preparation of future leaders. Business schools and training programs that continue to emphasize only traditional managerial skills will leave graduates ill-equipped for the realities of AI-driven governance. Curricula must expand to include data science, algorithmic accountability, and ethics of technology. Yet these technical skills alone are insufficient. Future leaders must also develop reflective judgment, empathy, and the capacity to navigate ambiguity—qualities that algorithms cannot replicate. The most effective managers will be those who can weave together technical acumen with human sensitivity, bridging the worlds of data and meaning.

The transition to AI-driven governance also forces reconsideration of the purposes of organizations. Traditional models were grounded in maximizing efficiency and profit. While these remain important, the growing role of algorithms highlights risks of short-termism, bias, and opacity that can undermine trust and resilience. Organizations must therefore reimagine their missions in broader terms: creating value that is sustainable, equitable, and socially legitimate. AI can be a powerful enabler of these goals if designed and governed responsibly. Conversely, it can accelerate inequality and fragility if left unchecked. The conclusion here is that management must expand its moral horizon: efficiency alone is no longer a sufficient benchmark for success.

The global dimension adds further complexity. AI is not deployed in a vacuum but within societies that have different traditions of governance, regulation, and cultural attitudes toward technology. In some regions, algorithmic decision-making is embraced enthusiastically as a path to modernization and control. In others, it is met with skepticism and demands for oversight. Multinational organizations must therefore navigate a mosaic of expectations and rules, adapting their governance models to local contexts without losing coherence. This requires cultural agility and institutional sensitivity. The future of management is not about a universal model of AI integration but about pluralism: the capacity to adapt hybrid governance systems to diverse environments while maintaining ethical standards.

The societal implications of this transition are equally important. Management is not confined to the firm; it shapes labor markets, social relations, and even political governance. As algorithms take on managerial functions, societies must grapple with the consequences for employment, equity, and citizenship. Will algorithmic governance displace workers, or will it create new forms of human-machine collaboration? Will it concentrate power in the hands of a few platform owners, or will it democratize access to knowledge and resources? The answers depend not only on technological design but also on the choices managers and policymakers make. Management in the age of AI is therefore inseparable from questions of democracy, justice, and the distribution of power.

Looking forward, several scenarios suggest themselves. In one scenario, organizations adopt AI uncritically, allowing algorithms to dominate governance. This may yield short-term efficiencies but risks long-term erosion of trust and legitimacy. In another scenario, organizations resist AI, clinging to traditional hierarchies. This may preserve familiar structures but at the cost of competitiveness and adaptability. The most promising scenario lies in the middle path: organizations that design hybrid models where algorithms provide analytical depth and efficiency, while humans ensure context, ethics, and accountability. Such models require ongoing experimentation, institutional innovation, and a willingness to embrace complexity rather than seek illusory certainty.

Another conclusion concerns resilience. The crises of recent decades—financial collapse, pandemics, climate disruptions—demonstrate that unpredictability is the rule rather than the exception. AI can help organizations become more resilient by detecting early warning signals, modeling alternative futures, and enabling rapid responses. Yet resilience cannot be outsourced to algorithms alone. It requires human judgment to interpret signals, to decide which futures matter, and to mobilize collective action. Hybrid governance, therefore, is not simply about efficiency but about resilience: the capacity to absorb shocks, adapt to change, and preserve legitimacy under conditions of uncertainty.

Finally, the conclusion must return to the human dimension. Management has always been about people: coordinating their efforts, aligning their goals, and shaping their experiences of work. AI does not change this reality; it reframes it. The challenge is not to choose between humans and machines but to design governance systems that allow both to contribute their strengths. Algorithms bring speed, scale, and precision; humans bring meaning, ethics, and imagination. Together, they can create organizations that are more adaptive and inclusive than those built on hierarchy alone. But this will not happen automatically. It will require conscious choices, deliberate design, and a commitment to values that extend beyond profit.

In sum, the future of management will be hybrid, plural, and contested. It will demand leaders who can integrate technical and ethical perspectives, organizations that balance efficiency with fairness, and societies that hold firms accountable for how they deploy AI. The conclusion of this chapter is therefore both cautionary and hopeful. Cautionary, because AI introduces risks of opacity, inequality, and dehumanization. Hopeful, because when integrated responsibly, AI offers unprecedented opportunities to enhance decision-making, resilience, and inclusivity. The path forward is not predetermined. It will be shaped by the choices organizations, leaders, and societies make. The task of management is to ensure that these choices create systems of governance that are not only efficient but also just, trustworthy, and humane.

REFERENCES

Balogun, J., & Johnson, G. (2004). Organizational restructuring and middle manager sensemaking. *Academy of Management Journal*, *47*(4), 523–549. DOI: 10.2307/20159600

Barney, J. (1991). Firm resources and sustained competitive advantage. *Journal of Management*, *17*(1), 99–120. DOI: 10.1177/014920639101700108

Barocas, S., Hardt, M., & Narayanan, A. (2019). *Fairness and machine learning: Limitations and opportunities*. MIT Press.

Bartlett, R., Morse, A., Stanton, R., & Wallace, N. (2022). Consumer-lending discrimination in the FinTech era. *Journal of Financial Economics*, *146*(2), 726–765. DOI: 10.1016/j.jfineco.2021.12.011

Binns, R. (2018). Fairness in machine learning: Lessons from political philosophy. *Proceedings of the 2018 Conference on Fairness, Accountability, and Transparency*, 149–159. DOI: 10.1145/3287560.3287572

Bogen, M., & Rieke, A. (2018). Help wanted: An examination of hiring algorithms, equity, and bias. *Upturn Report*.

Brynjolfsson, E., & McAfee, A. (2017). *Machine, platform, crowd: Harnessing our digital future*. W. W. Norton.

Bryson, J., & Winfield, A. (2017). Standardizing ethical design for artificial intelligence and autonomous systems. *Computer*, *50*(5), 116–119. DOI: 10.1109/MC.2017.154

Burrell, J. (2016). How the machine "thinks": Understanding opacity in machine learning algorithms. *Big Data & Society*, *3*(1), 1–12. DOI: 10.1177/2053951715622512

Chen, M., Zhang, Y., & Lee, D. (2023). Reinforcement learning in finance: Recent advances and future directions. *The Journal of Financial Data Science*, *5*(2), 1–20. DOI: 10.3905/jfds.2023.1.147

Choi, T. M., Wallace, S. W., & Wang, Y. (2021). Big data analytics in operations management. *Production and Operations Management*, *30*(6), 1819–1839. DOI: 10.1111/poms.13326

Chowdhury, G. (2020). Natural language processing. *Annual Review of Information Science & Technology, 54*(1), 1–42. DOI: 10.1002/aris.201900046

Cockburn, I. M., Henderson, R., & Stern, S. (2018). The impact of artificial intelligence on innovation. *NBER Working Paper No. 24449*. DOI: 10.3386/w24449

Crawford, K. (2021). *Atlas of AI: Power, politics, and the planetary costs of artificial intelligence*. Yale University Press.

Cummings, M. L. (2017). Artificial intelligence and the future of warfare. *Chatham House Report*.

Davenport, T. H., & Ronanki, R. (2018). Artificial intelligence for the real world. *Harvard Business Review, 96*(1), 108–116.

Dietvorst, B. J., Simmons, J. P., & Massey, C. (2015). Algorithm aversion: People erroneously avoid algorithms after seeing them err. *Journal of Experimental Psychology. General, 144*(1), 114–126. DOI: 10.1037/xge0000033 PMID: 25401381

Domingos, P. (2015). *The master algorithm: How the quest for the ultimate learning machine will remake our world*. Basic Books.

Drucker, P. (1954). *The practice of management*. Harper & Row.

Friedman, B., & Hendry, D. G. (2019). *Value sensitive design: Shaping technology with moral imagination*. MIT Press. DOI: 10.7551/mitpress/7585.001.0001

Goodfellow, I., Bengio, Y., & Courville, A. (2016). *Deep learning*. MIT Press.

Gouldner, A. W. (1954). *Patterns of industrial bureaucracy*. Free Press.

Government of Canada. (2020). *Directive on automated decision-making*. Treasury Board Secretariat.

Grewal, D., Hulland, J., Kopalle, P. K., & Karahanna, E. (2020). The future of technology and marketing: A multidisciplinary perspective. *Journal of the Academy of Marketing Science, 48*(1), 1–8. DOI: 10.1007/s11747-019-00711-4

Gunning, D., & Aha, D. W. (2019). DARPA's explainable artificial intelligence (XAI) program. *AI Magazine, 40*(2), 44–58. DOI: 10.1609/aimag.v40i2.2850

Huang, R., & Pierri, N. (2022). Fintech credit and shadow banking: Evidence from China. *Journal of Banking & Finance, 137*, 106441. DOI: 10.1016/j.jbankfin.2022.106441

Ivanov, D., & Dolgui, A. (2020). Viability of intertwined supply networks: Extending the supply chain resilience angles towards survivability. *International Journal of Production Research, 58*(10), 2904–2915. DOI: 10.1080/00207543.2020.1750727

Jordan, M. I., & Mitchell, T. M. (2015). Machine learning: Trends, perspectives, and prospects. *Science, 349*(6245), 255–260. DOI: 10.1126/science.aaa8415 PMID: 26185243

Kellogg, K. C., Valentine, M. A., & Christin, A. (2020). Algorithms at work: The new contested terrain of control. *The Academy of Management Annals, 14*(1), 366–410. DOI: 10.5465/annals.2018.0174

Kenney, M., & Zysman, J. (2016). The rise of the platform economy. *Issues in Science and Technology, 32*(3), 61–69.

Kleinberg, J., Ludwig, J., Mullainathan, S., & Sunstein, C. R. (2018). Discrimination in the age of algorithms. *The Journal of Legal Analysis, 10*(2), 113–174. DOI: 10.1093/jla/laz001

Kroll, J. A., Huey, J., Barocas, S., Felten, E. W., Reidenberg, J. R., Robinson, D. G., & Yu, H. (2017). Accountable algorithms. *University of Pennsylvania Law Review, 165*(3), 633–705.

Lee, M. K., Kusbit, D., Metsky, E., & Dabbish, L. (2015). Working with machines: The impact of algorithmic and data-driven management on human workers. *Proceedings of the 33rd Annual ACM Conference on Human Factors in Computing Systems*, 1603–1612. DOI: 10.1145/2702123.2702548

Long, D., & Magerko, B. (2020). What is AI literacy? Competencies and design considerations. *Proceedings of the 2020 CHI Conference on Human Factors in Computing Systems*, 1–16. DOI: 10.1145/3313831.3376727

Lum, K., & Isaac, W. (2016). To predict and serve? *Significance, 13*(5), 14–19. DOI: 10.1111/j.1740-9713.2016.00960.x

MacKenzie, D. (2021). *Trading at the speed of light: How ultrafast algorithms are transforming financial markets*. Princeton University Press.

Mateescu, A., & Nguyen, A. (2019). *Explainer: Workplace monitoring & surveillance*. Data & Society Research Institute.

Matthias, A. (2004). The responsibility gap: Ascribing responsibility for the actions of learning automata. *Ethics and Information Technology, 6*(3), 175–183. DOI: 10.1007/s10676-004-3422-1

Mehrabi, N., Morstatter, F., Saxena, N., Lerman, K., & Galstyan, A. (2021). A survey on bias and fairness in machine learning. *ACM Computing Surveys, 54*(6), 1–35. DOI: 10.1145/3457607

Möhlmann, M., & Zalmanson, L. (2017). Hands on the wheel: Navigating algorithmic management and Uber drivers' autonomy. *Proceedings of the International Conference on Information Systems*.

Monetary Authority of Singapore. (2018). *Principles to promote fairness, ethics, accountability and transparency in the use of AI and data analytics in financial services*.

Moore, P. V. (2018). Tracking affective labour for agility in the quantified workplace. *Body & Society, 24*(3), 27–55. DOI: 10.1177/1357034X18775203

Moore, P. V., Upchurch, M., & Whittaker, X. (2018). *Humans and machines at work: Monitoring, surveillance and automation in contemporary capitalism*. Palgrave Macmillan. DOI: 10.1007/978-3-319-58232-0

Narayanan, A. (2023). Regulating AI: The EU AI Act and its implications for financial services. *AI & Society, 38*(2), 567–581. DOI: 10.1007/s00146-022-01407-5

O'Neil, C. (2016). *Weapons of math destruction: How big data increases inequality and threatens democracy*. Crown.

O'Reilly, C. A.III, & Tushman, M. L. (2013). Organizational ambidexterity: Past, present, and future. *The Academy of Management Perspectives, 27*(4), 324–338. DOI: 10.5465/amp.2013.0025

Parent-Rocheleau, X., & Parker, S. K. (2021). Algorithms as work designers: How algorithmic management influences job design. *Human Resource Management Review*, *31*(4), 100763. DOI: 10.1016/j.hrmr.2020.100763

Raghavan, M., Barocas, S., Kleinberg, J., & Levy, K. (2020). Mitigating bias in algorithmic hiring: Evaluating claims and practices. *Proceedings of the 2020 Conference on Fairness, Accountability, and Transparency*, 469–481. DOI: 10.1145/3351095.3372828

Raisch, S., & Krakowski, S. (2021). Artificial intelligence and management: The automation–augmentation paradox. *Academy of Management Review*, *46*(1), 192–210. DOI: 10.5465/amr.2018.0072

Rajkomar, A., Dean, J., & Kohane, I. (2019). Machine learning in medicine. *The New England Journal of Medicine*, *380*(14), 1347–1358. DOI: 10.1056/NEJMra1814259 PMID: 30943338

Rolnick, D., Donti, P. L., Kaack, L. H., Kochanski, K., Lacoste, A., Sankaran, K., Ross, A. S., Milojevic-Dupont, N., Jaques, N., Waldman-Brown, A., Luccioni, A. S., Maharaj, T., Sherwin, E. D., Mukkavilli, S. K., Kording, K. P., Gomes, C. P., Ng, A. Y., Hassabis, D., Platt, J. C., & Bengio, Y. (2022). Tackling climate change with machine learning. *ACM Computing Surveys*, *55*(2), 1–96. DOI: 10.1145/3485128

Rosenblat, A. (2018). *Uberland: How algorithms are rewriting the rules of work*. University of California Press. DOI: 10.1525/9780520970632

Rudin, C., Chen, C., Chen, Z., Huang, H., Semenova, L., & Zhong, C. (2022). Interpretable machine learning: Fundamental principles and ten grand challenges. *Statistics Surveys*, *16*(none), 1–85. DOI: 10.1214/21-SS133

Schoemaker, P. J., & Tetlock, P. E. (2017). Building a more robust forecasting system: Lessons from the Good Judgment Project. *Harvard Business Review*, *95*(3), 72–77.

Shmueli, G., & Koppius, O. R. (2011). Predictive analytics in information systems research. *Management Information Systems Quarterly*, *35*(3), 553–572. DOI: 10.2307/23042796

Shrestha, Y. R., Ben-Menahem, S. M., & von Krogh, G. (2019). Organizational decision-making structures in the age of artificial intelligence. *California Management Review, 61*(4), 66–83. DOI: 10.1177/0008125619862257

Silver, D., Schrittwieser, J., Simonyan, K., Antonoglou, I., Huang, A., Guez, A., Hubert, T., Baker, L., Lai, M., Bolton, A., Chen, Y., Lillicrap, T., Hui, F., Sifre, L., van den Driessche, G., Graepel, T., & Hassabis, D. (2017). Mastering the game of Go without human knowledge. *Nature, 550*(7676), 354–359. DOI: 10.1038/nature24270 PMID: 29052630

Simon, H. A. (1947). *Administrative behavior*. Free Press.

Skitka, L. J., Mosier, K., & Burdick, M. (2000). Accountability and automation bias. *International Journal of Human-Computer Studies, 52*(4), 701–717. DOI: 10.1006/ijhc.1999.0349

Taylor, F. W. (1911). *The principles of scientific management*. Harper & Brothers.

Tooze, A. (2021). *Shutdown: How COVID shook the world's economy*. Viking.

Topol, E. (2019). *Deep medicine: How artificial intelligence can make healthcare human again*. Basic Books.

Wagner, B. (2018). Ethics as an escape from regulation: From ethics-washing to ethics-shopping? In Bayamlıoğlu, E., Baraliuc, I., Janssens, L., & Hildebrandt, M. (Eds.), *Being profiled: Cogitas ergo sum* (pp. 84–89). Amsterdam University Press. DOI: 10.2307/j.ctvhrd092.18

Weber, M. (1947). *The theory of social and economic organization*. Oxford University Press.

Weber, M. (1978). *Economy and society: An outline of interpretive sociology*. University of California Press.

Wilson, H. J., & Daugherty, P. R. (2018). *Human + machine: Reimagining work in the age of AI*. Harvard Business Review Press.

Womack, J. P., & Jones, D. T. (2003). *Lean thinking: Banish waste and create wealth in your corporation* (2nd ed.). Free Press.

Wood, A. J., Graham, M., Lehdonvirta, V., & Hjorth, I. (2019). Good gig, bad gig: Autonomy and algorithmic control in the global gig economy. *Work, Employment and Society*, *33*(1), 56–75. DOI: 10.1177/0950017018785616 PMID: 30886460

Zuboff, S. (2015). Big other: Surveillance capitalism and the prospects of an information civilization. *Journal of Information Technology*, *30*(1), 75–89. DOI: 10.1057/jit.2015.5

Zuboff, S. (2019). *The age of surveillance capitalism: The fight for a human future at the new frontier of power*. PublicAffairs.

Chapter 5
Predictive Auditing With AI and ML:
A Qualitative Investigation of Emerging Tools in the Accounting Sector

Tarun Sai Raavi
https://orcid.org/0009-0005-8947-656X
Vishwa Vishwani Institute of Systems and Management, India

Radhika Ramanchi
GITAM University, India

ABSTRACT

In today's rapidly evolving financial sector, integrating artificial intelligence and machine learning into auditing practices is not just a trend – it's a game-changer. The limitations of traditional auditing practices are the time-consuming nature of manual sample preparation, the struggle to detect complex fraud schemes, and managing vast amounts of transaction data, which have long plagued the auditor's profession. But now, in a new era of auditing, promises faster, more accurate, and predictive capabilities. Integrating artificial intelligence (AI) and machine learning (ML) into auditing practices reshapes the financial assurance landscape.

DOI: 10.4018/979-8-3373-3626-8.ch005

This chapter explores the technological revolution and how AI and ML are reshaping the auditing function, particularly at the Big Four accounting firms – Deloitte, PwC, EY, and KPMG.

1. INTRODUCTION

The modern financial market runs through technology which serves as the essential force for both marked improvements and increased operational effectiveness. The auditing profession has experienced a transformation because of two developing technologies which are Artificial Intelligence (AI) and Machine Learning (ML). Diverse audit approaches in the past were based on manual sampling with retrospective data analysis and standardized checklists. Although these traditional strategies fulfil basic regulatory needs and financial accuracy principles they lack the skill to detect sophisticated fraudulent activities and manage vast transactional data volumes in real-time situations.

AI and ML integration enables the automation of routine work and anomaly detection as well as continuous audit functions (Appelbaum et al., 2017). Academic studies have not fully examined how AI and ML benefit auditing operations specifically within real-life environments of major accounting companies such as Deloitte, PwC, EY, and KPMG.

AI and ML-driven predictive auditing has the potential to perform real-time audits for detecting fraud ahead of major damage occurrences while providing deep valuable insights to clients. Real-time auditing exists already and this technology is currently in operation.

1.1. Scope of the Chapter

This chapter AI and ML in the context of auditing explore how machine learning algorithms can process vast datasets, identify patterns, and flag anomalies with a level of speed and accuracy that was once thought impossible.The practical applications of AI and ML in audit practice, will discover how these technologies are being used for data extraction, contract analysis, fraud detection, and risk assessment.

It examine case studies that demonstrate the power of continuous auditing, showing how it improves audit efficiency and reduces human error, implementation of AI and ML technologies by the Big Four accounting firms. While public information on these initiatives is often limited, our qualitative investigation will provide unique insights into how these industry leaders are leveraging AI and ML to transform their audit processes. To explore platforms like PwC's "Halo" and Deloitte's "Argus," understanding their capabilities and the impact they're having on audit quality and efficiency.From issues with data quality to concerns about algorithmic bias, gain a nuanced understanding of the obstacles that need to be overcome, and discuss the cultural and ethical implications of embedding AI into legacy systems, and the resistance to change that often accompanies technological innovation. The use of AI and ML in fraud prediction and risk analytics. Machine learning models that are being used to classify high-risk transactions with remarkable accuracy. The world of neural networks and decision trees, understanding how these technologies are revolutionizing fraud detection in financial contexts. It's about how AI and ML are changing the day-to-day work of auditors and reshaping the auditing profession as a whole, the changing skill requirements for auditors in this new landscape, and how professionals can prepare themselves for the future of auditing.

Finally, the future, exploring emerging trends and technologies that could further revolutionize the field of auditing. From blockchain to quantum computing, how these innovations might intersect with AI and ML to create even more powerful auditing tools.

1.2. Research Problem / Research Gap

While the business world is increasingly digitalized, auditing practices still largely depend on conventional methods. These approaches are time-consuming, expensive, and often lack the agility to identify emerging financial risks. Research by Yoon et al. (2015) noted that despite advancements in data analytics, actual implementation of AI and ML in audit environments remains nominal and fragmented. Moreover, most existing studies either focus on data analytics broadly or lack empirical grounding in organizational case studies, mainly within top-tier firms. This research identifies a two-fold gap: first, the limited application of AI/ML in audit frameworks; and second, the lack of empirical studies investigating AI/ML implementation by major accounting firms.

1.3. Research Objectives and Questions

1. To explore how AI and ML technologies are presently being utilized in auditing.
2. To find out the specific tools adopted by Big Four firms for audit innovation.
3. To observe challenges in implementing AI and ML within audit frameworks.
4. To conclude whether AI/ML systems can predict risks and prevent financial fraud effectively.

1.4. Research Questions

1. How do AI and ML improve traditional auditing practices?
2. What specific technologies are the Big Four using to automate and improve audits?
3. What are the primary barriers to the adoption of AI and ML in auditing?
4. Can AI/ML systems reliably detect fraud and forecast financial risks?

2. LITERATURE REVIEW

One of the most notable impacts is the enhanced speed and scope of audits. ML algorithms enable full-population testing rather than limited sampling, increasing the reliability of audit findings (Laine, Minkkinen, & Mäntymäki, 2024). Real-time monitoring tools allow for continuous auditing, detecting fraud and financial irregularities almost as they occur (Birhane et al., 2024).

AI also enhances speed scope and accuracy, particularly in complex areas such as revenue recognition, lease accounting, and valuation, where traditional audits often relied heavily on professional judgment and manual verification.

Friday Jejeniwa (2023) developed a conceptual design revealing how Artificial Intelligence (AI) should integrate into financial auditing operations to transform measurements of efficiency and capabilities for fraud detection as well as data precision levels. Auditor uses Machine Learning algorithms combined with Natural Language Processing capabilities and Robotic Process computerization to discover unusual patterns in real-time data all throughout risk estimation processes. he implementation of artificial intelligence through auditing produces many benefits, but challenges such as data consistency and challenging malicious systems, restrictions from regulations, and labor skill shortages continue to be barriers to audit efficiency. Jejeniwa explains that AI tools must adhere to traditional audit principles in order to develop transparency accountability and compliance standards. The established framework has three essential components integrating artificial intelligence data management together with human-machine work collaboration coupled with risk operational systems. The Finance & Accounting Research Journal undertakes research on machine learning (ML) algorithm utilization during audits according to Adelakun et al. (2024). Throughout the paper it becomes evident that ML model technology brings superior data analytics while enabling anomaly detection along with predictive analytics and real-time fraud monitoring than conventional manual sampling systems.

However, it also identifies major challenges such as data integrity, algorithmic transparency, bias mitigation, and regulatory compliance. The authors argue that although ML enhances audit quality, continuous monitoring, model retraining, and auditor upskilling are essential to maintain ethical and effective AI integration. Their study offers practical case studies from Big Four firms (KPMG, Deloitte, EY, PwC), documenting real-world applications of intelligent audit tools. Birhane et al. (2024)in *arXiv Preprint Journal,* examine AI accountability challenges through the lens of auditing machine learning systems. Their research discusses how algorithmic biases, opacity, and flawed auditing standards compromise the trustworthiness of AI implementations in sensitive sectors like finance and auditing. The paper critiques current AI audit practices and emphasizes the need for independent, interdisciplinary auditing teams.

Recommendations include community-based standards for AI auditing, transparency reporting, and participatory evaluation models. Particularly relevant to AI in auditing, it highlights the risks when machine-driven systems lack clear explains ability and fairness benchmarks. Laine et al. (2024) in *Information & Management journal*, proposed a framework for ethics-based auditing of AI systems. They argue that traditional auditing standards are inadequate for assessing AI's societal impact, fairness, and transparency. The paper suggests integrating ethical evaluation metrics alongside technical ones in AI audits. The study is significant for auditing research as it encourages the development of holistic audit frameworks that include data governance, algorithmic bias detection, and accountability verification. They position ethics-based AI auditing as critical to restoring trust in intelligent financial systems and AI-augmented corporate audits.Ferrara (2024) in *Machine Learning with Applications Journal* discussed the "butterfly effect" in AI, where minor model inputs cause disproportionately large and unpredictable outcomes, challenging auditing practices. His paper emphasizes that AI auditing should not just focus on outputs but also consider system sensitivity, fairness, and long-term risks. Ferrara advocates for robust model risk management in AI-integrated audits, proposing resilience testing and adversarial audits. The insights are critical for auditors and regulators aiming to establish safe AI governance in financial reporting. Minkkinen et al. (2022) in *Digital Society Journal,*conceptualized continuous auditing of AI models. They argue that static audits are insufficient for dynamic AI systems, suggesting continuous real-time auditing using automated monitoring tools. In the context of AI-audited financial systems, they recommend integrating AI into audit frameworks for fraud detection, anomaly tracking, and real-time compliance. Their study outlines necessary skill sets for auditors: data science literacy, ethical AI comprehension, and critical evaluation skills, making a strong case for reskilling audit professionals. Laine, J et al. 2024 in *Information & Management* Analyzes ethics-based AI auditing frameworks. Identifies gaps in how principles like fairness and transparency are operationalized in audits.

Table 1. Literature Review

Costanza-Chock, S., Raji, I.D., Buolamwini, J.	2022	*ACM FAccT Conference*	Reviews algorithmic auditing ecosystem. Highlights gaps in auditing fairness and proposes field-level recommendations for ethical auditing.
Ferrara, E.	2024	*Machine Learning with Applications*	Surveys AI bias sources and fairness strategies. Focuses on "butterfly effect" risks where small biases cause systemic errors.
Laine, J., Minkkinen, M., Mäntymäki, M.	2024	*Information & Management*	Analyzes ethics-based AI auditing frameworks. Identifies gaps in how principles like fairness and transparency are operationalized in audits.
González-Sendino, R. et al.	2023	*Journal of Artificial Intelligence Research*	Summarizes fairness, accountability, and bias in AI. Reviews mitigation strategies and calls for integrating fairness into AI development from the start.
Fotoh, L.E., Lorentzon, J.I.	2023	*Accounting Horizons*	Reviews audit digitalization effects. Concludes that while automation enhances speed, it also exacerbates the audit expectation gap.
Duggineni, S.	2023	*Science and Technology*	Literature review on controls over data integrity and information systems in AI-driven environments, focusing on finance.
Wilson, C. et al.	2023	*ACM FAccT*	Reviews fairness auditing in automated candidate screening systems. Highlights how AI bias audits must be domain-specific.
Mökander, J. et al.	2022	*Minds and Machines*	Reviews conformity assessments in European AI governance proposals. Discusses role of audits in post-market AI monitoring.
Koshiyama, A. et al.	2024	*Royal Society Open Science*	Explores legal, ethical, and technological risks in AI. Advocates developing structured algorithm audit frameworks.
Jauhiainen, T., Lehner, O.M.	2022	*Artificial Intelligence in Accounting (Routledge)*	Analyzes how AI governance affects accounting practices. Reviews best practices for good governance in auditing algorithms.
Han, H.	2022	*PhD Dissertation, Brunel University*	Reviews AI and blockchain adoption impacts on corporate governance. Discusses auditing challenges related to data privacy and smart contracts.
Munoko, I., Brown-Liburd, H.L., Vasarhelyi, M.	2020	*Journal of Business Ethics*	Literature review on ethical risks of AI in auditing. Highlights transparency, bias, and fairness as critical future research areas.
Patel, P., Uddin, M.N.	2022	*International Journal of Social Analytics*	Reviews AI auditing tools for mitigating bias in big data systems. Advocates for ethical-by-design auditing technologies.
Díaz-Rodríguez, N. et al.	2023	*Information Fusion*	Review connecting AI principles, ethics, and regulation. Suggests auditing is essential for trustworthy AI deployment in sensitive fields like finance.

Source: Created by Authors from Different sources

3. HOW AI AND ML IMPROVE TRADITIONAL AUDITING PRACTICES

3.1. Introduction to AI and ML in Auditing

The traditional model of periodic auditing—conducted at fixed intervals—has increasingly shown limitations in an environment characterized by real-time transactions and high-speed financial operations.

Continuous auditing (CA) refers to an advanced technology system that attempts to completely transform auditing activities.

According to Minkkinen, Lain, and Mantimäki (2022), the predictive method of continuous auditing is driven by automated real-time monitoring and analysis of operations and transactions for control systems using ML and real-time analytics with AI.

The simulation of human intelligence tasks by machines strengthens artificial intelligence (AI), especially computer systems that demonstrate reasoning and self-correction as well as learning (Adelakun et al., 2024). Machine learning (ML) serves as a form of artificial intelligence (AI), which uses algorithms to help systems derive knowledge from information while discovering patterns through automated operations (Sarker, 2021). Auditing practices are being transformed by AI and ML technologies as these systems increase operational performance and increase accuracy levels along with their risk assessment capabilities. The auditing field uses AI technology for data mining processing and contract evaluation and performs fraud testing and risk assessment tasks according to Appelbaum et al. (2017). These technological processes allow for continuous auditing functions, which produce more efficient audits with reduced human error. ML-based anomaly detection systems excel in detecting unusual transactions through their application (Liu et al., 2020).

The traditional audit methodology used manual processes along with test samples because complete transaction review was impractical. These proven audit strategies from the past created circumstances where anomalies, errors and fraud would escape detection (Adelakun et al., 2024).

1. Comprehensive Data Analysis

The implementation of AI and ML technology allows auditors to analyze entire population data sets as well as detect irregularities instantly in addition to conducting predictive analyses along with automation functions. ML algorithms process complete datasets quickly with a high accuracy level while traditional auditing methods generally rely on limited transaction samples (Adelakun et al., 2024).

ML systems analyze big data repositories that contain structured and unstructured formats to detect system-wide patterns beyond human ability. Random Forests and Decision Trees algorithms work as part of a system to examine extensive financial data in order to identify unusual transactions along with outliers which need additional examination (Ali et al., 2022).

Thus, comprehensive data analysis:

- Reduces sampling risk,
- Enhances audit coverage,
- Improves the reliability of audit findings.

As noted by Brown, Davidovic, and Hasan (2021), full data analysis minimizes the possibility of oversight and introduces a more holistic approach to auditing financial records.

2. Enhanced Anomaly and Fraud Detection

Through AI and ML technology auditors become more effective at identifying both irregularities and cases of fraud. Machine learning models acquire ability to detect normal operational patterns by undergoing training with historical transaction data. The system marks deviations from previous statistical norms as potential anomaly signals (Adelakun et al., 2024).

Support Vector Machines (SVM) along with Artificial Neural Networks (ANN) serve as advanced algorithms which identify abnormal patterns within big transactional databases (Ali et al., 2022). These models help auditors to:Identify suspicious transactions,

- Investigate potential cases of financial misstatement,
- Detect fraudulent schemes early.

According to Seligson and Lehner (2022), AI-based anomaly detection models offer auditors a powerful tool to prioritize audit procedures and allocate resources to high-risk areas, thus increasing audit effectiveness and fraud prevention capabilities. Also Reviews digitization of auditing. Finds that AI in accounting brings new ethical challenges about data safety and professional roles.

3. Predictive Analytics for Risk Assessment

Another development over traditional audit practices is the employ of predictive analytics. ML models can predict potential risks by examining historical and real-time financial data (Adelakun et al., 2024). These predictive models allow auditors to anticipate issues before they materialize, thereby changing the auditing paradigm from reactive to proactive.

Predictive analytics improves traditional risk evaluation in several ways:

- Identifies emerging risk patterns,
- Predicts areas prone to financial misstatements,
- leads auditors in focusing their procedures on high-risk accounts or transactions (Cheng, Varshney, & Liu, 2021).

For example, Deloitte has integrated predictive analytics tools in its audits to assess client risks improved and planed more effective audit responses (Adelakun et al., 2024).

4. Automation of Repetitive and Manual Tasks

Traditional auditing methods contain several time-consuming operations which include data extraction together with validation and reconciliation activities with basic analytical tasks. Automatic functions of AI and ML technologies enable auditors to dedicate their efforts to complex judgmental areas (Chen, Wu, & Wang, 2023).

The implementation of automation in auditing brings various examples into practice as follows:

- Robotic Process Automation (RPA) for data gathering and processing,
- ML-based classification algorithms for transaction categorization,
- Automated risk scoring systems for audit planning.

According to Fedyk et al. (2022), in *Review of Accountign Studies Journal*, automation not only increases efficiency and reduces errors but also enables auditors to conduct more thorough audits within tighter deadlines. AI's impact on financial auditing processes. AI improves error detection but cautions about regulatory and transparency challenges.

Automated systems enable audit services to scale as they provide simultaneous auditing for businesses operating on a global scale without excessive resource growth.

5. Improvement in Auditor Judgment and Decision-Making

The implementation of AI and ML tools functions to assist auditors in making their professional judgments during audits. Such technologies enhance the investigation of complex data patterns which enables auditors to base their decisions on factual evidence instead of relying solely on intuition or small-size sample examination.

Auditors who leverage AI and ML technologies can interpret meaningful conclusions through patterns and trends which their models identify according to Zakaria (2021). Such systems help in:

- Identifying high-risk areas,
- Prioritizing audit tasks,
- Suggesting tailored audit procedures based on client-specific risks.

Thus, AI-enhanced auditing improves both the quality and credibility of auditors' decisions.

6. Scalability and Flexibility in Audit Procedures

Traditional auditing faces challenges when dealing with large datasets or highly dynamic businesses. ML algorithms offer scalability, allowing auditors to adapt to growing volumes and complexities of client data (Adelakun et al., 2024).

ML models can be quickly retrained and adjusted to audit different types of industries and operational environments. This scalability ensures that auditors can maintain high audit quality regardless of the client's size or data complexity.

Additionally, the flexibility of AI tools enables auditors to:

- Conduct audits remotely,
- Analyze real-time data feeds,
- Adjust audit procedures dynamically based on emerging findings (Fotoh & Lorentzon, 2023).

Such flexibility is crucial in today's digital economy, where business environments are increasingly volatile.

7. Enhancement of Real-Time Continuous Auditing

Traditional audit processes mostly review financial transactions and activities which happened several months previously. AI and ML systems enable organizations to adopt real-time audit monitoring and continuous auditing methods according to Birhane et al. (2024).

Continuous auditing operates in the course of constant financial data stream monitoring to spot irregularities whenever they come out.

This approach:

- Reduces the time lag between occurrence and detection of errors or fraud,
- Allows immediate corrective actions,
- Enhances organizational accountability.

Real-time anomaly detection systems based on ML, such as those implemented by EY, enable the firm to provide clients with ongoing assurance services (Adelakun et al., 2024).

8. Data-Driven Audit Planning and Scoping

AI and ML make easy smarter audit planning and scoping decisions. Traditional audits rely a lot on manual risk assessments conducted at the commencement of the engagement. AI tools examine historical, operational, and environmental data to dynamically judge risks and inform audit plans (Adelakun et al., 2024).

By leveraging AI-driven insights, auditors may:

- Identify key risk indicators earlier,
- Tailor audit procedures to address client-specific risks,
- Allocate resources more effectively to high-risk areas.

This data-driven approach enhances audit efficiency and increases the likelihood of detecting material misstatements.

9. Standardization and Consistency in Audit Quality

Audit procedures that involve human labor produce inconsistent results through mistakes made by auditors and different evaluation approaches between them. AI and ML systems maintain standardization by using similar rules to evaluate every piece of information in the dataset (Munoko, Brown-Liburd, & Vasarhelyi, 2020).

A machine learning model which categorizes transactions uses uniform criteria for every item by eliminating emotional judgment from such processes.

This consistency:

- Enhances the reliability of audit outcomes,
- Facilitates regulatory compliance,

- Supports auditors in meeting international audit standards (ISA) requirements.

10. Ethical Auditing and Bias Mitigation

A critical area where AI and ML improve traditional auditing is ethical auditing and the mitigation of biases. Traditional auditing practices risk bias contamination through unconscious mental biases that affect both risk assessment and judgment activities.

The appropriate training and monitoring of ML models reduces biases during operations. The audit firm EY developed continuous frameworks to recognize and solve audit biases which resulted in equitable audit findings according to Adelakun et al. (2024).

The combination of bias detection algorithms together with fairness audits allows for these benefits:

Bias detection algorithms and fairness audits provide:

- Ethical auditing practices,
- Greater trust in audit outcomes,
- Improved stakeholder confidence (Geiger et al., 2023).

However, it must be noted that ML models themselves must be carefully trained to avoid perpetuating historical biases in data.

11. Improvement in Fraud Risk Management

AI-powered fraud detection tools look up traditional auditing's advance to managing fraud risks. Traditional audits rely on auditors' experience and limited analytical tools, whereas ML systems will identify suspicious transactions and user behaviors investigate fraud.

Key improvements:

- Early detection of fraud schemes,
- Enhanced scrutiny of high-risk transactions,
- Advanced predictive models for fraud risk assessment (Wilson et al., 2021).

KPMG, for instance, successfully implemented ML-based fraud detection models that scan massive datasets in real time for fraud indicators (Adelakun et al., 2024).

12. Advancement in Natural Language Processing (NLP) for Document Review

Auditing through traditional methods requires incessant manual checking of contracts and invoices as well as communication records. Unstructured documents can be analyzed and information extracted through the automated process provided by Natural Language Processing (NLP) within AI techniques (Zakaria, 2021). Chatterjee, M. et al 2022 ICICC Proceedings Literature review on biases in NLP applications. The study presents direct consequences regarding AI audit fairness which demonstrates the way audit algorithms inherit biases present in societies.

Through NLP:

- Contracts can be reviewed for compliance breaches,
- Emails can be analyzed for fraud risks,
- Invoice data can be validated automatically against accounting entries.

This progression substantially reduces the auditor's work and improves the comprehensiveness of file reviews.

13. Realization of Cost Efficiency

By automating labor-intensive tasks and improving audit focus, AI and ML provides to considerable cost efficiencies. Firms such as PwC and Deloitte have realized cost savings while simultaneously increasing audit quality by adopting AI-based solutions (Adelakun et al., 2024).

These cost efficiencies arise from:

- Reduced time spent on manual testing,
- Faster data processing,

- Fewer resource requirements for large audits.

Thus, AI and ML enable audit firms to provide high-quality services at competitive costs.

Table 2. How AI and ML improve traditional auditing practices

Aspect	Traditional Auditing	AI/ML-Enhanced Auditing	Benefit/Improvement
Data Analysis	Sample-based testing	Full-population testing using ML	Comprehensive, risk-reducing analysis
Anomaly Detection	Manual anomaly identification	ML models detecting anomalies automatically	Early fraud and error detection
Risk Assessment	Historical, manual assessment	Predictive analytics forecasting future risks	Proactive risk management
Routine Task Automation	Manual data entry, validation	RPA and ML automate repetitive tasks	Efficiency, reduced human error
Auditor Judgment Support	Reliance on limited samples	Data-driven insights supporting decisions	Better-informed auditor judgment
Scalability	Limited by human resources	ML models scale easily to big data	Adaptable to complex organizations
Real-Time Auditing	Retrospective audits	Continuous auditing with real-time ML monitoring	Immediate anomaly detection
Audit Planning and Scoping	Static risk assessments	Dynamic, data-driven audit planning	Targeted and efficient audit focus
Consistency	Prone to inconsistencies	Standardized ML procedures	Consistent, unbiased audit outcomes
Ethical Auditing	Susceptible to human bias	Bias detection and mitigation algorithms	Fairer and more ethical audits
Fraud Risk Management	Experience-based fraud detection	ML models flag high-risk activities early	Stronger fraud prevention
Document Review	Manual document examination	NLP automates unstructured data analysis	Faster, thorough document reviews
Cost Efficiency	Labor-intensive and costly	Automation reduces time and resources needed	Cost-effective, scalable audits

Source: Summary Created by Authors

3.2 Real-World Implementations

1. Implementation in the Big Four

While all Big Four firms have initiated AI-driven platforms—such as PwC's "Halo" and Deloitte's "Argus"—public academic literature documenting their performance is limited. Studies like those of Warren Jr. et al. (2015) emphasize the need for empirical evaluation, particularly through case-based and interview-driven methods.

EY, one of the Big Four auditing firms, deployed real-time fraud detection systems powered by ML to analyze transactional data streams and flag irregularities immediately (Adelakun et al., 2024).

Similarly, IBM's AI auditing systems incorporate both supervised and unsupervised learning to continuously monitor financial transactions for signs of fraud, using advanced techniques such as Hidden Markov Models (HMM) to detect complex temporal fraud patterns (Han, 2022).

Accenture implemented predictive fraud analytics across banking clients, significantly reducing internal fraud cases by flagging anomalous employee behaviors and irregular account activities (Bandari, 2023).

Specific Tools Adopted by Big Four Firms for Audit Innovation

Case Study 1: KPMG's Smart Audit Platform

Overview

KPMG, one of the Big Four firms, introduced its Clara Smart Audit Platform integrating AI, ML, and continuous auditing principles into its financial audit processes (Adelakun et al., 2024). The audit processes at KPMG employ strategic machine learning (ML) algorithm applications for fraud detection along with audit quality improvement. Their main work involves the estimate of big financial transaction datasets with designed ML models leads to track unusual patterns marking potential fraud. KPMG achieved better audit accuracy together with higher efficiency which enabled auditors to provide their clients with improved insights.

Impact on Audit Efficiency

The regular review of client transactions powered by real-time data entry along with continuous analysis would allow KPMG auditors to provide dynamic risk assessment performance upgrades relative to adopting static annual review snapshots.

Clara performed 70 percent automation on typical audit operations which included journal entry examination and control command validation (Bakare et al., 2024).

Efficiency improvements included:

- Faster identification of risk areas,
- Reduced rework due to earlier error detection,
- Improved allocation of audit resources to higher-risk transactions.

Reduction of Human Error

Before Clara, auditors often missed anomalies due to delayed data access and fatigue during busy seasons. Clara's real-time alerts and predictive analytics reduced oversight errors by 40%, according to internal KPMG assessments (Kumar et al., 2023).

1. KPMG's Audit Innovation Tools

Specifically, KPMG employed the following tools and approaches:

- Machine Learning-Based Fraud Detection Models: These models automatically detect unusual patterns in large datasets.
- Anomaly Detection Algorithms: Used to flag irregular financial behaviors that require further investigation.
- Predictive Analytics Systems: To foresee potential risk areas based on historical transaction data .

2. Deloitte's Audit Innovation Tools

Case Study 2: Deloitte's CortexAI for Audit

Overview

Deloitte implemented CortexAI, a platform incorporating continuous auditing capabilities, particularly in transaction-intensive industries like banking and insurance. Deloitte has also implemented ML algorithms to support its audit innovation goals, focusing particularly on enhancing risk assessment procedures. Deloitte's ML models analyze historical financial and operational data to predict potential risks and provide auditors with targeted mitigation strategies.

Impact on Audit Efficiency

With CortexAI:

- Data ingestion and reconciliation were performed continuously across millions of transactions,
- Auditors were provided near-instant anomaly alerts and risk flagging,
- Dynamic audit planning adjusted focus areas automatically based on transaction patterns (Adelakun et al., 2024).

Time spent on manual sampling and validation decreased by 45%, allowing more thorough audit coverage within shorter timelines.

Reduction of Human Error

Manual sampling traditionally led to sampling bias and missed errors. Deloitte's continuous audit platform achieved:

- A 30% reduction in audit opinion revisions,
- Improved detection of small but cumulative anomalies, such as unauthorized approvals below materiality thresholds (Laine et al., 2024).

Deloitte's key tools and strategies include:

- Risk Prediction Models: Algorithms that forecast potential high-risk areas within audited entities.
- Pattern Recognition Systems: ML tools that identify recurring risk patterns and emerging trends.
- Automated Decision Support Systems: Assisting auditors in making quicker and more accurate risk assessments .

These ML integrations have improved Deloitte's ability to deliver high-quality, customized audit services tailored to the specific risk profiles of their clients.

3. PwC's Audit Innovation Tools

Case Study 3: PwC's Halo for Journals

Overview

PwC launched Halo for Journals, a continuous auditing tool designed to analyze 100% of journal entries across client systems using AI and machine learning (Adelakun et al., 2024). PwC encountered challenges primarily related to data quality and transparency when adopting ML into their audit processes. To overcome these challenges, PwC introduced several innovations:

Impact on Audit Efficiency

Instead of manually testing samples of journal entries, auditors could analyze every journal posting:

- Suspicious patterns (e.g., weekend entries, odd approvers) were flagged immediately,
- Segregation of duties violations were detected proactively.

This improved risk assessment accuracy and reduced substantive testing requirements by 35% (Ferrara, 2024).

Reduction of Human Error

Halo's automation decreased human-dependent selection biases and sampling errors:

- Entry-level auditors reported 25% fewer errors in journal risk assessments,
- Experienced auditors could focus on interpreting flagged results, improving judgment quality.

- Robust Data Quality Control Frameworks: Systems designed to ensure the cleanliness, completeness, and accuracy of data inputs used by ML models.
- Machine Learning Transparency Documentation: PwC mandated detailed documentation explaining the functioning and outcomes of ML algorithms to satisfy both internal auditors and external regulators .

The specific tools adopted by PwC include:

- Validation and Testing Frameworks for ML Models: To ensure predictive accuracy and eliminate biases.
- Explainable AI (XAI) Tools: Enhancing auditor and stakeholder understanding of ML-driven audit outcomes.
- Bias Detection and Mitigation Algorithms: Special emphasis was placed on reducing algorithmic bias that could compromise audit fairness and credibility .

4.EY's Audit Innovation Tools

Case Study 4: EY's Blockchain-Based Real-Time Auditing

Overview

EY leveraged blockchain technology to build continuous auditing capabilities into clients' accounting systems, especially for cryptocurrency firms and digital asset management companies (Odeyemi et al., 2024). EY implemented ML with a significant focus on improving fraud detection and managing algorithmic bias, recognizing bias as a crucial challenge in the application of machine learning models .

Impact on Audit Efficiency

Blockchain's immutable ledger allowed auditors to:

- Verify transactions instantly without repeated client confirmation,
- Maintain audit trails in real-time,
- Perform continuous assurance on asset ownership, movement, and valuation.

This reduced fieldwork hours by approximately 50% in complex asset auditing contexts (Geiger et al., 2023).

Reduction of Human Error

Blockchain eliminated risks associated with:

- Manual ledger verifications,
- Misstatements due to record inconsistencies,
- Data duplication across systems.

EY reported a 65% improvement in error detection rates for blockchain-enabled audits compared to traditional reconciliations.

EY's primary tools and methods include:

- Bias Detection and Mitigation Techniques: Regular audits and evaluations of ML models to ensure fairness and avoid skewed audit outcomes.
- Real-time Fraud Detection Systems: ML algorithms analyzing transactional data in real-time to uncover suspicious activities.
- Continuous Monitoring Tools: Automated systems to regularly assess the performance and fairness of deployed ML models .

These strategies have enabled EY to improve audit accuracy, enhance fraud detection capabilities, and strengthen the credibility of their auditing outputs.

Common Themes Across Big Four Firms' Audit Innovations

Machine Learning-Based Anomaly Detection

All Big Four firms adopted ML-based anomaly detection tools. These tools enable auditors to go beyond traditional sampling techniques, allowing analysis of entire datasets for rare and hidden anomalies .

Predictive Analytics

Another recurring theme is the use of predictive analytics models. These models analyze historical data to forecast future risks, thus enabling a proactive audit approach, rather than a reactive one .

Automation of Routine Tasks

The Big Four firms have adopted ML and AI to automate routine tasks like:

- Data extraction,
- Categorization,
- Preliminary risk assessments.

This shift allows human auditors to focus on complex and high-value tasks, enhancing the strategic value of audits .

Focus on Explainable AI (XAI)

Given the need for transparency in audits, Big Four firms have prioritized Explainable AI tools that allow auditors and stakeholders to understand how machine learning models arrive at specific conclusions .

Bias Monitoring and Ethical AI

Organizations frequently address problems associated with biased algorithms as a primary concern. EY and other firms have integrated bias detection frameworks together with continuous model evaluation processes to achieve unbiased results from their ML models

Table 3. Tools and Technologies used by Big Four

Firm	Tools/Technologies	Purpose
KPMG	ML Fraud Detection, Predictive Analytics, Anomaly Detection,	Fraud detection and audit enhancement
Deloitte	Risk Prediction Models, Automated Decision Support Pattern Recognition Systems,	Enhanced risk assessment and custom-made auditing
PwC	Data Quality Control, Explainable AI, Bias Mitigation Algorithms	Improved transparency, data accuracy, and fairness
EY	Bias Detection Techniques, Real-time Fraud Continuous Monitoring Tools Detection Systems,	Fraud detection and fairness in auditing results

Source: Created by Authors

Specific Algorithms and Techniques Used

Table 4. Several machine learning techniques adopted in auditing innovations in addition to firm-specific tools

Technique	Description	Application in Auditing
Support Vector Machine (SVM)	Used for classification tasks.	Classifying financial transactions or anomalies as fraudulent or legitimate.
Hidden Markov Models (HMM)	For modeling complex random processes in financial data.	Modeling sequences of financial data to detect hidden states or patterns in fraud.
Artificial Neural Networks (ANN)	Mimicking human cognitive functions to analyze intricate financial patterns.	Detecting intricate patterns in financial data, such as fraud or irregular behavior.
Fuzzy Logic	Handling uncertainty in data interpretation during audits.	Managing uncertain or imprecise data during audit analysis.
K-Nearest Neighbors (KNN)	For grouping similar financial transactions for analysis.	Grouping transactions based on similarity to detect anomalies or outliers.
Decision Trees	Used in risk prediction and anomaly detection.	Identifying risky financial transactions and predicting potential fraud.
Genetic Algorithms	Optimization tools for identifying the best audit strategies.	Optimizing auditing strategies and identifying efficient detection methods.
Ensemble Methods	Combining multiple models for higher predictive accuracy.	Increasing the robustness and accuracy of fraud detection systems.
Logistic Regression	Applied in fraud detection classifications.	Classifying financial activities into fraud/no fraud categories.
Clustering Techniques	For unsupervised grouping of similar financial activities.	Grouping similar transactions to identify unusual patterns or anomalies.
Random Forest	Ensemble of decision trees for stronger, more robust audit models.	Enhancing fraud detection by combining multiple decision trees for stronger predictions.
Naïve Bayes	For probability-based classification in detecting anomalies.	Detecting financial anomalies based on probabilistic classification.

Source: created by Authors

4. CHALLENGES IN APPLYING AI AND ML WITHIN AUDIT FRAMEWORKS

During fast industrial revolution auditing joins other sectors where Artificial Intelligence (AI) and Machine Learning (ML) act as catalysts. A conventional auditing process depended on manual verification together with sampling and judgmental decision-making which created conditions for human errors alongside unnoticed fraud that resulted from inadequate sampling methods. Auditing practices now benefit from ML algorithms included in audit frameworks because they boost efficiency and improve accuracy and enable comprehensive audit procedures (Adelakun et al., 2024). AI and ML technologies face multiple fundamental obstacles that prevent their complete use in auditing practice. Financial auditors encounter a series of implementation obstacles including poor information quality, unclear algorithmic processes, biased data analysis, regulatory compliance issues, workforce skill shortages and expensive technology operations together with employee resistance to operational changes. This paper examines these barriers through review of recent research while suggesting approaches to address them. Most organizations fail to adequately recognize the cultural as well as ethical aspects which arise from placing AI into their existing systems according to Ransbotham et al. (2017).

1. Data Quality and Integrity Issues

The principal hurdle in implementing ML for auditing is managing the quality as well as maintaining the integrity of adopted data collection methods. The data used for training machine learning algorithms holds direct influence on their operational capabilities. The model outputs tend to reflect the same quality errors found in the training data because of incomplete or inaccurate or outdated or biased data (Adelakun et al., 2024). Data of poor quality leads to inaccurate risk assessments as well as missed frauds and distorted audit reports.

Auditors must ensure robust data management practices, including data cleaning, preprocessing, and continuous data quality assessments (Akinrinola et al., 2024). However, establishing and maintaining such rigorous data controls is time-consuming and requires specialized tools and expertise, making it a significant challenge for audit firms, especially small and mid-sized ones.

2. Algorithmic Transparency and Explainability

The "black box" nature of many ML algorithms presents another substantial hurdle. Complex ML models, particularly deep learning networks, often operate without easily interpretable decision-making processes (Adelakun et al., 2024). For auditors, transparency is paramount; they must not only trust the outputs but also explain them to clients, regulators, and other stakeholders.

Lack of explainability can undermine stakeholder trust and regulatory compliance, particularly under standards like the General Data Protection Regulation (GDPR) and International Standards on Auditing (ISA) (Varona & Suárez, 2022). Techniques such as model interpretation, visualization tools, and Explainable AI (XAI) have been suggested (Zakaria, 2021), but implementing them remains technically challenging and resource-intensive.

3. Algorithmic Bias and Fairness

Another profound issue is algorithmic bias. If historical data contains biases—such as underreporting certain types of frauds or reflecting human prejudices—then ML models will likely perpetuate these biases (Costanza-Chock et al., 2022). Audit results that contain bias will produce incorrect risk analyses that result in penalties and damage professional reputations.

Auditors need to implement bias detection platforms and data management approaches which include fairness measurements in model assessments as well as model updates to admit unbiased information (Mehrabi et al., 2021). Researchers continue to work for complete bias elimination although achieving it proves particularly difficult.

4. Regulatory and Compliance Challenges

Compliance with regulatory standards such as GDPR, ISA, and emerging AI-specific regulations like the EU Artificial Intelligence Act is critical when implementing ML in auditing (Ayling & Chapman, 2022). Organizations must follow specific rules that address data protection requirements together with mandatory disclosure of decision mechanisms and measurable AI system functionality and unbiased assurance processes.

Auditors need to ensure that ML-based auditing follows existing frameworks through extra documentation along with independent audits and continuous compliance assessments as reported by Mökander et al. (2022). Rules that change frequently force audit firms to maintain constant practice evolution which generates operational expenses for the company.

Skills Gap and Training Needs

A substantial deficiency exists within auditing practice concerning professionals' understanding of AI and ML technological applications. The skills needed to perform traditional auditing differ from those required for ML-driven audits because modern ML-driven audits need data science expertise along with statistical modeling proficiency as well as programming knowledge and algorithm evaluation understanding according to Hu et al. (2021).

The process of upskilling current auditors together with the hiring of data scientists who specialize in audit-related ML applications demands both financial strain and extended time periods (Al-dahabi et al., 2024). Integrating domain experience with technological abilities stands as an essential requirement which auditing rarely addresses adequately thus slowing down AI implementation in auditing processes.

5. INFRASTRUCTURE COSTS AND INVESTMENT BARRIERS

Organizations must spend major resources to deploy ML technologies because they need cloud computing platforms along with high-performance servers and advanced software licenses and robust cybersecurity protection (Duggineni, 2023). Such expenses are highly challenging to manage especially for companies with small or medium audit firm operations.

Regular costs for maintaining models together with cybersecurity upgrades and compliance assessments and model retraining expenses increase overall financial responsibility in auditing. Capacity to expand through cloud options creates data ownership issues and dependence on single suppliers become primary hurdles for organizations.

6. Resistance to Change and Organizational Culture

Auditing professionals actively oppose the integration of new technology which creates substantial hurdles for ML admission to auditing practice. Laborers in auditing show reluctance because they believe ML instruments will replace them while questioning the impact on their expert judgment and doubting AI-based assessment (Aldemİr & Uçma Uysal, 2024).

Cultural institutions that follow traditional business models generally oppose the adoption of new technological solutions. Overcoming this requires change management strategies, including education programs, pilot projects, and highlighting success stories that show how AI complements, rather than replaces, human auditors (Fotoh & Lorentzon, 2023).

7. Data Privacy and Security Concerns

ML algorithms require vast volumes of sensitive financial data for training and operational use. Protecting this data against breaches, theft, and unauthorized access is a significant challenge. Auditors must implement strict encryption, anonymization, and access control measures (Galdon Clavell et al., 2020).

Moreover, under regulations such as GDPR, organizations must ensure that customer data used for model training complies with consent and data minimization principles (Ayling & Chapman, 2022). Data protection audits become mandatory, adding another layer of complexity and cost.

8. Integration Complexity

Integrating ML tools into existing audit workflows, enterprise systems (like ERP), and compliance reporting frameworks is a complex task. ML systems need to interact seamlessly with legacy systems without disrupting ongoing audit operations (Minkkinen et al., 2022).

Many audit firms have customized workflows, and fitting ML models into these flows often requires bespoke integrations, custom APIs, and continuous IT support. Integration challenges can delay projects, inflate budgets, and lower ROI from ML initiatives.

9. Ethical and Accountability Issues

Ensuring that ML models act ethically—avoiding discriminatory practices, respecting client confidentiality, and maintaining auditor independence—is a growing concern. ML outputs must be aligned with ethical auditing standards and professional codes of conduct (Birhane et al., 2024).

Accountability questions also arise: If an ML model's mistake leads to an audit failure, who is responsible—the model developer, the auditor using it, or the audit firm? Clear lines of responsibility must be established, and legal liabilities clarified before widespread adoption.

10.Strategies for Addressing Challenges

Table 5. Strategies to mitigate challenges

Recommendation	Description	Source
Robust Data Governance	Establish stringent data quality, data lineage, and validation protocols.	Islam, 2024
Explainable AI (XAI)	Incorporate explainability tools to demystify ML outputs.	Zakaria, 2021
Bias Audits	Regular audits to detect and correct algorithmic biases.	Laine et al., 2024
Regulatory Compliance Monitoring	Build dedicated teams for compliance assurance and legal reviews.	
Training Programs	Upskill auditors in data science basics, ML concepts, and AI ethics.	Hu et al., 2023
Cost-effective ML Tools	Utilize cloud-based, scalable ML solutions that minimize upfront investment.	

continued on following page

Table 5. Continued

Recommendation	Description	Source
Change Management Initiatives	Engage auditors early, provide continuous learning opportunities, and emphasize how AI can empower their roles.	
Privacy-by-Design	Embed privacy considerations into every stage of ML model development and deployment.	Galdon Clavell et al., 2020
Pilot Projects	Start with small-scale deployments to test feasibility and refine strategies before scaling.	
Ethical Governance Frameworks	Create internal guidelines to govern AI usage responsibly.	Cumming et al., 2024

Source: created by Authors

6. PREDICTIVE RISK AND FRAUD ASSESSMENT THROUGH AI AND ML

AI and ML systems can predict financial risks by using historical and real-time datasets to identify patterns associated with risky activities. Predictive analytics involves the use of statistical techniques and ML models to forecast future outcomes based on past data (Cheng, Varshney, & Liu, 2021).

ML models have demonstrated potential in fraud detection and predictive analytics in financial contexts. For example, neural networks and decision trees have been used to classify high-risk transactions with considerable accuracy (Cokina & Davenport, 2017). However, these models still require domain expertise for interpretation and validation.

In auditing contexts, ML models like:

- Random Forests,
- Support Vector Machines (SVMs),
- Logistic Regression,
- Artificial Neural Networks (ANNs),

are usually used to model and forecast risk factors (Ali et al., 2022).

These models operate by:

- Learning from historical financial records,
- Identifying features associated with past fraudulent activities,
- Generating predictive scores for new transactions or entities.

According to Adelakun et al. (2024), predictive models built using supervised learning algorithms have shown significant accuracy in forecasting audit risks, credit defaults, misstatements, and fraudulent behaviors in financial statements.

Examples of Predictive Success

- By using predictive ML algorithms Deloitte measures client transactions and forecasts potential risk zones as part of their substantive audit procedures (Adelakun et al., 2024). AI models evaluate financial trends that focus on irregular revenue recognition and unexplained expenses together with rapid balance sheet alterations for future misstatement projection.
- KPMG used ML-based tools to assess extensive financial data which identified likely future financial reporting issues within its client base thereby helping auditors to distribute resources optimally (Bakare et al., 2024).
- The data explains that Artificial Intelligence/Machine Learning systems demonstrate success in risk prediction for finance applications when they method quality data sets and receive ongoing updates for changing financial situations.
- Financial Fraud Prevention Using AI and ML
- The process of audit prevention goes beyond identifying threats since it requires immediate awareness of fraudulent activities before substantial financial losses occur. The ability of ML models to find unusual patterns enables them to stop fraudulent payments in automatic real-time (Adelakun et al., 2024).
- The detection of fraud systems require multiple machine learning approaches for their operation.
- Anomaly Detection Models: Identify outliers or unusual behaviors that deviate from normal financial activity.

- Clustering Algorithms: Group similar transactions to spot anomalies.
- Classification Models: Categorize transactions as legitimate or potentially fraudulent based on previous fraud cases.

Seligson and Lehner (2022) note that AI systems can process millions of transactions instantaneously, spotting subtle patterns that human auditors or traditional rule-based systems might overlook.

6.1 Mechanisms Through Which AI/ML Enhance Fraud Prediction and Prevention

Risk prediction alongside fraud prevention gets improved through various mechanisms which AI and ML systems deliver.

1. Continuous Learning and Adaptation

The evolution of ML models depends on new data input because they learn from ongoing information intake. By analyzing new fraud patterns the systems update their parameters for remaining methodical of scam artists (Fedyk et al., 2022).

A supervised ML fraud detection system becomes more effective through the addition of new examples that label fraudulent and non-fraudulent transactions.

2. Real-Time Monitoring

Transaction monitoring as a service with AI systems provides instant capabilities that help organizations detect and prevent fraud in real-time (Adelakun et al., 2024). Continuous ML-powered auditing systems warn organizations about unusual transactions right away thus enabling them to stop suspicious activities before financial losses happen.

3. Advanced Pattern Recognition

AI systems with ML express remarkable skill to extract complex patterns existing in multidimensional data sets. Frauds in transaction layering between different accounts and currencies and jurisdictions become detectable with ensemble modeling and deep neural networks according to Ali et al. (2022).

The models search for discreet patterns which standard rule-based programs and traditional human audits are unable to identify.

4. Risk Scoring and Prioritization

The analytical decisions of Artificial Intelligence (AI) generate risk ratings for financial transactions together with banking records as well as business clients according to established patterns found in past occurrences and environmental aspects (Chatterjee et al., 2022). Auditors determine which entities present high risks so their investigation efforts can be focused strategically to key trouble areas.

The optimized resource distribution enables better capabilities in preventing fraud.

6.2 Limitations and Challenges in AI/ ML-Based Fraud Prediction

1. Dependence on Data Quality

AI/ML systems are heavily reliant on high-quality, labeled datasets for training (Adelakun et al., 2024). Inaccurate, incomplete, or biased datasets can compromise the predictive accuracy of models, leading either to missed fraud cases or false positives.

KPMG reported that data quality control mechanisms were crucial when integrating ML models into their audit systems (Bakare et al., 2024).

2. Model Interpretability and Transparency

Many ML models, especially deep learning networks, operate as "black boxes," making it difficult for auditors and regulators to understand how fraud decisions are made (Laine, Minkkinen, & Mäntymäki, 2024).

Explainable AI (XAI) frameworks are being developed to address this issue, but full transparency remains a challenge, particularly when legal and compliance justifications are needed.

3. Evolving Fraud Tactics

Fraudsters continually adapt their methods to bypass detection systems. ML models must be frequently updated and retrained to remain effective against new fraud schemes (Mökander et al., 2022).

Without continuous monitoring and re-tuning, even the most sophisticated models can become obsolete quickly.

4. Resource and Cost Constraints

Developing, implementing, and maintaining advanced AI/ML fraud detection systems requires significant investment in technology infrastructure, skilled personnel, and continuous model training (Fotoh & Lorentzon, 2023).

Small and mid-sized audit firms may find it challenging to afford comprehensive AI-based solutions, limiting widespread adoption.

- Comparative Effectiveness of AI/ML vs. Traditional Methods
- Studies reveal that AI/ML-based methods outperform conventional auditing methods together with rule-based fraud detection solutions for risk identification and fraud prevention responsibilities.
- According to Zakaria (2021) machine learning algorithms outperform traditional audit methods in financial fraud detection but only when models reach 90% accuracy in designated industries while manual auditing can only detect less than 1/2of fraud.
- Tests show Random Forest combined with Logistic Regression produces superior true positive results as compared to static rule-based systems when assessing credit card fraud activities (Ali et al., 2022).

- AI and ML systems demonstrate superior competence to traditional methods both for fraud detection and predictive analysis and fraud prevention scope.
- Ethical and Regulatory Considerations
- When organizations depend more on AI and ML to detect fraud it generates significant ethical problems about data privacy and algorithmic fairness (Costanza-Chock, Raji, & Buolamwini, 2022).
- Collection models need to build prevention mechanisms which stop particular population groups or specific entities from being excluded. The examination of personal financial data for fraud expertise does require auditor verification which ensures GDPR compliance throughout the process.
- The emerging concept of AI governance needs ongoing model auditing to maintain ethical standards of AI technology-based fraud detection systems (Ferrara, 2024).

6. Research Philosophy: Paradigm and Realm

- The authors choose an interpretivist paradigm because they wish to determine how auditors experience and make sense of artificial intelligence and machine learning systems during their auditing processes. Constructivism functions as the basis for knowledge development because development occurs through social contexts.
- In the AI/ML audit domain:
- Auditors construct understanding of machine outputs,
- Organizations interpret AI systems based on internal culture and external pressures,
- Regulators co-construct standards around AI audit technologies (Ferrara, 2024).

The interpretive-constructivist view thus informs the decision to pursue qualitative methodologies such as semi-structured interviews, case studies, and thematic analysis, aiming to derive rich, contextually embedded insights rather than generalized, quantitative patterns.

This philosophical orientation is crucial for revealing how AI/ML is not merely a tool but a co-actor that shapes and is shaped by auditing practice (Mökander, 2023).

7. ROADMAP FOR AI/ML ADOPTION IN AUDITING

Through empirical case studies, the research outlines a practical roadmap for organizations seeking to embed AI/ML into audit workflows, including:

- Selecting appropriate audit-specific AI tools (e.g., risk prediction engines, fraud detection models),
- Ensuring data governance to support model accuracy,
- Balancing automation with professional judgment,
- Building interdisciplinary teams combining audit expertise and data science skills (Adelakun et al., 2024).

Such a roadmap addresses a key industry concern: many audit firms express enthusiasm about AI/ML yet lack structured guidance for successful implementation (Duggineni, 2023).

1. Full Integration of Continuous Auditing in Financial Reporting

Future audits will not be annual events but continuous assurance engagements, providing stakeholders with real-time audit updates, particularly in volatile industries like cryptocurrency, fintech, and e-commerce (Han, 2022).

2. Rise of Continuous Auditing Dashboards

Auditors and clients will use real-time dashboards, visualizing:

- Anomalies,
- Risk scores,
- Regulatory compliance statuses (Ferrara, 2024).

These dashboards will drive more informed decision-making throughout the financial year.

3. Skillset Evolution

Auditors will require:

- Data science knowledge,
- AI/ML literacy,
- Real-time analytics interpretation capabilities (Minkkinen et al., 2022).

Professional bodies like the AICPA and ICAEW are already updating curricula to reflect these emerging demands.

4. Regulatory Evolution

Continuous auditing demands:

- Updates to International Standards on Auditing (ISAs),
- Specific guidelines for real-time audit evidence,
- Ethical codes around AI usage in audits (Owolabi et al., 2024).

Global regulators must keep pace with continuous assurance technologies to maintain public trust.

8. KEY MECHANISMS THROUGH WHICH CONTINUOUS AUDITING IMPROVES AUDIT EFFICIENCY

1. Real-Time Monitoring

Continuous auditing replaces point-in-time reviews with ongoing transaction monitoring.

This allows:

- Immediate anomaly detection,
- Faster issue resolution before financial close,
- Dynamic risk reassessments (Birhane et al., 2024).

2. Automation of Routine Tasks

Continuous auditing tools automate:

- Data extraction,
- Validation,
- Risk scoring.

This drastically cuts down the time spent on manual work, allowing auditors to focus on strategic tasks (Fedyk et al., 2022).

3. Dynamic Risk Assessment

Traditional audits fix risk profiles at planning stages.
Continuous auditing enables:

- Adjusting risk assessments based on live data,
- Detecting emergent risks unnoticed during initial planning (Koshiyama et al., 2024).

8.1 Redefining Auditor Roles and Skills

AI does not replace auditors but redefines their roles. Auditors increasingly need competencies in:

- Interpreting AI outputs,
- Managing data science workflows,
- Applying professional skepticism to algorithmic results (Munoko, Brown-Liburd, & Vasarhelyi, 2020).

Firms like PwC and EY are already investing in upskilling auditors in AI literacy, blending technological fluency with traditional accounting expertise (Adelakun et al., 2024).

8.2 Key Ways Continuous Auditing Reduces Human Error

1. **Elimination of Sampling Bias**

Continuous auditing examines entire datasets rather than small, selected samples:

- Errors that would have gone unnoticed under traditional sampling are now visible,
- Statistical representativeness is no longer a concern (Zakaria, 2021).

2. **Reduction in Fatigue-Related Errors**

Auditors no longer need to manually sift through massive datasets for low-probability anomalies.

Instead, AI-powered continuous audits:

- Prioritize anomalies,
- Reduce decision fatigue,
- Improve judgment consistency (Laine et al., 2024).

8.3 Objective and Standardized Decision-Making

Machine learning models:

- Apply the same logic to all transactions,
- Reduce subjective inconsistencies between different auditors.

Thus, audit quality and reliability are enhanced (Costanza-Chock et al., 2022).

9. CONCLUSION

AI and ML technologies represent not merely a disruptive innovation but an evolutionary leap in the auditing profession. By augmenting auditors' capabilities to process vast datasets, detect hidden anomalies, and predict emerging risks, these technologies have begun reshaping audit practices in profound ways (Adelakun et al., 2024). 10. Conclusion

AI and ML are not just disruptive technologies; they represent an evolutionary leap in how audits are conducted. By enhancing speed, scope, and accuracy, they hold the potential to redefine the auditing profession. This research aims to map this transition through grounded qualitative inquiry, offering both scholarly insights and practical implications.

REFERENCES

Adelakun, O., Akinrinola, B. T., & Islam, R. (2024). Applications of machine learning models in auditing: Opportunities and challenges. *Finance & Accounting Research Journal.*

Ali, I., Mehreen, A., & Shah, S. (2022). The role of machine learning algorithms in fraud detection: A financial sector perspective. *International Journal of Financial Studies*, *10*(3), 45–62.

Appelbaum, D., Kogan, A., & Vasarhelyi, M. (2017). Big Data and analytics in the modern audit engagement: Research needs. *Auditing*, *36*(4), 1–27. DOI: 10.2308/ajpt-51684

Bakare, A. O., Odeyemi, O., & Kumar, M. (2024). Audit automation: Impact of AI platforms like Clara in Big Four firms. *Journal of Auditing Technology Research*, *12*(1), 34–50.

Birhane, A. (2024). Auditing artificial intelligence systems: Challenges and solutions. *arXiv preprint arXiv:2401.00001.*

Brown, C., Davidovic, N., & Hasan, S. (2021). Enhancing audit reliability through full dataset analysis. *Accounting and Information Systems Research*, *20*(2), 85–105.

Chatterjee, M., Bose, S., & Banerjee, P. (2022). Biases in natural language processing applications: Consequences for audit fairness. *ICICC Proceedings 2022.*

Cheng, J., Varshney, K. R., & Liu, H. (2021). Predictive analytics in financial risk assessment: A survey. *Decision Support Systems*, *146*, 113539.

Costanza-Chock, S., Raji, I. D., & Buolamwini, J. (2022). Towards ethical algorithm auditing: Recommendations for the field. *Proceedings of the ACM Conference on Fairness, Accountability, and Transparency (FAccT).*

Cumming, D., Hou, W., Lee, E., & Wei, J. (2024). Ethical governance frameworks for AI auditing. *Journal of Business Ethics.*

Duggineni, S. (2023). Challenges in auditing AI-driven financial environments. *Science and Technology Journal*, *22*(4), 77–92.

Ferrara, E. (2024). Understanding the butterfly effect in AI auditing. *Machine Learning with Applications, 10*, 100214.

Fotoh, L. E., & Lorentzon, J. I. (2023). The digitalization of audit: Expectations versus realities. *Accounting Horizons, 37*(1), 71–90.

Galdon Clavell, G. (2020). Data protection and AI in the auditing sector. *Technology and Regulation, 10*(1), 22–31.

Geiger, T. J. (2023). Enhancing audit trust through continuous monitoring and AI fairness. *Journal of Accounting and Organizational Change, 19*(2), 289–309.

González-Sendino, R., Fernández-Llamas, C., & García-Díaz, V. (2023). Fairness, accountability, and bias in AI systems: Implications for auditing. *Journal of Artificial Intelligence Research, 76*, 1–25.

Han, H. (2022). AI and blockchain in corporate governance: Implications for auditing. (Doctoral dissertation, Brunel University).

Hartmann, F., Moers, F., & van Staden, C. (2024). Future standards for AI-enabled auditing. *International Journal of Auditing, 28*(1), 15–30.

Hu, H., Shao, H., & Zhang, Y. (2021). Upskilling auditors for AI-based audit technologies: A systematic review. *Journal of Accounting Education, 57*, 100748.

Islam, R. (2024). Data governance strategies for AI audits. *Information Systems Management, 41*(1), 45–59.

Jauhiainen, T., & Lehner, O. M. (2022). AI governance and the transformation of accounting practices. In *Artificial Intelligence in Accounting* (pp. 103–124). Routledge.

Koshiyama, A., Kazim, E., & Preece, A. (2024). Algorithmic auditing and governance: A comprehensive framework. *Royal Society Open Science, 11*(1), 210534.

Kumar, M., Sharma, S., & Bakare, A. (2023). Evaluating the impact of real-time auditing platforms: The case of KPMG's Clara. *Audit Innovation Journal, 9*(2), 64–82.

Laine, J., Minkkinen, M., & Mäntymäki, M. (2024). Ethics-based auditing frameworks for AI systems. *Information & Management, 61*(2), 103624.

Liu, Y., Li, M., & Liu, B. (2020). Anomaly detection techniques for financial fraud detection: A review. *ACM Computing Surveys, 53*(4), 1–36. DOI: 10.1145/3357375

Mehrabi, N., Morstatter, F., Saxena, N., Lerman, K., & Galstyan, A. (2021). A survey on bias and fairness in machine learning. *ACM Computing Surveys, 54*(6), 1–35. DOI: 10.1145/3457607

Minkkinen, M., Laine, J., & Mäntymäki, M. (2022). Continuous auditing of AI systems: Toward dynamic audit processes. *Digital Society : Ethics, Socio-Legal and Governance of Digital Technology, 1*(1), 1–17.

Mökander, J. (2023). The interpretive turn in AI auditing: Human-machine collaboration. *AI and Ethics, 3*(1), 79–98.

Mökander, J. (2022). Conformity assessments and audits in European AI governance. *Minds and Machines, 32*(1), 123–149.

Munoko, I., Brown-Liburd, H. L., & Vasarhelyi, M. A. (2020). The ethical implications of using artificial intelligence in auditing. *Journal of Business Ethics, 167*(2), 209–234. DOI: 10.1007/s10551-019-04407-1

Odeyemi, O., Bakare, A., & Kumar, M. (2024). Blockchain-based assurance in EY's auditing practices. *Accounting and Blockchain Review, 5*(1), 12–33.

Owolabi, I. (2024). Regulation and assurance of AI in financial auditing: A global perspective. *International Journal of Accounting Information Systems, 44*, 100614.

Patel, P., & Uddin, M. N. (2022). Ethical AI auditing tools for big data systems. *International Journal of Stochastic Analysis, 4*(1), 1–16.

Ransbotham, S., Kiron, D., & Prentice, P. (2017). Cognitive technologies in auditing: Early lessons. *MIT Sloan Management Review, 58*(4), 1–12.

Sarker, I. H. (2021). Machine learning: Algorithms, real-world applications and research directions. *SN Computer Science, 2*(3), 160. DOI: 10.1007/s42979-021-00592-x PMID: 33778771

Seligson, A., & Lehner, O. M. (2022). AI's role in fraud detection and risk management: Challenges and opportunities. *Journal of Financial Crime*, *29*(3), 745–761.

Varona, J., & Suárez, J. P. (2022). Transparency in AI decision-making: An imperative for auditors. *Information Systems Frontiers*, *24*(2), 425–439.

Warren, J. D.Jr, Moffitt, K. C., & Byrnes, P. (2015). How Big Data will change accounting. *Accounting Horizons*, *29*(2), 397–407. DOI: 10.2308/acch-51069

Wilson, C., Denton, E., & Williams, M. (2023). Domain-specific fairness auditing for automated candidate screening systems. *Proceedings of the ACM FAccT Conference*.

Zakaria, I. (2021). The impact of artificial intelligence on auditing practices: An ethical perspective. *Journal of Accounting and Organizational Change*, *17*(2), 254–274.

Chapter 6
Enhancing Fraud Detection With AI in International Systems

Mustafa Kayyali

https://orcid.org/0000-0003-3300-262X

Maaref University of Applied Sciences, Syria

ABSTRACT

Fraud, in its evolving digital forms, poses an immense challenge to global financial stability. This chapter explores how artificial intelligence, particularly machine learning, is reshaping the way fraud is detected and prevented across international financial systems. By tracing the shift from traditional rule-based approaches to dynamic, data-driven methods, the authors examine the integration of AI tools within diverse accounting frameworks. The chapter also navigates the ethical and legal complexities surrounding algorithmic oversight and cross-border data governance. In doing so, it presents a critical look at both the promise and peril of relying on intelligent systems in a domain as sensitive as financial integrity. Ultimately, this work advocates for a balanced, collaborative future—where innovation in fraud detection is met with global regulatory alignment and a firm commitment to transparency.

DOI: 10.4018/979-8-3373-3626-8.ch006

INTRODUCTION

Fraud, much like a virus, adapts to its environment. It mutates in response to scrutiny, evolves past regulations, and exploits gaps in oversight wherever it finds them. In today's hyper-connected global economy—where billions of transactions occur daily across digital platforms, jurisdictions, and currencies—the mechanisms of fraud have grown more elusive, more sophisticated, and, ultimately, more dangerous. And despite decades of reform, compliance upgrades, and whistleblower protections, fraud continues to siphon off trillions of dollars annually from institutions, governments, and citizens alike. What we are witnessing is not merely the persistence of an old enemy—it is the emergence of fraud as a shape-shifting, data-driven adversary, requiring tools of a similarly adaptive kind. This is where artificial intelligence enters the frame, not as a silver bullet, but as an evolving ally.

Artificial intelligence (AI), and particularly its subset of machine learning (ML), is not new to the financial sector (Mahalakshmi et al, 2022). Algorithms have long powered credit scoring, algorithmic trading, and automated customer service. Yet only recently have we begun to grasp the potential of AI to detect fraud not just after the fact, but in real time—and in many cases, before it unfolds. At its best, AI can parse through oceans of data at speeds that outmatch human capability, identify hidden patterns invisible to the naked eye, and "learn" from each incident it encounters (Valavanidis, 2023). But deploying AI in the realm of fraud detection—especially across international systems—is not without its challenges. The path forward is riddled with complexities, ranging from inconsistent regulatory standards and ethical ambiguities to data privacy concerns and the risk of algorithmic bias.

This chapter begins with a contextual grounding in the scale and scope of fraud, particularly in transnational contexts. It then explores the transition from conventional fraud detection techniques—largely rule-based and reactive—to dynamic, AI-powered systems capable of self-improvement. We will delve into the technical underpinnings of these systems, such as anomaly detection, neural networks, and behavioral analytics, and examine case studies where AI tools have either succeeded or failed in the fight against financial misconduct. The chapter also interrogates the ethical dilemmas posed by autonomous systems: Can a machine accuse a human of wrongdoing without oversight? What happens when AI makes an error? How can we ensure transparency in black-box models?

As fraud becomes increasingly global, the call for collaborative, standardized approaches to AI regulation grows louder (Asad, 2025). The chapter ends by proposing a roadmap for cross-border cooperation—a shared ethical framework, guided by accountability, interoperability, and cultural sensitivity. Ultimately, enhancing fraud detection with AI is not just a technical challenge—it is a governance issue, a philosophical dilemma, and a collective test of our willingness to protect the integrity of financial systems in a world spinning ever faster on digital rails.

THE GLOBAL COST OF FRAUD: A PROBLEM BEYOND BORDERS

Fraud doesn't knock politely. It seeps. It slithers. It disguises itself in official signatures, cloaks itself in corporate jargon, weaves through supply chains, and smiles through polished PowerPoint decks (Banerjee, 2024). Unlike petty theft, which operates in shadows and margins, fraud knows how to hold a meeting. It knows how to wear a suit. It doesn't just break the rules—it rewrites them midgame. And when it spreads, it doesn't respect borders. In fact, it thrives on the spaces between them: the jurisdictional loopholes, the regulatory blind spots, the bureaucratic delays that make international oversight feel like trying to catch fog with bare hands.

The global cost of fraud is staggering—and yet strangely abstract (Dyck et al, 2024). Every few years, a report surfaces. The Association of Certified Fraud Examiners (ACFE), for instance, estimates that organizations lose roughly 5% of their annual revenues to fraud (Adeniyi, 2025). Just sit with that. Five percent. In a world where multinational corporations move billions every quarter, and public budgets are stretched threadbare, this isn't a rounding error—it's a haemorrhage. Add to this the sprawling dark economy of cyber fraud, offshore laundering, procurement corruption, trade misinvoicing, cryptocurrency scams, embezzlement, fake NGOs, shell companies, identity theft, invoice manipulation—the list grows like an unchecked tumor—and what you end up with isn't just a financial issue (Yarovenko, 2024). It's a structural erosion of trust. It's disbelief becoming institutional. And unlike natural disasters, fraud has no epicenter. There's no seismic zone to map. No geographic logic to its spread. It originates anywhere and affects everywhere—an Indonesian procurement fraud rippling into Australian real estate; a forged Swiss invoice padding a contract in Zambia; a Russian ransomware attack locking up American hospitals. It mutates in response to regulation. And as we digitize faster—more mobile payments, more blockchain applications, more digital banking in unregulated spaces—we're simultaneously creating new vectors of vulnerability (Martino, 2021). The speed and complexity of modern financial systems have outpaced the guardrails meant to protect them. As a result, fraudsters are no longer outsiders—they're system surfers. But maybe the real damage isn't just in the dollar value lost. It's in the paranoia that follows. Fraud breeds suspicion—between governments, within institutions, among citizens. It corrodes public trust, the kind you can't quantify in spreadsheets. When people start believing that systems are rigged, that the rules apply selectively, that money and power always find a way to cheat—something unravels. Call it civic glue, social cohesion, moral consensus—it thins. The fallout isn't just economic; it's existential. Fraud, at scale, makes honesty feel naïve.

Take development finance. Billions flow every year from global north to south in the name of infrastructure, health, education (Hildyard, 2023). But somewhere along the way, large chunks vanish—into inflated project costs, ghost workers, bribed auditors, fictitious vendors. The aid still arrives; the impact doesn't. And so donors grow cynical, locals grow disillusioned, and governments retreat into defensive posturing (Lopes, 2024). Meanwhile, schools go unbuilt, clinics remain shells, and communities continue to wait for promises that were funded, signed, and swallowed.

Or consider financial inclusion. Mobile money platforms like M-Pesa in Kenya or Paytm in India have revolutionized access for millions (Suri et al, 2023). But with inclusion comes exposure. Fraudsters now impersonate customer service agents. They phish SMS messages. They hijack wallets with social engineering techniques. These aren't elite hackers—they're often local actors, nimble, adaptive, and operating faster than regulation can chase. And when people lose their savings to fraud—even just once—their trust in digital finance collapses, and with it, the larger push for inclusion stalls. Progress doesn't only depend on innovation; it leans heavily on security.

International banking paints a darker picture still. The 1MDB scandal in Malaysia—a case so brazen it reads like financial fiction—saw billions siphoned from a national development fund into luxury apartments, Hollywood films, and personal jetliners (Tan, 2021). But the theft wasn't localized. The money passed through Swiss accounts, American firms, Singaporean banks, and Caribbean tax havens. It was dressed up in legal contracts, shielded by front companies, and laundered through institutions that should've known better. The enablers weren't always criminals; many were just compliant functionaries, too passive or too disincentivized to ask deeper questions. And that's the quiet tragedy. Fraud often hides in the cracks of plausible deniability. In the grey zones. In the silence of the unverified assumption. It doesn't always announce itself with a red flag. More often, it walks in wearing the uniform of normalcy, blends in with compliance reports, and flourishes in places where people are too busy, too afraid, or too jaded to care.

One of the cruellest ironies is that the better we get at tracing fraud, the more we realize how little we've done to prevent it (Sawyer, 2024). Data leaks like the Panama Papers or the Pandora Papers have exposed the global machinery of evasion—how law firms, banks, and shell companies work together to help the ultra-wealthy hide assets (Cockfield, 2021). These are not "illegal" in the traditional sense; they are masterclasses in legal arbitrage. But the effect is the same: a siphoning of public resources, an intensification of inequality, and a deepening of public distrust. What makes this especially corrosive is that those hit hardest by fraud—small businesses, everyday taxpayers, underfunded public services—are the ones least able to recover from its effects. And yet, somehow, we keep playing catch-up. Fraudsters innovate faster than regulators. They crowdsource tactics on the dark web, rent botnets by the hour, and experiment with AI-generated identities. Meanwhile, compliance systems remain burdened by legacy software, overwhelmed by false positives, and mired in procedural inertia. The average fraud detection system in a multinational bank still relies heavily on rule-based mechanisms—static lists, threshold triggers, basic pattern recognition. But fraud has moved on. It's agile now. It's probabilistic. It doesn't behave according to old rules. It learns from its failures—and from ours.

So what do we do in the face of such a globalized, shapeshifting threat? Do we throw more rules at it? Build higher walls, stronger passwords, more complex protocols? Maybe. But that only works if those walls are the same height everywhere. One country's firewall is meaningless if its neighbor's gate is wide open. One bank's integrity means little if the next ten are vulnerable. Fraud doesn't need unanimity—it just needs inconsistency. A single point of entry. A jurisdiction with lax controls. A loophole left unpatched.

Which is why fighting fraud globally requires more than technology (Achim et al, 2021). It requires coordination. Harmonized regulatory frameworks. Shared data protocols. Cross-border whistleblower protections. Real-time information exchange. These things sound bureaucratic—and they are—but they're also essential. Because in the absence of a shared defense, fraudsters will always find the weakest link. And in a world this interconnected, the weakest link isn't someone else's problem. It's everyone's.

What's equally urgent is the moral reckoning we need around fraud. We tend to talk about it in technical terms—controls, audits, risk exposure. But fraud is also a story about values. About what people think they can get away with (Knechel & Mintchik, 2022). About what kind of behavior institutions tolerate, excuse, or incentivize. There's a reason so many high-level fraud cases involve insiders—people on the payroll, trusted actors, credentialed professionals. These aren't rogue players; they're products of the culture. And when internal reporting structures are weak, when misconduct is rationalized away as "just business," fraud becomes not an aberration but a symptom.

To address the global cost of fraud, we need a shift not just in tools but in mindsets (Lee, 2024). We need to treat integrity as infrastructure—not optional, not cosmetic, but foundational. And that means investing not just in systems, but in people. Ethical training. Transparent leadership. Cultures that reward accountability rather than performance at any cost.

We also need to shed the illusion that fraud is a problem "over there"—in developing countries, in shady firms, in rogue states. Fraud is everywhere. It just takes different shapes. In the global south, it may wear the face of petty corruption or contract manipulation. In the global north, it shows up in creative accounting, tax evasion, insider trading (Kristianto et al, 2021). The methods vary, but the motive remains the same: to game the system for personal gain at collective expense.

Ultimately, the global cost of fraud is more than a line item on a balance sheet. It's a tax on trust. A drain on public confidence. A slow, corrosive force that eats away at the legitimacy of institutions, the fairness of markets, and the credibility of global cooperation. And unless we confront it with the seriousness it deserves—not just through punitive measures, but through smarter design, ethical AI, international solidarity, and cultural renewal—it will continue to outpace us. Always one step ahead. Always just out of reach. But maybe, just maybe, we're beginning to catch up.

SHIFTING PARADIGMS: FROM MANUAL DETECTION TO INTELLIGENT AUTOMATION

For decades, fraud detection felt like playing an eternal game of hide and seek—with a blindfold (Olushola & Mart, 2024). Compliance officers would comb through spreadsheets late into the night, manually cross-referencing invoices, scrutinizing bank statements, flipping through expense reports with the faint hope that anomalies might betray themselves through sheer visibility. Detection was more art than science, a matter of instinct, pattern familiarity, and sheer persistence. Fraud wasn't found—it was stumbled upon. And once exposed, its discovery often arrived too late, like a burnt match trailing smoke in an empty room.

Back then, systems weren't designed for nuance. They were built on rules—if-then conditions, threshold flags, binary triggers. If a transaction exceeded a certain amount, raise a red flag. If an employee logged in at an odd hour from an unexpected location, send a warning. If an invoice number was duplicated, halt the process (Horan, 2024). These were not flawed methods; they were simply limited, like a city map drawn in crayon. They worked—until they didn't. Fraud evolved, but the systems remained largely static. They couldn't account for context, intention, or ingenuity. And fraud, being what it is—a shape-shifter, a mimic, a parasite—learned quickly how to sidestep these predictable barriers. The more we relied on rigid detection mechanisms, the easier it became for fraudsters to write around the rules. They knew which flags to avoid. They knew the thresholds. They learned how to play just beneath them, hiding in plain sight, disguised as normality. Eventually, it wasn't just the manual labor that failed us. It was the philosophy. We were fighting 21st-century fraud with 20th-century thinking. Something had to give.

Enter intelligent automation. Not as a sudden messiah, but as a creeping transformation—quiet at first, experimental, even mistrusted. Algorithms began showing up in compliance meetings. Machine learning models arrived in pilot programs (Kalusivalingam et al, 2022). Neural networks started analyzing transaction patterns. There wasn't a sudden revolution. There was, instead, a slow erosion of the old ways, replaced bit by bit with something more fluid, more adaptive, more curious.

Intelligent automation doesn't "detect" in the way humans do. It doesn't get tired. It doesn't overlook small deviations. It doesn't care about narrative consistency or personal biases. What it does is inhale data—massive volumes of it—and find patterns we wouldn't know to look for. It sees the frequency of an address used across multiple accounts. It notices a vendor whose invoicing has changed ever so slightly. It recognizes the rhythm of financial behavior—the cadence of normalcy—and flags the faintest stutter in its beat. But let's be honest: we didn't trust it at first.

There's something unnerving about machines telling humans what's suspicious. An algorithm doesn't explain itself. It doesn't say *why* it flagged a transaction; it just does (Gigerenzer, 2022). And for auditors trained in reasoning, causality, and evidence trails, this black-box logic felt alien, even threatening. What if it was wrong? What if it flagged too much? Or worse—what if it missed the obvious?

These fears weren't unfounded. Early AI systems stumbled frequently. They flagged false positives at alarming rates. They were brittle, sensitive to noise, and often failed to adapt to organizational changes. And because they were trained on historical data, they often absorbed the very biases they were meant to correct. In some cases, they over-flagged certain demographics, under-flagged others, and reinforced patterns of institutional oversight. AI, it turned out, wasn't neutral. It reflected the flaws of its teachers. But failure, for machines, is a form of growth. Unlike traditional systems, intelligent automation learns. Through supervised learning, systems are fed both fraudulent and legitimate examples, allowing them to discern subtle differences that no human could articulate (Barocas et al, 2023). Through unsupervised learning, they identify clusters of behavior that "don't belong," even without prior examples. Through reinforcement learning, they adapt dynamically to changing tactics.

What this means is that fraud detection is no longer about *rules*—it's about *probabilities*. It's about heat maps, anomalies, behavioral scoring. A transaction isn't suspicious because it violates a rule; it's suspicious because it deviates from an evolving, context-aware model of what "normal" looks like. And that shift—from deterministic logic to probabilistic inference—is the heart of the paradigm change.

Consider this: in the old world, if a manager signed off on an invoice from a known vendor, it passed without question. But in the new world, an AI system might flag it—not because of the vendor or the amount, but because the IP address from which the approval was made deviates from the manager's norm. Or because the language in the invoice carries subtle linguistic inconsistencies. Or because the timing of the transaction aligns with a network of suspicious activity occurring elsewhere in the organization. The signal is not always visible. It's emergent. And machines, more than humans, are built to detect emergence.

Of course, not everything that deviates is fraudulent. And that's where human oversight returns—not as a final arbiter, but as a collaborator. Intelligent automation doesn't replace auditors; it amplifies them (Grigonytė, 2023). It does the heavy lifting, the tireless monitoring, the thousand-mile stare into databases. But the final judgment, the moral calibration, the understanding of context—that remains human, as it should. The best fraud detection systems today are hybrids: machines for scale, humans for sense-making.

There's also a shift in how we visualize risk. Traditional systems treated it as static—red, yellow, green. But intelligent automation understands risk as fluid. A vendor's risk profile today is not the same as yesterday. A bank's exposure changes with geopolitical shifts, cybersecurity events, or even viral misinformation. AI systems ingest these signals in real time.

They adapt risk models dynamically (Verma & Singhal, 2023). Fraud detection is no longer an audit function—it's an ecosystem monitor.

This shift also forces us to rethink the architecture of accountability. When a human auditor misses a fraudulent transaction, we ask: what went wrong? Were they undertrained? Overworked? Negligent? But when an AI system misses fraud—or falsely flags a legitimate one—where does responsibility lie? With the data? The model developers? The institution that deployed it? These questions are not hypothetical. They're already in courtrooms, in regulatory hearings, in board meetings. Intelligent automation brings not just efficiency, but a new layer of ethical and legal complexity (Kunkel, 2022). And yet, for all its complications, this shift is not optional. The scale of modern financial systems, the speed of fraud's innovation, and the growing complexity of global transactions have made manual detection obsolete. It's not a matter of if organizations will automate, but how wisely they do it. The real danger isn't in using AI—it's in using it poorly, blindly, or without ethical scaffolding.

There's also the temptation to treat intelligent automation as a one-time investment: install the software, train the model, and walk away. But these systems require nurturing. They require constant retraining, diverse data inputs, rigorous bias testing, and contextual re-evaluation. Fraud tactics evolve. So must the defenses. Intelligent automation is not a product. It's a process. A relationship between technology, data, and human insight that needs ongoing maintenance and mutual respect (Magliocca et al, 2024). And perhaps that's the most important lesson: this shift isn't just technological. It's cultural. It asks institutions to let go of rigid control, to embrace ambiguity, to trust in systems that see more than we can—but that still need our moral compass. It demands collaboration between data scientists and compliance officers, between machine logic and human ethics (Cañas, 2022). It requires us to question not just what we're detecting, but why—and whether our metrics for "success" in fraud detection reflect the realities of those affected. Because at the end of the day, behind every detected fraud is a real-world consequence: a pension drained, a public fund misused, a reputation destroyed. Intelligent automation helps us get there faster. But the goal isn't speed. It's justice. Fairness. Resilience. And if we can keep those north stars in mind—if we can resist the allure of automation for its own sake, and instead channel it toward a more transparent, accountable, and ethical future—then this shift in paradigm might just be our most meaningful one yet.

MACHINE LEARNING AND ANOMALY DETECTION IN FINANCIAL ECOSYSTEMS

It starts, sometimes, with a flicker. A single transaction. A number slightly off. A timestamp that doesn't quite fit. Nothing obvious, nothing screaming danger. Just a sliver of something *other*. A signal lost in a sea of patterns, an outlier dressed as routine. In manual systems, this might never be seen. But in machine learning ecosystems—where every whisper of data is listened to, mapped, tested, remembered—it's exactly these glimmers that catch the algorithm's eye.

Anomaly detection, at its core, is about honoring the strange. It's about listening harder when something *doesn't* look right, even if you can't quite explain why (Fährmann et al, 2024). And in financial systems—where transactions tick by in their billions, flowing silently from account to account, nation to nation, card swipe to blockchain—it's the subtle divergences that matter. Because fraud, particularly the smart kind, hides in the smooth. It camouflages itself within routine. It mimics the expected so flawlessly that it can glide undetected for months, sometimes years. But machine learning? It remembers. It compares. It notices when something breaks the rhythm.

What makes machine learning such a revelation in this context isn't just its speed or scale—it's its capacity for pattern intimacy (Murugan, 2023). It doesn't rely on fixed rules. It doesn't need a checklist. Instead, it absorbs the behavior of users, vendors, regions, accounts—each with its own set of fingerprints. It watches how they breathe financially. How they act on weekends. How they handle invoices at quarter's end. How they withdraw cash in clusters, how they round their payments, how often they log in, and from where. It creates living, adaptive portraits of "normal," and flags anything that slips out of frame.

Of course, not all anomalies are malicious. Sometimes they're just noise. A new vendor with a different billing structure. A travel expense submitted late (Dewi, 2022). A promotion that skews customer purchase trends. Machine learning knows this. It doesn't just scream at every deviation—it learns which ones matter. That's the beauty of unsupervised learning: it doesn't come in with assumptions. It just notices. Clusters, densities, distributions. It maps the unseen geometry of data and looks for the holes, the bulges, the awkward shapes that don't quite belong.

Still, this isn't magic. Behind every well-performing anomaly detection model lies a messy birth: raw data cleaned obsessively, features engineered by patient analysts, algorithms tested, tweaked, retrained. There's no one-size-fits-all solution. A model that catches insider fraud in a North American investment bank may fail completely in a Nigerian mobile payment platform (Ayodeji, 2024). Context is everything. Culture, behavior, regulation, even local holidays—they all inform what "normal" looks like. That's the paradox of global financial systems: they run on universal infrastructure but are deeply shaped by local patterns.

Consider supervised learning for a moment. Here, the system is trained with labeled examples—clear-cut fraud cases and clean transactions. This kind of learning can be powerful, especially when historical fraud data is rich. But fraud is a moving target. Train your model too well on yesterday's scam, and it'll miss tomorrow's. Supervised learning is most effective when paired with a continuous feedback loop, where flagged anomalies—whether true or false—are cycled back into the training set, making the model smarter over time. But again, it's messy. You need reliable labeling, responsive feedback mechanisms, and a team that actually learns with the machine.

There's also the challenge of rarity. Fraud, thankfully, is rare in proportion to total transactions. But that makes it harder for models to learn what fraud *looks* like (Olushola & Mart, 2024). Class imbalance is a major issue in machine learning—when the thing you're trying to detect is a tiny sliver of the data. It's like training a dog to bark at ghosts when it's only ever seen squirrels. So we use tricks: resampling methods, synthetic data generation, cost-sensitive learning. We give the algorithm more "ghosts" to practice on. But these tricks have limits. They simulate risk, but they don't *feel* it. Only humans understand the weight of a missed fraud—what it costs, what it breaks.

Anomaly detection models must also contend with noise. Finance is noisy. Human behavior is inconsistent (Hilal et al, 2022). A well-meaning employee might suddenly approve a high-value transaction because their boss is out sick. A customer might buy gift cards in strange denominations because they're traveling and want to tip in local currency. These are anomalies, yes, but not malicious ones. The job of machine learning isn't just to catch everything—it's to *discern*. To weigh. To doubt itself. A model that flags everything is useless. Precision matters. So does recall. Balancing the two is a delicate art.

What adds another layer of complexity is that fraudsters, too, are learning. They test the system. They probe its thresholds. They feed in small transactions to see what gets flagged, then scale up once they've mapped the blind spots. It's a feedback loop, a cat-and-mouse game, a war of adaptation. In this game, machine learning is both sword and shield. It's not just watching what happens—it's anticipating what *could* happen, based on tiny shifts, early warning signs, behavioral tremors.

Behavioral analytics, in particular, has become a frontier space (Tariq et al, 2021). It's not just about what was done, but *how*. How fast was a form filled out? How long was a mouse hovered over a button? Was the typing cadence consistent with the account holder's usual rhythm? Did the user switch devices mid-session? These micro-patterns—imperceptible to humans—can be golden signals for fraud detection. But they also raise uncomfortable questions about privacy, surveillance, and digital autonomy. Are we detecting fraud, or are we just watching people too closely?

This is where ethical machine learning becomes more than an afterthought. Financial ecosystems are trust systems. You can't maintain public confidence if users feel like they're being watched by invisible algorithms, judged for every click, punished for straying outside a statistical average (Sinnreich & Gilbert, 2024). Transparency is crucial. So is explainability. If a transaction is flagged, the institution must be able to say *why*. Not just "the model said so," but a human-readable rationale. And that's hard. Deep learning models, especially, are notorious for their opacity. Neural networks don't explain—they just perform. So we build interpretability layers. We develop explainable AI. We train our models to not only be smart, but also legible.

The financial ecosystem, by nature, is high-stakes. One missed fraud case can destroy a small business (Koffman, 2024). One false positive can cost a customer their mortgage approval. The pressure to be right isn't academic—it's real, personal, consequential. That's why machine learning in this context must be held to a different standard than, say, movie recommendation algorithms. Lives are impacted. Livelihoods, reputations, freedoms. The stakes are too high for complacency.

There's also a geostrategic dimension to consider. As machine learning-based fraud detection tools become more sophisticated, they're also becoming tools of influence (Njoku et al, 2024). A bank with superior fraud models isn't just safer—it's more trusted, more competitive, more globally viable. Countries that adopt intelligent financial infrastructure gain soft power. Those that lag risk becoming havens for illicit flows. This is not just a tech race—it's a new kind of regulatory arms race. And like all races, it risks leaving the vulnerable behind. But perhaps the most profound implication of machine learning and anomaly detection in financial systems isn't technical or political—it's philosophical. These systems force us to reimagine what "normal" is. They ask us to quantify behavior, to abstract identity, to turn trust into a calculus of signals. That's both thrilling and terrifying. Because when algorithms decide what's legitimate, we're no longer just enforcing rules—we're redefining them in real time.

So maybe the real question isn't just how well machine learning can detect fraud. Maybe it's: Can we live with the world it reveals? A world where intention is inferred from patterns, where risk is calculated probabilistically, where trust is mediated by models, and where deviation—any deviation—is suspect until proven otherwise. Can we accept that? Should we? Or must we insist, as guardians of both innovation and ethics, that the human element never disappears—that behind every model, every anomaly score, every flagged transaction, there's still someone watching with curiosity, humility, and just enough doubt to ask the unasked question? Machine learning can help us see better. But only if we're still willing to look.

CHALLENGES, RISKS, AND ETHICAL BOUNDARIES IN AI-POWERED FRAUD DETECTION

There's something quietly seductive about the promise of AI in fraud detection (Johora et al, 2024). The clean dashboards. The glowing graphs. The elegant code that slices through noise to find meaning—subtle, powerful, indifferent. It feels like control. Like clarity in the chaos. You feed in terabytes of messy, sprawling data, and out comes... insight. Suspicion with statistical backing. Fraud mapped into metrics. But underneath that shine—just beneath the polished veneer of artificial intelligence—lie murky waters. Waters filled with missteps, blind spots, and ethical quicksand we're only beginning to recognize. Let's begin with a hard truth: AI is not neutral. It may compute without fatigue, but it learns from us—our data, our decisions, our prejudices, even the ones we never admit aloud (Mitchell, 2021). And when we ask it to detect fraud, it does so with our fingerprints all over it. Biased input? Biased output. It's simple, brutal math.

Take historical fraud data, for instance. It reflects more than fraud—it reflects what *was caught*. Which means it reflects who was surveilled, which behaviors were scrutinized, which patterns were deemed suspicious in the first place. If your dataset overrepresents fraud from small vendors or certain regions or minority customers, the model will learn to be suspicious of them (Mutemi & Bacao, 2023). It won't ask why. It won't consider context. It'll just flag. Again and again. Until people who were once merely disadvantaged are now also algorithmically targeted. And here's the kicker—no one might even notice. Because when a system works at scale and with statistical justification, it's terrifyingly easy to trust it. And trust is dangerous when it's unearned.

There's also the issue of opacity. Many AI fraud detection models, especially those powered by deep learning, function like black boxes (Chaquet-Ulldemolins et al, 2022). They give you a score, a signal, a red flag—but not an explanation. Not one you can read and understand, anyway. Try asking a neural network *why* it flagged a transaction. You won't get a story. You'll get weights, matrices, gradients. Which makes accountability a problem. If a customer's account is frozen because of an algorithmic decision, who do they turn to? The bank? The developer? The model? And how do you appeal to a system that can't explain itself?

This lack of interpretability isn't just inconvenient—it's existential. Financial decisions are not minor. When someone is denied a mortgage, flagged as a criminal, or investigated by a compliance team, their life shifts. Their reputation, sometimes their freedom, hangs in the balance. And yet the engine making these calls might be little more than a statistical soup stirred by yesterday's data and today's best guesses.

Even explainable AI—our noble attempt to pull back the curtain—has limits (Wasserman-Rozen et al, 2024). Sure, we can highlight which features mattered most in a decision. We can say that an address, or a device ID, or a transaction time contributed heavily to a fraud flag. But correlation isn't explanation. And humans crave *why*. Not just what. Without narrative, we flail.

Then there's the matter of false positives. AI is powerful, but it's not perfect. And in fraud detection, the cost of being wrong cuts both ways (Kamuangu, 2024). Miss a fraudster, and damage is done. Flag an innocent, and trust is shattered. The margin for error is slim, and the fallout asymmetrical. A fraudster might shrug off detection as bad luck. But a wrongly accused customer—someone whose transactions were genuine, whose intentions were clean—might never trust the system again. They might close accounts, tell their networks, shift to cash. The cost isn't just individual—it's systemic. A single false positive can ripple through brand reputation, user adoption, even regulatory scrutiny. And yet, the fear of false negatives pushes institutions to be aggressive. To widen the net. To set the sensitivity high. Better to catch ten innocent fish than miss one shark. But at what cost? What happens when our fraud detection becomes overzealous? When we teach our systems to be paranoid? We don't just detect fraud—we begin to treat everyone like a suspect. Suspicion becomes default. Innocence becomes an outlier.

That paranoia has cultural implications, too. AI-powered fraud detection is increasingly global. It crosses borders, reads across languages, compares behaviors from wildly different cultural and economic contexts (Shan, 2025). But what's anomalous in one place may be normal elsewhere. A vendor in Indonesia might operate with cash-heavy transactions due to infrastructure gaps. A farmer in Nigeria might rotate SIM cards due to unreliable networks. A small business in Egypt might have sporadic invoices due to seasonal rhythms. These aren't red flags—they're realities. But to an algorithm trained on Western financial patterns, they look... off.

This is how AI becomes imperial without meaning to. It takes one context and treats it as universal. It normalizes certain behaviors and penalizes deviations. And when those deviations align with race, geography, class, or religion, the system doesn't just detect fraud—it perpetuates inequity. And not loudly. Quietly. Algorithmically. Disguised as "risk scoring." What makes this worse is how automation can dull human skepticism. Once a system is in place, once it delivers consistent output, there's a tendency to defer to it. To stop asking hard questions. To trust the machine over the messiness of human intuition. This is automation bias. It's seductive. It's easy. But it's also dangerous.

There's a line somewhere—blurry, shifting, uncomfortable—between using AI to augment human judgment and using it to *replace* it. And once we cross that line, we lose something. We stop asking if the flag makes sense. We stop looking at the context. We become custodians of systems we no longer understand. And then there's privacy. Fraud detection systems, especially the advanced ones, don't just look at transactions (Hilal et al, 2022). They look at behavior. Devices. IP addresses. Typing patterns. Location histories. Sometimes even voice data or facial patterns. The deeper they go, the better they get. But also—the creepier they feel.

When does detection become surveillance? When does protection become intrusion? This is not a theoretical concern. In a world already grappling with data breaches, corporate espionage, and digital authoritarianism, the idea of financial institutions monitoring behavior at such granular levels is unsettling. Especially when that data is stored, sold, or shared. The line between fraud detection and surveillance capitalism is paper-thin.

Regulation tries to keep up. GDPR, CCPA, various banking oversight bodies—they all try to draw the boundaries (Yusuff et al, 2023). But enforcement is patchy. Laws lag behind technology. And multinational banks operate across jurisdictions, some strict, some lax. What's ethical in Berlin may be legal but unprincipled in Dubai. What's standard in New York may be scandalous in Nairobi. And in the absence of universal standards, companies tend to adopt the *lowest* common denominator. The path of least resistance. The rules that are easiest to follow. Ethics becomes a matter of compliance, not conscience. And what about transparency? Do users know when AI is judging them? Do they understand what data is being used, how it's stored, how long it's kept? Rarely. Consent is buried in pages of legalese. Opt-outs are obscure, if they exist at all. And even when people know they're being monitored, they rarely grasp the extent.

That asymmetry—between what the system knows and what the user understands—is a power imbalance (Stefanija, 2023). And power, when invisible, is easily abused. So what do we do? We question more. We demand explainability. Not just from the developers, but from the institutions deploying these systems. We build ethics teams that aren't ornamental. We test models for bias. We audit outputs, not just inputs. We ask how the data was collected, labeled, processed, and what stories it tells—and which ones it silences. We train our models on diverse datasets. We include edge cases. We listen to people who've been wrongly flagged. We treat mistakes as opportunities for moral recalibration, not just technical tuning. And most of all—we stay human. We don't let the thrill of precision blind us to the cost of overreach. We don't confuse confidence scores with truth. We remember that behind every anomaly score is a person—sometimes a fraudster, yes. But sometimes, just a glitch in the system. A mistake. A human quirk. AI can help us see sharper, deeper, faster. But ethics? That's still our job. Always will be.

TOWARD RESILIENT SYSTEMS: CROSS-BORDER COLLABORATION AND POLICY ALIGNMENT

Resilience—it's a word that gets tossed around like confetti in policy papers and press briefings (Merkel, 2023). But in the real world, in the clunky, entangled, jurisdictionally fragmented machinery of international finance, resilience isn't just a virtue. It's a survival strategy. Not the sleek kind found in thought-leader keynotes, but the messy, weather-beaten kind forged through mistrust, miscommunication, and the slow, painful work of building bridges across borders that were never meant to be crossed by algorithms.

Fraud doesn't care about sovereignty. It doesn't recognize national flags or respect institutional silos. It flows where the gaps are. Where one country's regulation ends and another's begins. Where data stops being protected in Brussels and starts being exploited in a backroom server in São Paulo. The transnational nature of financial fraud is both its strength and our Achilles' heel (Cheliatsidou et al, 2023). Because while money moves fluidly, rules do not. And AI, for all its power, can't fix what geopolitics won't face.

So, when we talk about building resilient systems, we're not just talking about upgrading our servers or buying the latest threat-detection software. We're talking about reimagining governance. We're talking about humility—about institutions learning to trust one another, share what they'd rather hide, and align in ways that often feel... unnatural. Because resilience, in the age of AI-enhanced fraud detection, isn't about who has the best tech. It's about who's willing to collaborate—even when it's inconvenient, even when it's uncomfortable. But here's the thing: collaboration is messy. It runs into everything. Culture, language, politics, pride. What's a priority for one nation barely registers for another. A suspicious financial behavior flagged in Tokyo may not even raise an eyebrow in Lagos (Ajiola, 2025). A fraud typology common in Dubai might not exist in San Francisco. There are gaps in legal definitions, in taxonomies, in enforcement strategies. What constitutes "suspicious activity" is anything but universal. And yet, we keep pretending there's a one-size-fits-all framework. We write glossy documents filled with acronyms and standardized benchmarks. We convene summits, sign memoranda, build coalitions. But when push comes to shove, institutions still hoard data like treasure. They fear reputational damage, litigation, national scrutiny. No one wants to be the weak link. So silence wins. And fraud slips through.

Let's talk data sharing—because that's where everything starts and stops. AI fraud detection lives on data. Not just volume, but richness. Context. Nuance. Behavior over time. The kind of data that can't be captured in a one-off report or a compliance checklist. But cross-border data sharing is a regulatory minefield. Privacy laws vary wildly. GDPR sets the tone in Europe—rigorous, protective, wary (Leiser & Lodder, 2024). The U.S. is fragmented, with federal and state-level tensions. Other regions operate in legal grey zones, or simply lack robust data governance altogether. So how do we build systems that can learn across borders when the very data needed to fuel those systems can't legally cross them?

One approach has been federated learning—training models locally and sharing the insights rather than the raw data (Zhang et al, 2021). It's promising, technically. But it's also new, under-tested, and difficult to implement at the scale and consistency global fraud detection requires. And even if the data never moves, the political suspicion remains. Who owns the model? Who decides what it learns? And who takes the blame if it fails? Blame, of course, is the unspoken anchor in all of this. Institutions hesitate to align because alignment means accountability. Shared systems mean shared responsibility. If one node in the network fails—if one country's lax enforcement allows a fraud ring to flourish—who answers for the consequences? Without mutual legal assistance treaties that are nimble, responsive, and actually honored, coordination remains aspirational.

Then there's the issue of technological disparity. Not all countries have the infrastructure, funding, or expertise to develop and deploy AI-powered fraud systems. When collaboration does occur, it's often lopsided. Larger, wealthier nations dominate the architecture, set the parameters, and dictate the standards. Smaller nations are expected to comply, to contribute what they can, and to adapt—fast. That kind of imbalance breeds resentment. It creates systems that may be technically "resilient," but politically brittle.

True resilience requires more than coordination. It requires trust. And trust, in the world of global finance, is in short supply. Decades of economic exploitation, unequal trade agreements, and post-colonial hangovers have left scars. So when a multinational bank proposes a new global fraud detection model, or when a Western regulatory body suggests a set of AI ethics principles, the response isn't always enthusiasm. Sometimes it's skepticism. Sometimes it's silence.

Building resilience, then, means rebuilding trust. Not through declarations, but through lived transparency (Lansing et al, 2023). Through systems that are open, explainable, and inclusive by design. Through feedback loops that aren't just technical but human. Through frameworks that allow for local adaptation, cultural sensitivity, and legal plurality—without sacrificing the shared goal of financial integrity. We need harmonization, yes—but not homogenization. We need common protocols for flagging suspicious activity, for alerting partners, for responding to breaches. But those protocols must leave room for difference. A resilient system isn't one that forces everyone into the same mold. It's one that can bend, adapt, and absorb shocks without breaking.

Take real-time fraud alerts, for instance. They sound great in theory. One country detects a fraud vector—say, a new phishing strategy targeting fintech apps—and sends a rapid alert across its network. Other countries update their models, adjust their thresholds, warn their citizens. It's fast, efficient, preventative. But it also requires trust that the alert is valid, that the source is credible, that the data hasn't been politicized. It requires interoperability of systems, agreement on risk thresholds, and, crucially, the ability to respond quickly—something many nations struggle with. Now imagine doing that across 100 countries, in 30 languages, with 50 legal systems in play. Hard? Absolutely. Impossible? Not necessarily.

What's needed is more than technology. It's governance. Human-centered, equity-driven, globally coordinated governance. Not just of AI systems, but of the financial and regulatory environments they inhabit. We need international AI ethics boards with teeth—bodies that can audit models, investigate failures, and penalize misuse (Schiff et al, 2024). We need cross-border regulatory sandboxes where nations can experiment, share, and co-create fraud detection tools in controlled environments. We need open-source models, open-access research, and global talent mobility to reduce the North-South knowledge divide.

We also need language—not just technical language, but moral language—that helps us frame what we're doing. Fraud detection isn't just about security. It's about fairness. It's about stewardship. It's about building systems that don't just catch the corrupt but protect the honest. Systems that don't trade civil liberties for efficiency. Systems that understand that resilience without justice is just a prettier kind of failure. Somewhere in all this, we need a new kind of imagination (Walker, 2023). One that doesn't separate technology from humanity, or regulation from culture. One that understands that AI is not just a tool we use, but a mirror we hold up to our institutions. A resilient system doesn't just survive attacks. It survives self-deception. It survives apathy. It survives our tendency to build walls instead of bridges.

So, what would such a system look like? Maybe it's one where a Kenyan bank can instantly share a fraud pattern with a Swedish fintech startup—and both can understand what it means. Maybe it's one where regulators from Bogotá, Jakarta, and Berlin can sit at the same table—not as competitors, but as co-authors of a global risk map. Maybe it's one where the smallest credit union and the largest investment firm operate under AI systems that are not just powerful, but accountable, auditable, and fair. Resilience isn't just bouncing back. It's bouncing forward. Learning from what broke. Anticipating what's next. Protecting what matters (Kirsop-Taylor, 2022). And what matters, at the end of the day, is people. Their trust. Their dignity. Their right to financial systems that work for them—not just efficiently, but ethically. That's the future worth building. Not perfect. But possible.

CONCLUSION

There is something unsettlingly poetic about the nature of fraud: its reliance on illusion, its quiet manipulation of trust, and its mimicry of legitimacy until the moment it unravels. In many ways, fraud exploits the same vulnerabilities that make human systems so powerful—interconnectedness, delegation, belief. It slips through the cracks of bureaucracy, hides behind complex transactions, and thrives in ambiguity. For decades, our defenses were reactive, clunky, slow. We waited for red flags. We followed rules written for yesterday's schemes. But today, artificial intelligence offers a different approach—not only faster and more flexible but more anticipatory, more nuanced, more relentless in its pursuit of patterns and possibilities.

Yet even as we celebrate the potential of AI to transform fraud detection, we must remain vigilant about what we're building—and how. Machine learning models are trained on historical data, and history is riddled with bias, blind spots, and institutional prejudice. An AI system trained to detect fraud in one region may falsely flag legitimate behaviors in another. A neural network that optimizes for accuracy may sacrifice fairness. And the more we automate, the more we risk losing human judgment—the critical pause, the moral filter, the capacity to question the logic of the machine. If left unchecked, AI may not only replicate injustice—it may institutionalize it at scale.

Moreover, international systems pose their own unique complications. What counts as fraud in one jurisdiction may be viewed differently elsewhere. Data protection laws, transparency requirements, and legal definitions of accountability vary widely across borders. Without a shared regulatory framework, the deployment of AI in fraud detection risks becoming fragmented, inconsistent, and susceptible to exploitation. We may end up with pockets of advanced oversight surrounded by swathes of digital wilderness—regions where fraud flourishes precisely because no common standard exists. This isn't a technical failure; it's a policy one.

So, where does that leave us? It leaves us at a crossroads. We can choose to build isolated tools and treat fraud detection as a competitive advantage hoarded by the most technologically advanced institutions. Or we can treat it as a collective responsibility—an area where collaboration is not just desirable but essential. That means designing AI systems that are explainable and auditable. It means pushing for global dialogues between governments, developers, and civil society. It means investing not just in smarter algorithms, but in smarter governance.

Ultimately, AI will not "solve" fraud. But it can help us build financial systems that are more transparent, responsive, and fair—if we approach it with humility, caution, and a willingness to confront both our technical limitations and our ethical responsibilities. In the end, enhancing fraud detection with AI is not about eliminating risk entirely; it is about learning to manage it with wisdom, foresight, and a renewed commitment to trust.

REFERENCES

Achim, M. V., Borlea, S. N., & Văidean, V. L. (2021). Does technology matter for combating economic and financial crime? A panel data study. *Technological and Economic Development of Economy*, *27*(1), 223–261. DOI: 10.3846/tede.2021.13977

Adeniyi, E. O. (2025). Occupational Fraud: A Quantitative Study on the Impact of Enhancing Anti-Fraud Controls With Forensic Accounting (Doctoral dissertation, South College).

Ajiola, F. O. (2025). Urban Crime in the Lagos Traffic: An Ethnography at the Crossroads of Multiple Codes of Ethics. *Journal of African Cultural Studies*, *37*(1), 127–144. DOI: 10.1080/13696815.2024.2376544

Asad, F. (2025). AI-Driven Strategies for Fraud Risk Management in Emerging Markets: Enhancing Regulatory Oversight and Digital Transparency.

Ayodeji, I. A. (2024). Fraud Detection and Prevention in the Nigerian Financial Industry (Doctoral dissertation, Walden University).

Banerjee, R. (2024). *Who Cheats and How: Scams, Frauds and the Dark Side of the Corporate World*. Penguin Random House India Private Limited.

Barocas, S., Hardt, M., & Narayanan, A. (2023). *Fairness and machine learning: Limitations and opportunities*. MIT press.

Cañas, J. J. (2022). AI and ethics when human beings collaborate with AI agents. *Frontiers in Psychology*, *13*, 836650. DOI: 10.3389/fpsyg.2022.836650 PMID: 35310226

Chaquet-Ulldemolins, J., Gimeno-Blanes, F. J., Moral-Rubio, S., Muñoz-Romero, S., & Rojo-Álvarez, J. L. (2022). On the black-box challenge for fraud detection using machine learning (ii): Nonlinear analysis through interpretable autoencoders. *Applied Sciences (Basel, Switzerland)*, *12*(8), 3856. DOI: 10.3390/app12083856

Cheliatsidou, A., Sariannidis, N., Garefalakis, A., Azibi, J., & Kagias, P. (2023). The international fraud triangle. *Journal of Money Laundering Control*, *26*(1), 106–132. DOI: 10.1108/JMLC-09-2021-0103

Cockfield, A. (2021). Secrets of the Panama papers: How tax havens exacerbate income inequality. Colum. *J. Tax L.*, *13*(1), 45–76. DOI: 10.52214/cjtl.v13i1.8979

Dewi, I. (2022). Process of Vendor Bill Payment. *Lead Journal of Economy and Administration*, *1*(1), 8–13. DOI: 10.56403/lejea.v1i1.33

Dyck, A., Morse, A., & Zingales, L. (2024). How pervasive is corporate fraud? *Review of Accounting Studies*, *29*(1), 736–769. DOI: 10.1007/s11142-022-09738-5

Führmann, D., Martín, L., Sánchez, L., & Damer, N. (2024). Anomaly detection in smart environments: A comprehensive survey. *IEEE Access : Practical Innovations, Open Solutions*, *12*, 64006–64049. DOI: 10.1109/ACCESS.2024.3395051

Gigerenzer, G. (2022). *How to stay smart in a smart world: Why human intelligence still beats algorithms*. MIT Press.

Grigonytė, G. (2023). Assessing the influence of artificial intelligence on the auditor profession: a qualitative study (Doctoral dissertation, Kauno technologijos universitetas.).

Hilal, W., Gadsden, S. A., & Yawney, J. (2022). Financial fraud: A review of anomaly detection techniques and recent advances. *Expert Systems with Applications*, *193*, 116429. DOI: 10.1016/j.eswa.2021.116429

Hildyard, N. (2023). Licensed larceny: Infrastructure, financial extraction and the Global South. In *Licensed larceny*. Manchester University Press. DOI: 10.7765/9781526169457.00009

Horan, D. J. (2024). The Finer Points. In The Retailer's Guide to Loss Prevention and Security (pp. 145-218). Routledge. DOI: 10.4324/9781003575092-13

Johora, F. T., Hasan, R., Farabi, S. F., Alam, M. Z., Sarkar, M. I., & Al Mahmud, M. A. (2024, June). AI Advances: Enhancing Banking Security with Fraud Detection. In *2024 First International Conference on Technological Innovations and Advance Computing (TIACOMP)* (pp. 289-294). IEEE. DOI: 10.1109/TIACOMP64125.2024.00055

Kalusivalingam, A. K., Sharma, A., Patel, N., & Singh, V. (2022). Enhancing Corporate Governance and Compliance through AI: Implementing Natural Language Processing and Machine Learning Algorithms. *International Journal of Artificial Intelligence and Machine Learning*, *3*(9).

Kamuangu, P. (2024). A Review on Financial Fraud Detection using AI and Machine Learning. Journal of Economics. *Finance and Accounting Studies*, *6*(1), 67–77.

Kirsop-Taylor, N. (2022). Leaping forwards, bouncing forwards, or just bouncing back: Resilience in environmental public agencies through after the austerity decade. *Environmental Management*, *70*(5), 697–709. DOI: 10.1007/s00267-022-01701-z PMID: 36008627

Knechel, W. R., & Mintchik, N. (2022). Do personal beliefs and values affect an individual's "fraud tolerance"? Evidence from the World Values Survey. *Journal of Business Ethics*, *177*(2), 1–27. DOI: 10.1007/s10551-020-04704-0

Koffman, T. (2024). *Myth of money: breaking out of the failing financial system*. John Wiley & Sons.

Kristianto, A. H., Widya, P. R., & Nadapdap, J. P. (2021). The portrait of the underground economy and tax evasion: descriptive analysis from border region.

Kunkel, R. J. (2022). Artificial intelligence, automation, and proletarianization of the legal profession. *Creighton Law Review*, *56*, 69.

Lansing, A. E., Romero, N. J., Siantz, E., Silva, V., Center, K., Casteel, D., & Gilmer, T. (2023). Building trust: Leadership reflections on community empowerment and engagement in a large urban initiative. *BMC Public Health*, *23*(1), 1252. DOI: 10.1186/s12889-023-15860-z PMID: 37380973

Lee, H. (2024). Enhancing the world by mitigating fraud and emphasizing the significance of ethics.

Leiser, M., & Lodder, A. R. (2024). The GDPR at a Crossroads: From Pioneering to Uncertainty.

Lopes, C. (2024). The Disappointing Discussion About Aid Effectiveness. In *The Self-Deception Trap: Exploring the Economic Dimensions of Charity Dependency within Africa-Europe Relations* (pp. 39–57). Springer Nature Switzerland. DOI: 10.1007/978-3-031-57591-4_3

Magliocca, P., Canestrino, R., Carayannis, E. G., & Gagliardi, A. R. (2024). Understanding human–technology interaction: Evolving boundaries. *European Journal of Innovation Management*. Advance online publication. DOI: 10.1108/EJIM-04-2024-0341

Mahalakshmi, V., Kulkarni, N., Kumar, K. P., Kumar, K. S., Sree, D. N., & Durga, S. (2022). The role of implementing artificial intelligence and machine learning technologies in the financial services industry for creating competitive intelligence. *Materials Today: Proceedings*, *56*, 2252–2255. DOI: 10.1016/j.matpr.2021.11.577

Martino, P. (2021). *Blockchain and banking: How technological innovations are shaping the banking industry*. Springer Nature. DOI: 10.1007/978-3-030-70970-9

Merkel, W. (2023). What Is Democratic Resilience and How Can We Strengthen It. *Policy Brief*, (169), 1–15.

Mitchell, M. (2021). Why AI is harder than we think. arXiv preprint arXiv:2104.12871. DOI: 10.1145/3449639.3465421

Murugan, M. S., & T, S. K. (2023). Large-scale data-driven financial risk management & analysis using machine learning strategies. *Measurement. Sensors*, *27*, 100756. DOI: 10.1016/j.measen.2023.100756

Mutemi, A., & Bacao, F. (2023). A numeric-based machine learning design for detecting organized retail fraud in digital marketplaces. *Scientific Reports*, *13*(1), 12499. DOI: 10.1038/s41598-023-38304-5 PMID: 37532696

Njoku, D. O., Iwuchukwu, V. C., Jibiri, J. E., Ikwuazom, C. T., Ofoegbu, C. I., & Nwokoma, F. O. (2024). Machine learning approach for fraud detection system in financial institution: A web base application. Machine Learning, 20(4), 1-12.

Olushola, A., & Mart, J. (2024). Fraud Detection using Machine Learning. ScienceOpen *Preprints*.

Sawyer, K. R. (2024). Scams: Blaming the Victims.

Schiff, D. S., Kelley, S., & Camacho Ibáñez, J. (2024). The emergence of artificial intelligence ethics auditing. *Big Data & Society, 11*(4), 20539517241299732. DOI: 10.1177/20539517241299732

Shan, W. (2025). AI-powered fraud detection in banking: innovations, challenges and preventive strategies (Doctoral dissertation).

Sinnreich, A., & Gilbert, J. (2024). *The secret life of data: Navigating hype and uncertainty in the age of algorithmic surveillance.* MIT Press. DOI: 10.7551/mitpress/14040.001.0001

Stefanija, A. P. (2023). Power asymmetries, epistemic imbalances and barriers to knowledge: the (im) possibility of knowing algorithms. In *Handbook of Critical Studies of Artificial Intelligence* (pp. 563–572). Edward Elgar Publishing. DOI: 10.4337/9781803928562.00058

Suri, T., Aker, J., Batista, C., Callen, M., Ghani, T., Jack, W., & Sukhtankar, S. (2023). Mobile money. *VoxDevLit, 2*(2), 3.

Tan, J. (2021). *Survival Kit for Stressful Times.* Jackie Tan.

Tariq, M. U., Babar, M., Poulin, M., Khattak, A. S., Alshehri, M. D., & Kaleem, S. (2021). Human behavior analysis using intelligent big data analytics. *Frontiers in Psychology, 12*, 686610. DOI: 10.3389/fpsyg.2021.686610 PMID: 34295289

Valavanidis, A. (2023). Artificial intelligence (ai) applications. Department of Chemistry, National and Kapodistrian University of Athens, University Campus Zografou, 15784.

Verma, A., & Singhal, N. (2023, September). Integrating Artificial Intelligence for Adaptive Decision-Making in Complex System. In International Conference on Advances in Data-driven Computing and Intelligent Systems (pp. 95-105). Singapore: Springer Nature Singapore.

Walker, S. (2023). *Design for resilience: Making the future we leave behind.* MIT Press. DOI: 10.7551/mitpress/14924.001.0001

Wasserman-Rozen, H., Gilad-Bachrach, R., & Elkin-Koren, N. (2024). Lost in translation: The limits of explainability in AI. *Cardozo Arts & Ent. LJ*, *42*, 391.

Yarovenko, H. (2024). Digital transformation: economy development and fighting against illegal practices. Publishing House "Baltija Publishing".

Zhang, C., Xie, Y., Bai, H., Yu, B., Li, W., & Gao, Y. (2021). A survey on federated learning. *Knowledge-Based Systems*, *216*, 106775. DOI: 10.1016/j.knosys.2021.106775 PMID: 34909232

Chapter 7
Strategic Management in the Age of AI: Redefining Financial Decision-Making

Diana Andreea Mândricel
https://orcid.org/0009-0009-0179-7887
Titu Maiorescu University, Romania

ABSTRACT

Strategic management is undergoing a profound transformation as artificial intelligence (AI) reshapes the foundations of financial decision-making. Traditional approaches, built on human judgment, hierarchical coordination, and historical forecasting, are increasingly complemented—and at times challenged—by algorithmic models capable of real-time analysis and adaptive learning. AI enhances strategic decision-making by uncovering hidden patterns, simulating multiple futures, and optimizing resource allocation under conditions of uncertainty. At the same time, it raises concerns around accountability, transparency, and ethical legitimacy. This chapter examines how AI redefines strategic management in finance, highlighting opportunities for efficiency and resilience while addressing risks of bias and opacity. It argues that the future of strategy lies in hybrid models that combine human oversight with algorithmic intelligence.

DOI: 10.4018/979-8-3373-3626-8.ch007

INTRODUCTION

Strategic management has always been about anticipating change, navigating uncertainty, and guiding organizations toward sustainable advantage. From the planning systems of the mid-twentieth century to the agile approaches of the digital age, the discipline has consistently evolved alongside economic, political, and technological transformations. The arrival of artificial intelligence (AI) represents one of the most profound disruptions in this trajectory. Unlike earlier innovations, which expanded managerial tools incrementally, AI fundamentally alters the ways organizations gather information, model uncertainty, and make financial decisions. It is not simply another technology to be adopted; it reshapes the epistemological foundations of decision-making, challenging managers to rethink how strategy is designed, implemented, and evaluated.

The global context intensifies the importance of this shift. Organizations operate in a landscape marked by interdependence, volatility, and systemic shocks. Financial crises, geopolitical instability, climate risks, and pandemics have underscored how quickly markets can change and how fragile traditional models of analysis can be (Talwar & Koury, 2017). In such an environment, the capacity to respond dynamically is critical. AI offers new ways of perceiving and navigating complexity by integrating diverse data sources, learning from patterns, and simulating multiple futures. For strategic management, this means moving from static analysis toward adaptive systems of decision-making that can evolve in real time.

Financial decision-making exemplifies the challenges and opportunities of this transition. Historically, managers relied on accounting reports, macroeconomic indicators, and econometric models to inform investment and risk strategies. While effective in stable environments, these tools are less suited to contexts characterized by rapid shifts and nonlinear dynamics. AI allows firms to analyze high-frequency market data, alternative datasets such as satellite imagery or geolocation patterns, and unstructured information from news or social media (Nash et al., 2022). These capabilities enable earlier detection of emerging risks and more granular identification of opportunities. Yet they also demand a rethinking of strategic frameworks: decisions are no longer grounded solely in human interpretation but increasingly shaped by algorithmic processes.

This transformation redefines the role of information in strategy. In the past, data was often scarce, costly, and delayed. Today, information is abundant, continuous, and multifaceted. The challenge is not access but interpretation. AI systems excel at processing vast amounts of information, identifying hidden correlations, and generating probabilistic forecasts. However, their outputs are shaped by data quality, model design, and contextual assumptions. For managers, the strategic task shifts from collecting information to curating data ecosystems and overseeing algorithmic interpretations (Paschen et al., 2020). The value of strategy in the AI age lies not only in analyzing the past but in orchestrating futures based on dynamic, evolving signals.

AI also alters the temporal logic of strategic management. Traditional planning cycles often operated on annual or multi-year horizons. AI enables continuous strategy, where decisions are revised dynamically as new data flows in. Financial markets, in particular, illustrate the importance of speed: algorithmic trading systems react to signals in milliseconds, while reinforcement learning models adapt to evolving conditions. This acceleration requires strategic managers to reconcile two tempos: the instantaneous pace of machine learning and the slower rhythms of human deliberation. The art of strategy in this environment lies in balancing short-term adaptability with long-term vision (Longoni & Cian, 2022).

At the organizational level, AI challenges established notions of authority and accountability. In hierarchical models, decisions could be traced to specific managers, supported by rules and reporting lines. In AI-mediated governance, accountability becomes distributed across algorithms, data scientists, managers, and regulators. This raises questions about legitimacy: when financial decisions are informed by opaque models, how can stakeholders be assured of fairness and responsibility? Scholars have argued for the importance of explainability and contestability, suggesting that transparency must be built into AI systems to maintain trust (Raisch & Krakowski, 2021). For strategic management, legitimacy is not a secondary concern but a central factor in sustaining competitive advantage in markets that value trust as much as efficiency.

The integration of AI into financial strategy also highlights geopolitical dynamics. Nations and firms compete not only for market share but also for leadership in AI development. Data resources, computational infrastructures, and regulatory regimes shape the contours of competition. For example, AI adoption in financial services has progressed differently in North America, Europe, and Asia, reflecting variations in institutional priorities, cultural attitudes, and regulatory frameworks (Bughin et al., 2018). Strategic management in global firms must therefore navigate a patchwork of approaches, adapting governance systems to local contexts while leveraging global capabilities. This demands cultural agility and institutional sensitivity, qualities that extend beyond technical expertise.

Another dimension concerns organizational learning. AI does not simply provide answers; it transforms how organizations learn. Traditional learning models emphasized feedback loops between strategy, performance, and adjustment. AI accelerates these loops by generating continuous feedback and detecting weak signals early. Yet rapid feedback can overwhelm organizations or create overreliance on short-term optimization. Strategic managers must therefore design learning systems that integrate AI insights without losing sight of broader goals. This involves embedding reflection, context, and ethical reasoning alongside computational analysis (Haefner et al., 2021).

The ethical dimension cannot be overlooked. Financial decision-making affects not only shareholders but also employees, customers, and societies. Algorithms trained on biased data may reproduce inequalities in lending, investment, or credit scoring. Opaque models may privilege efficiency over fairness, undermining trust. Strategic managers must therefore integrate ethical considerations into their frameworks, ensuring that AI serves not only performance but also legitimacy and inclusivity. The question is not whether AI can optimize decisions but whether those decisions align with the values and responsibilities of organizations in society (Daugherty & Wilson, 2018).

The introduction of AI also compels a reconsideration of education and skills. Managers trained in classical finance and strategy must develop new literacies: the ability to interpret algorithmic outputs, to question assumptions embedded in data, and to collaborate with technical experts. Business schools are beginning to adapt curricula, integrating courses on data analytics, AI ethics, and digital strategy (Leiponen, 2021). Yet beyond technical skills, managers must cultivate reflexivity and judgment, recognizing the limits of algorithmic reasoning and the enduring importance of human interpretation. The future of strategy will depend not only on machines that learn but on humans who learn to govern machines responsibly.

The long-term implications extend beyond firms to entire industries and societies. AI-enabled financial decision-making has the potential to reshape competitive landscapes, concentrating advantage in firms with superior data and computational resources. This raises concerns about inequality, monopolization, and systemic risk. Strategic managers must anticipate these dynamics, balancing firm-level advantage with system-level stability. The future of strategy may thus require greater engagement with regulators, policymakers, and civil society, ensuring that AI-driven governance contributes to resilient and inclusive financial systems (Galaz et al., 2021).

In light of these dynamics, the purpose of this chapter is threefold. First, it examines how AI redefines strategic analysis and forecasting in financial contexts, highlighting the tools and methods that reshape decision-making. Second, it explores how AI alters organizational capabilities and governance structures, requiring new forms of leadership and accountability. Third, it considers the broader implications for industries and societies, situating AI-driven financial decision-making within global, ethical, and institutional contexts. Together, these themes underscore that the age of AI is not merely an extension of existing strategy but a redefinition of its foundations.

ARTIFICIAL INTELLIGENCE AND THE TRANSFORMATION OF STRATEGIC FORECASTING: FROM DATA ECOSYSTEMS TO GLOBAL GOVERNANCE

Strategic analysis and forecasting are undergoing a profound transformation as artificial intelligence (AI) becomes embedded in the infrastructure of decision-making. At its core, forecasting has always depended on access to relevant information and the ability to process it into meaningful patterns. What differentiates the AI era is not only the expansion of available data but also the capability to integrate diverse sources and transform them into continuously updated insights. This expansion redefines what counts as strategic knowledge and changes the nature of foresight in organizations.

The first domain where AI exerts influence is the transformation of data ecosystems. Financial and strategic analysis were once limited to structured, periodic data: balance sheets, macroeconomic reports, and performance statistics. These datasets were standardized, curated, and often backward-looking. By contrast, AI enables organizations to incorporate vast flows of alternative data, including geospatial information, online search patterns, sentiment analysis from social media, and signals from Internet of Things (IoT) devices. Such data offers a timelier and more granular view of economic activity. For instance, the analysis of shipping routes via satellite imagery can reveal supply chain disruptions before they appear in official trade statistics, offering managers a strategic advantage in anticipating risks (Ghosh et al., 2019). The key transformation lies not simply in volume but in the richness and diversity of signals, turning forecasting into a holistic exercise rather than one confined to conventional indicators.

The ability to draw on alternative data also changes the epistemology of forecasting. Instead of relying on a single explanatory model, AI systems identify correlations across multidimensional datasets. Natural language processing allows analysts to extract meaning from unstructured documents such as earnings calls or regulatory filings. These capacities create opportunities for discovering weak signals that may precede market shifts or policy changes. The broader implication for strategy is that organizations can move from retrospective interpretation to anticipatory governance, identifying emerging trends as they unfold rather than after the fact (Kenton & Mulligan, 2021). By leveraging these insights, strategic managers can reposition assets, reallocate resources, and design contingency plans with greater precision.

The second transformation occurs in the modeling of forecasts. Traditional econometric models often assume linear relationships, stationarity, and relatively stable dynamics. AI-based models challenge these assumptions by capturing non-linear, adaptive, and high-dimensional relationships. Deep learning architectures, for example, can detect complex dependencies in financial time series, while reinforcement learning frameworks continuously optimize strategies as new data arrives (Fischer & Krauss, 2018). This capacity for adaptivity redefines forecasting: predictions are no longer static outputs but dynamic processes that evolve with each new input. Such models align more closely with the realities of volatile markets, where shocks and discontinuities are not exceptions but structural features.

In portfolio management, this adaptivity translates into continuous rebalancing. Reinforcement learning agents adjust asset allocations in response to shifting risk–return profiles, integrating signals from global markets, macroeconomic policies, and firm-level performance. Unlike traditional strategies that rely on periodic reviews, AI-driven systems create "living forecasts" that remain updated throughout the trading day. For strategic management, this capacity introduces a new logic: instead of formulating strategy as a fixed plan, organizations can cultivate strategies as ongoing, self-adjusting processes embedded in digital infrastructures (Goodell et al., 2021). This does not diminish the role of human oversight but reframes it, positioning managers as curators of adaptive systems rather than sole authors of strategic plans.

A third domain of transformation is the simulation of scenarios. Scenario planning has been a cornerstone of strategy, particularly in uncertain environments, yet it has been constrained by the imagination and bandwidth of human planners. AI multiplies the scale and scope of this practice by generating thousands of plausible scenarios across multiple dimensions. Natural language processing can analyze policy debates, public opinion, and news to identify emergent risks; machine learning then integrates these signals into scenario trees that capture divergent futures. This capability allows organizations to stress-test strategies against a wider range of contingencies, from geopolitical conflicts to environmental shocks (Nguyen et al., 2021). In finance, AI-enabled scenario simulations improve stress testing of portfolios, ensuring resilience not only against historical shocks but also against novel disruptions that may not have precedents.

The implications extend beyond efficiency. By broadening the horizon of what is thinkable, AI challenges organizations to confront uncomfortable futures. It expands the boundary of strategic imagination, forcing managers to consider scenarios that would otherwise remain outside traditional planning exercises. In doing so, it democratizes foresight, making it possible for mid-level teams as well as executives to explore and evaluate alternative trajectories. This diffusion of foresight throughout the organization can increase adaptability, aligning daily decisions with long-term resilience.

A further innovation is the integration of human and AI judgment. Forecasting is not only about accuracy but also about interpretation and legitimacy. AI systems can produce highly precise outputs, yet without human contextualization these outputs risk being misapplied or misunderstood. Research suggests that hybrid systems—where algorithms generate forecasts and humans interpret and act upon them—outperform either humans or machines alone (Rahwan et al., 2019). The manager's role in such systems is not diminished but transformed: from producer of forecasts to interpreter of algorithmic signals. This requires new literacies, including the ability to interrogate model assumptions, identify contextual mismatches, and integrate computational outputs with qualitative judgment.

This hybridization has organizational implications. It requires new forms of collaboration between technical experts and strategic leaders. Data scientists must understand the strategic contexts in which their models are deployed, while managers must acquire enough technical literacy to engage critically with AI outputs. This co-evolution of skills fosters a culture of "collaborative intelligence" where human intuition and machine learning complement each other (Wilson & Daugherty, 2018). Such cultures reshape not only forecasting but also organizational learning more broadly, embedding continuous adaptation into the DNA of firms.

Organizational learning itself is accelerated by AI-based forecasting. Traditionally, firms learned through cycles of planning, execution, and review. Feedback was often slow, tied to reporting periods. AI compresses these cycles by providing continuous feedback and real-time updates. This acceleration enables firms to detect weak signals earlier, experiment with alternative strategies, and refine actions more quickly. However, accelerated learning also requires careful governance: organizations must avoid the temptation to prioritize short-term adjustments at the expense of long-term vision. The challenge for strategic management is to design learning systems where AI-driven forecasts enhance both tactical agility and strategic coherence (George et al., 2021).

Another emerging trend is the use of AI to analyze interconnected systems. Financial decision-making increasingly depends on complex interdependencies—between markets, sectors, and geopolitical contexts. AI allows organizations to model these interdependencies more effectively, identifying systemic risks that might otherwise remain hidden. Network analysis powered by machine learning can reveal vulnerabilities in global supply chains, financial linkages, or regulatory environments. This systemic perspective broadens the function of forecasting: it becomes not just a tool for predicting isolated outcomes but an instrument for mapping relational dynamics across entire ecosystems (Acemoglu et al., 2022). For managers, this provides a richer understanding of how shocks propagate and where interventions may be most effective.

The systemic dimension also introduces ethical and political considerations. Forecasting based on AI is not neutral; it shapes decisions that affect employees, customers, and societies. The power to predict implies the power to prioritize, raising questions about whose futures are being envisioned and whose risks are being managed. For example, credit scoring models that incorporate alternative data may expand access for some groups while excluding others. Strategic forecasting in the AI era must therefore incorporate considerations of fairness, inclusivity, and legitimacy. The challenge is not only to predict more accurately but to ensure that predictions align with organizational values and social expectations (Lepri et al., 2018).

The cumulative effect of these transformations is a redefinition of strategic analysis and forecasting as continuous, adaptive, and systemic processes. AI reshapes the sources of data, the models of prediction, the imagination of scenarios, the roles of managers, and the culture of learning. Financial decision-making, once constrained by periodic reports and limited datasets, becomes an ongoing practice of sense-making across diverse signals and multiple futures. This redefinition does not eliminate uncertainty but transforms how it is navigated. Strategy in the AI age is less about controlling the future and more about co-evolving with it, guided by hybrid systems of human and machine intelligence.

If the first wave of AI-driven forecasting in strategic management concentrated on reconfiguring data sources and computational models, a second wave is emerging that expands the scope of application to global, interdisciplinary, and societal domains. Forecasting is no longer limited to firm-level outcomes such as portfolio optimization or market entry timing; it increasingly engages with complex, interconnected phenomena that shape the global environment of business. In this sense, AI does not simply add predictive accuracy to existing models but transforms the very object of strategic foresight, broadening it to encompass geopolitical dynamics, regulatory landscapes, climate trajectories, and socio-cultural change.

A major development in this expansion is the rise of multi-scenario forecasting. Traditional scenario planning often worked with three archetypal futures—optimistic, pessimistic, and baseline. AI systems can now generate thousands of plausible pathways by combining variables across domains: shifts in global trade patterns, regulatory reforms in emerging markets, technological adoption rates, demographic transitions, or climate-related disruptions. For example, natural language processing applied to parliamentary debates, central bank reports, and policy papers can identify subtle shifts in regulatory priorities long before they are codified into law. Machine learning models can then integrate these signals with macroeconomic data and environmental indicators to forecast regulatory–economic interactions that shape financial markets. This ability to create richly textured, cross-domain scenarios is particularly valuable for organizations exposed to systemic shocks, such as energy firms navigating both decarbonization policies and volatile commodity prices.

The growing sophistication of scenario simulations highlights the interdisciplinary character of AI forecasting. Whereas strategic forecasting was once dominated by economists and financial analysts, AI-driven foresight requires collaboration between data scientists, political scientists, climate modelers, sociologists, and ethicists. Each discipline contributes different datasets, interpretive frameworks, and validation criteria. Strategic managers are thus placed in the role of orchestrators, coordinating diverse expertise around AI platforms that can integrate disparate inputs. This interdisciplinarity strengthens the resilience of forecasts, as blind spots from one perspective may be mitigated by insights from another. Yet it also challenges traditional hierarchies of knowledge within organizations, requiring humility from managers and openness to alternative epistemologies.

Education and skill development emerge as crucial enablers of this interdisciplinary turn. Managers trained in classical finance may not be prepared to interpret AI-driven forecasts that draw on climate models or socio-political sentiment analysis. Business schools and executive programs are beginning to incorporate modules on data analytics, machine learning, and algorithmic governance, but the challenge goes beyond technical literacy. Leaders must develop narrative competence—the ability to craft strategic stories from complex, probabilistic data—and ethical sensitivity, ensuring that forecasts are not only accurate but also legitimate in the eyes of stakeholders. Strategic foresight in the AI age is as much about communication and persuasion as about computation. Forecasts must be translated into narratives that inspire action without overstating certainty.

The educational dimension extends into organizational culture. Firms that succeed with AI forecasting often cultivate cultures of experimentation and continuous learning, where forecasts are treated not as definitive predictions but as tools for exploration. This stands in contrast to traditional organizations that demand definitive answers before making commitments. The iterative, probabilistic nature of AI outputs demands a shift in expectations: forecasts provide guidance under uncertainty rather than guarantees of outcomes. Embedding this cultural shift requires sustained investment in training, leadership role-modeling, and alignment of incentives to reward adaptability rather than rigid adherence to plans.

At the global level, AI-driven forecasting is increasingly central to financial governance. International institutions such as the International Monetary Fund, the Bank for International Settlements, and regional development banks are experimenting with AI tools to anticipate systemic risks, monitor capital flows, and detect early warning signs of crises. These institutions face the challenge of integrating heterogeneous data from multiple jurisdictions, often with varying levels of transparency and reliability. AI can help by identifying anomalies, clustering similar patterns across countries, and highlighting outliers that warrant attention. Yet this also raises questions of sovereignty and trust: should global forecasts generated by AI influence national policies, and how can legitimacy be maintained when algorithms operate across borders? Strategic managers in multinational firms must navigate these dynamics, balancing the authority of global forecasts with sensitivity to local contexts.

Geopolitics adds another layer of complexity. Competition for AI leadership has become a defining feature of global power relations. The United States, China, and the European Union each promote distinct models of AI development and governance, with implications for strategic forecasting. U.S.-based systems often emphasize market-driven innovation, Chinese initiatives integrate AI into state-led planning, and European frameworks foreground ethics and human rights. For global firms, this means that AI forecasts may not be portable across jurisdictions: an algorithm trained on U.S. data may misinterpret patterns in China, while forecasts aligned with European ethical norms may conflict with practices elsewhere. Strategic foresight thus requires contextualization: managers must interpret AI outputs through the lens of local institutional, cultural, and political conditions.

Beyond geopolitics, AI forecasting is reshaping societal expectations of corporate responsibility. Stakeholders increasingly demand that organizations not only anticipate risks to profits but also consider social and environmental impacts. AI forecasting enables firms to simulate the consequences of strategic decisions for employment, inequality, carbon emissions, and community resilience. Investors, regulators, and civil society groups use these forecasts to hold organizations accountable, pressing them to integrate environmental, social, and governance (ESG) considerations into strategic planning. As a result, strategic forecasting becomes a site of contestation over corporate purpose: is the goal merely to maximize shareholder returns, or to balance financial outcomes with broader contributions to society?

The societal role of forecasting raises normative questions about inclusion. Forecasts based on AI are not neutral—they reflect the data they draw upon and the assumptions embedded in their models. If data from marginalized communities is scarce or of poor quality, forecasts may systematically neglect their realities. Strategic managers must therefore address representational justice in forecasting: ensuring that the data incorporated into AI models captures diverse perspectives and experiences. This expands the ethics of forecasting from avoiding harm to actively promoting fairness. Organizations that neglect these issues risk reputational damage and erosion of trust, while those that address them may differentiate themselves as responsible innovators.

The expansion of AI forecasting into global and societal domains also forces a reconsideration of temporality. While AI excels at short-term predictions, the most pressing strategic challenges—climate change, demographic transitions, technological disruptions—unfold over decades. Strategic forecasting must therefore integrate short-term adaptability with long-term vision. This requires combining AI models that generate immediate insights with frameworks that preserve intergenerational responsibility. Financial institutions are beginning to experiment with such combinations, linking AI-powered risk assessments with sustainability models that project decades into the future. The challenge for managers is to hold these temporalities together, avoiding the myopia of short-term optimization without losing responsiveness to immediate opportunities and threats.

Finally, the expansion of AI forecasting compels organizations to rethink their legitimacy in democratic societies. Forecasts shape expectations, allocate resources, and influence policy debates. When algorithms generate forecasts that appear authoritative but are opaque, public trust may be undermined. Strategic managers must therefore prioritize transparency not only within organizations but also in communication with stakeholders. This includes explaining the assumptions behind forecasts, acknowledging uncertainty, and engaging stakeholders in interpreting results. Legitimacy in the AI era depends not only on accuracy but also on openness, humility, and responsiveness to public concerns.

Together, these dynamics reveal that AI in strategic analysis and forecasting is more than a technical innovation. It is a reconfiguration of how organizations imagine the future, how they distribute authority across disciplines and geographies, and how they engage with societal expectations. Forecasting in the AI age becomes a practice of co-creation between humans and machines, firms and societies, local contexts and global systems. The challenge for strategic management is to embrace this expanded horizon, cultivating the skills, cultures, and institutions necessary to use AI forecasting not only for competitive advantage but also for sustainable, inclusive, and legitimate governance of the future.

One of the most overlooked aspects of artificial intelligence in strategic forecasting is its ability to reconfigure attention itself. In an environment saturated with signals, not every piece of information is equally valuable. Traditional analysts often struggled with the dilemma of selecting which indicators to prioritize, a task inevitably colored by personal experience and cognitive biases. AI reframes this dilemma by ranking, clustering, and filtering signals across vast datasets, essentially curating the flow of organizational attention. This raises an important insight: forecasting is not simply about predicting outcomes but about shaping what organizations choose to notice. The strategic significance of AI lies not only in accuracy but also in its power to direct attention toward weak signals, hidden correlations, or unconventional data sources that may otherwise remain invisible.

Beyond filtering, AI also transforms the creativity of strategy. Forecasting has long been considered a largely analytical activity—an effort to extrapolate from known variables into plausible futures. Generative models complicate this narrative. They are capable of creating new scenarios, synthesizing possibilities by combining signals across domains in unexpected ways. When such models suggest futures no human team had imagined, they broaden the space of strategic creativity. Instead of being restricted to linear extrapolation, organizations can explore counterintuitive or even provocative futures. This capability does not replace human imagination but augments it, acting as a catalyst for brainstorming, scenario workshops, and visioning exercises. The imaginative potential of AI challenges the stereotype of machines as purely rational calculators and invites us to see them as partners in creative exploration.

Closely tied to creativity is the relationship between AI forecasts and managerial intuition. Intuition has always played a significant role in strategy, often celebrated as the mark of visionary leadership. Yet in the AI era, intuition is neither eliminated nor simply confirmed by data; it is redefined. Managers must learn to reinterpret their intuitive judgments in light of algorithmic outputs, sometimes overriding their instincts, at other times questioning the limits of models. This dialectic between human intuition and machine learning creates a dynamic form of foresight, where intuition is sharpened rather than sidelined. When a forecast aligns with intuition, confidence is reinforced; when it contradicts intuition, reflection is stimulated. Either way, AI ensures that intuition is no longer a solitary act but a dialogue between human experience and machine-generated insights.

Equally significant is the emotional dimension of AI forecasting. Predictions do not exist in a vacuum; they shape the moods, anxieties, and confidence levels of organizational actors. A forecast suggesting downturns can trigger caution, slow investment, and generate defensive strategies. Conversely, optimistic forecasts can build confidence, accelerate commitments, and stimulate risk-taking. The novelty of AI forecasting is the aura of authority it carries. Because machine-generated predictions are perceived as highly objective, they may exert greater emotional influence than human forecasts. Organizations must therefore acknowledge that forecasts are not only technical tools but also emotional instruments, shaping the psychological climate in which strategies are debated and enacted. Managing this emotional impact becomes part of the strategic task.

Another new frontier is the possibility of participatory foresight. Historically, forecasting was an elite function, concentrated among analysts and executives. AI lowers barriers by providing tools that can be accessed and interpreted by a wider range of stakeholders. Dashboards, visualization platforms, and interactive scenario models allow employees, customers, or even community representatives to engage in shaping the interpretation of futures. When diverse actors contribute to foresight, the result is not just broader legitimacy but also richer content, as multiple perspectives surface different priorities and concerns. Participatory foresight supported by AI can democratize strategy, aligning organizational directions with stakeholder expectations in ways that traditional top-down forecasting rarely achieved.

AI also opens the possibility of extreme horizons in forecasting. While most organizations plan within a five-to-ten-year window, the challenges of the twenty-first century increasingly require foresight over much longer spans. Climate change, demographic shifts, and technological disruptions unfold over decades. AI models, especially when combined with scientific simulations, can project trends across 50 or even 100 years. Though uncertainty increases with time, the purpose of such extreme horizon forecasting is not precision but awareness. It helps organizations situate themselves in intergenerational contexts, prompting reflection on responsibilities that extend beyond immediate profit cycles. By stretching the time horizon, AI anchors strategy in the long-term survival and flourishing of organizations and societies alike.

The interplay between attention, creativity, intuition, emotion, participation, and temporality shows that AI reshapes forecasting at multiple levels simultaneously. It is not only a tool for better predictions but a medium that transforms how organizations perceive, imagine, and feel about the future. Strategic managers must therefore expand their understanding of forecasting from a technical exercise into a socio-technical practice. They are no longer just interpreters of signals but stewards of collective imagination and emotion, facilitators of participatory dialogue, and custodians of long-term responsibilities.

Such an expansion carries profound implications for organizational design. If AI broadens foresight, then structures must evolve to accommodate this breadth. Decision-making forums may need to include new roles—data curators, scenario facilitators, ethical interpreters—alongside traditional executives. Governance systems must incorporate protocols not only for validating predictions but also for reflecting on their emotional and social consequences. Performance metrics must account for long-term resilience and stakeholder legitimacy, not just short-term accuracy. In this sense, the architecture of the forecasting function itself becomes strategic, shaping how organizations relate to their futures.

The most transformative implication, however, may be cultural. When AI forecasting becomes embedded in everyday practice, organizations may gradually internalize a new attitude toward the future. Instead of seeking certainty, they may learn to live with multiplicity. Instead of fearing uncertainty, they may see it as a source of creativity. Instead of treating foresight as the privilege of a few, they may cultivate it as a collective competence. This cultural transformation could redefine what it means to be a strategic organization in the twenty-first century: not one that controls the future but one that thrives by continuously co-evolving with it.

CONCLUSIONS AND FUTURE DIRECTIONS

The integration of artificial intelligence (AI) into strategic management and financial decision-making represents one of the most significant transformations in contemporary organizational practice. Across this chapter, we have explored how AI reshapes analysis, forecasting, and the allocation of resources, highlighting the way it expands the horizons of strategic thought. Drawing conclusions from these developments requires a recognition that we are not merely witnessing incremental change but a redefinition of management's epistemological foundations. AI alters the nature of knowledge itself in organizations, enabling new forms of foresight, adaptivity, and systemic awareness. At the same time, it compels managers, regulators, and societies to confront normative questions about legitimacy, fairness, and inclusivity in algorithmically mediated governance.

One of the central conclusions is that AI has changed the relationship between data and strategy. In earlier decades, strategy depended on relatively scarce, structured, and delayed forms of information—financial reports, market analyses, or industry surveys. AI transforms this relationship by enabling organizations to access abundant, continuous, and multidimensional streams of data. These include alternative sources such as mobility patterns, geospatial imagery, and real-time consumer behavior. The shift is not simply quantitative but qualitative: what counts as strategic information has been radically expanded. Strategic managers must therefore cultivate the ability to curate data ecosystems, ensuring that the right signals are captured without being overwhelmed by noise. This curatorial role is central to maintaining coherence in decision-making.

Another conclusion concerns the temporal logic of strategy. AI enables continuous forecasting and adaptive learning, challenging the traditional cycle of annual or multi-year planning. Strategy becomes a living process rather than a static document. This shift has implications for leadership: managers must learn to balance short-term responsiveness with long-term orientation. They must operate in what has been described as a "dual temporality," reconciling the fast pace of algorithmic insights with the slower rhythms of institutional change and human deliberation (Susskind, 2022). The art of management increasingly lies in integrating these temporalities rather than privileging one over the other.

Equally important is the conclusion that AI redefines organizational learning. Forecasts and analyses generated by machine learning models provide constant feedback, enabling rapid experimentation and adjustment. Firms become laboratories where strategies are tested in real time, with outcomes feeding back into models. Yet accelerated learning can generate risks of myopia, as organizations optimize for immediate performance without considering long-term consequences. The strategic task is therefore to design learning systems that preserve depth and reflection alongside speed. This requires embedding deliberative practices—such as scenario planning and stakeholder consultation—into AI-enabled environments, ensuring that the search for efficiency does not eclipse the broader mission of resilience.

The diffusion of AI also changes the role of managers themselves. In traditional contexts, managers were the principal interpreters of information and the final decision-makers. In the AI age, they are increasingly curators, mediators, and translators. Their authority derives not from possessing superior information but from their ability to integrate algorithmic outputs with contextual judgment, ethical awareness, and organizational vision. This does not diminish the importance of leadership; it reframes it. Leaders must now demonstrate not only technical literacy but also the capacity to explain, justify, and contest AI-generated insights in ways that maintain legitimacy and trust (Shneiderman, 2020).

From these conclusions flow several future directions for research and practice. The first concerns the design of hybrid governance models. Purely algorithmic systems risk opacity and overreliance, while purely human systems may be overwhelmed by complexity. The future lies in carefully calibrated combinations, where humans and machines collaborate in complementary ways. Future research should investigate the most effective forms of this collaboration: when should decisions be automated, when should they remain human-driven, and how can oversight be designed to ensure accountability? Empirical studies across industries and regions could provide valuable insights into how hybrid systems function in practice.

A second direction concerns the education and training of future leaders. Business schools and professional programs must adapt curricula to ensure that managers develop both technical literacy and ethical reflexivity. Understanding machine learning models, data governance, and algorithmic accountability will be essential for strategic decision-making. Yet equally important is cultivating the ability to communicate probabilistic forecasts, manage uncertainty, and align technological capabilities with human values. Future research could explore pedagogical innovations in management education, including interdisciplinary training that bridges finance, computer science, and philosophy (Levin & Madsbjerg, 2022).

A third direction involves the integration of AI forecasting into global governance. Financial systems are deeply interconnected, and shocks propagate rapidly across borders. International institutions such as the International Monetary Fund or the World Bank increasingly rely on AI-driven models to monitor systemic risks. However, the legitimacy of such models depends on their inclusivity and transparency. Future research should examine how global forecasts can be designed to respect national sovereignty while providing credible early warnings of crises. Comparative studies of regulatory frameworks could also shed light on how different jurisdictions balance innovation with oversight (OECD, 2021).

A fourth direction concerns the incorporation of sustainability into AI-driven strategic forecasting. Climate change, biodiversity loss, and resource constraints represent long-term risks that cannot be addressed through short-term optimization. AI models can contribute by integrating environmental data into financial decision-making, enabling firms to anticipate regulatory shifts, consumer preferences, and physical disruptions. Yet this requires developing models that are not only technically accurate but also normatively aligned with sustainability goals. Future research should focus on the methodological and ethical challenges of embedding environmental, social, and governance (ESG) considerations into AI systems (Rockström et al., 2021).

Another promising avenue involves the geopolitics of AI in finance. As nations compete for leadership in AI development, their regulatory choices and technological investments shape global competition. The United States, China, and the European Union promote distinct models of AI governance, each with implications for strategic management. Understanding how these models interact and how multinational firms navigate them will be a critical area of study. Future directions should include cross-national analyses of AI adoption in financial decision-making, exploring how institutional diversity shapes outcomes (Miller & Raji, 2022).

The ethics of forecasting also demands further exploration. Forecasts are not neutral; they shape expectations, influence behaviors, and allocate resources. When AI-driven forecasts exclude marginalized groups or reflect biased datasets, they perpetuate inequalities. Future research should investigate mechanisms for ensuring representational justice in forecasting: how can AI models incorporate diverse perspectives and experiences, and how can organizations ensure that forecasts promote inclusion rather than exclusion? This inquiry intersects with broader debates on fairness, accountability, and transparency in AI governance (Whittlestone et al., 2019).

At the organizational level, a key future direction lies in the development of cultures that embrace uncertainty as a condition rather than a problem to be solved. AI forecasting enhances the ability to anticipate multiple futures, but managers must learn to live with ambiguity rather than eliminate it. This requires cultural shifts toward experimentation, adaptability, and resilience. Research could explore how organizations cultivate such cultures, what leadership practices support them, and how they influence performance.

Finally, future directions must address the political economy of AI forecasting. Access to data and computational resources is unevenly distributed, raising concerns about concentration of power in a few firms or regions. Strategic management scholarship must engage with these dynamics, examining how asymmetries in data access shape competitive advantage, innovation, and global inequality. Understanding the implications of such asymmetries is crucial for ensuring that AI-driven forecasting contributes not only to firm-level success but also to broader social well-being.

In conclusion, the integration of AI into strategic analysis and forecasting redefines the foundations of management. It expands the scope of data, accelerates organizational learning, and reshapes the role of managers. It also raises new questions about legitimacy, fairness, and inclusivity. The future of strategic management lies in hybrid systems where humans and machines collaborate, in educational reforms that prepare leaders for algorithmic environments, in global governance frameworks that balance innovation with responsibility, and in ethical commitments that ensure AI serves not only efficiency but also sustainability and justice. By pursuing these directions, research and practice can help shape a future where strategic forecasting enhances resilience and inclusivity in financial decision-making.

REFERENCES

Acemoglu, D., Ozdaglar, A., & Tahbaz-Salehi, A. (2022). Systemic risk and stability in financial networks. *The American Economic Review*, *112*(3), 991–1034. DOI: 10.1257/aer.20191479

Bughin, J., Seong, J., Manyika, J., Chui, M., & Joshi, R. (2018). Notes from the AI frontier: Modeling the impact of AI on the world economy. *McKinsey Global Institute Report*.

Daugherty, P. R., & Wilson, H. J. (2018). *Human + machine: Reimagining work in the age of AI*. Harvard Business Review Press.

Fischer, T., & Krauss, C. (2018). Deep learning with long short-term memory networks for financial market predictions. *European Journal of Operational Research*, *270*(2), 654–669. DOI: 10.1016/j.ejor.2017.11.054

Galaz, V., Centeno, M. A., Callahan, P. W., Causevic, A., Patterson, T., Brass, I., & Levy, K. (2021). Artificial intelligence, systemic risks, and sustainability. *Technology in Society*, *67*, 101741. DOI: 10.1016/j.techsoc.2021.101741

George, G., Haas, M. R., & Pentland, A. (2021). Big data and management. *Academy of Management Journal*, *64*(3), 584–590. DOI: 10.5465/amj.2021.4003

Ghosh, A., Choudhury, S. R., & Bhadury, A. (2019). Satellite data and economic forecasting: A review. *Economic Modelling*, *80*, 43–54. DOI: 10.1016/j.econmod.2019.05.002

Goodell, J. W., Kumar, S., & Lim, W. M. (2021). Artificial intelligence and machine learning in financial forecasting. *Journal of Behavioral and Experimental Finance*, *32*, 100574. DOI: 10.1016/j.jbef.2021.100574

Haefner, N., & Sternberg, R. (2020). AI-enabled innovation management: Opportunities and challenges. *Technovation*, *98*, 102176. DOI: 10.1016/j.technovation.2020.102176

Haefner, N., Wincent, J., Parida, V., & Gassmann, O. (2021). Artificial intelligence and innovation management: A review, framework, and research agenda. *Technological Forecasting and Social Change*, *162*, 120392. DOI: 10.1016/j.techfore.2020.120392

Hendershott, T., Li, H., & Zhang, M. (2021). FinTech credit risk modeling using alternative data. *Journal of Financial Services Research*, *59*(2-3), 195–227. DOI: 10.1007/s10693-020-00339-w

Jordan, M. I., & Russell, S. J. (2020). Artificial intelligence: The revolution has not happened yet. *Harvard Data Science Review*, *2*(1), 1–19. DOI: 10.1162/99608f92.f06c6e61

Kenton, W., & Mulligan, C. (2021). Alternative data in finance: The rise of nontraditional sources. *Journal of Investment Management*, *19*(1), 33–48.

Kozlowski, A. C., Taddy, M., & Evans, J. A. (2022). The geometry of culture: Word embeddings and cultural analysis. *American Sociological Review*, *87*(5), 947–981. DOI: 10.1177/00031224221107354

Leiponen, A. (2021). Digital platforms and management education: Re-thinking curriculum design in the age of AI. *Academy of Management Learning & Education*, *20*(4), 443–456. DOI: 10.5465/amle.2020.0059

Lepri, B., Oliver, N., Letouzé, E., Pentland, A., & Vinck, P. (2018). Fair, transparent, and accountable algorithmic decision-making processes. *Philosophy & Technology*, *31*(4), 611–627. DOI: 10.1007/s13347-017-0279-x

Levin, C., & Madsbjerg, C. (2022). *The rise of techno-strategy: Managing in an algorithmic age*. Harvard Business Press.

Lim, B., & Zohren, S. (2020). Time-series forecasting with deep learning. *Philosophical Transactions of the Royal Society A*, *378*(2164), 20190147. DOI: 10.1098/rsta.2019.0147

Longoni, C., Bonezzi, A., & Morewedge, C. K. (2019). Resistance to medical artificial intelligence. *The Journal of Consumer Research*, *46*(4), 629–650. DOI: 10.1093/jcr/ucz013

Longoni, C., & Cian, L. (2022). Artificial intelligence in strategy: Implications for managers and consumers. *Journal of the Academy of Marketing Science*, *50*(5), 930–950. DOI: 10.1007/s11747-021-00842-8

Mikalef, P., Pappas, I. O., Krogstie, J., & Giannakos, M. (2020). Big data analytics capabilities: A systematic literature review. *Information Systems and e-Business Management*, *18*(3), 547–574. DOI: 10.1007/s10257-017-0362-y

Miller, H., & Raji, I. D. (2022). Out of one, many: Using AI for financial inclusion globally. *Patterns (New York, N.Y.)*, *3*(7), 100542. DOI: 10.1016/j.patter.2022.100542

Nash, J., Smith, C., & Zhao, Y. (2022). Alternative data in financial decision-making: The role of artificial intelligence. *The Journal of Financial Data Science*, *4*(3), 12–29. DOI: 10.3905/jfds.2022.1.089

Nguyen, T., Yoon, J., & Lee, J. (2021). AI-based scenario simulation for strategic decision-making. *Technological Forecasting and Social Change*, *171*, 120963. DOI: 10.1016/j.techfore.2021.120963

OECD. (2021). *AI in society: Implications for finance and governance*. OECD Publishing.

Paschen, J., Pitt, C., & Kietzmann, J. (2020). Artificial intelligence in business-to-business marketing. *Journal of Business Research*, *116*, 209–220. DOI: 10.1016/j.jbusres.2020.05.001

Paschen, J., Wilson, M., & Ferreira, J. J. (2020). Collaborative intelligence: How human and artificial intelligence create value along the B2B sales funnel. *Business Horizons*, *63*(3), 403–414. DOI: 10.1016/j.bushor.2020.01.003

Rahwan, I., Cebrian, M., Obradovich, N., Bongard, J., Bonnefon, J.-F., Breazeal, C., Crandall, J. W., Christakis, N. A., Couzin, I. D., Jackson, M. O., Jennings, N. R., Kamar, E., Kloumann, I. M., Larochelle, H., Lazer, D., McElreath, R., Mislove, A., Parkes, D. C., Pentland, A. S., & Wellman, M. (2019). Machine behaviour. *Nature*, *568*(7753), 477–486. DOI: 10.1038/s41586-019-1138-y PMID: 31019318

Raisch, S., & Krakowski, S. (2021). Artificial intelligence and management: The automation–augmentation paradox. *Academy of Management Review, 46*(1), 192–210. DOI: 10.5465/amr.2018.0072

Rockström, J., Gupta, J., Lenton, T. M., Qin, D., Lade, S. J., Abrams, J. F., … Xu, J. (2021). Identifying a safe and just corridor for people and the planet. *Earth's Future, 9*(4), e2020EF001866. DOI: 10.1029/2020EF001866

Russell, S., & Norvig, P. (2021). *Artificial intelligence: A modern approach* (4th ed.). Pearson.

Schoemaker, P. J. H., Day, G. S., & Snyder, S. A. (2013). Integrating organizational networks, weak signals, strategic radars, and scenario planning. *Technological Forecasting and Social Change, 80*(4), 815–824. DOI: 10.1016/j.techfore.2012.10.020

Shneiderman, B. (2020). Human-centered artificial intelligence: Reliable, safe & trustworthy. *International Journal of Human-Computer Interaction, 36*(6), 495–504. DOI: 10.1080/10447318.2020.1741118

Sjödin, D., Parida, V., Leksell, M., & Petrovic, A. (2021). Smart factory implementation and process innovation: A study of AI-enabled manufacturing. *Technovation, 102*, 102222. DOI: 10.1016/j.technovation.2020.102222

Susskind, D. (2022). *A world without work: Technology, automation, and how we should respond.* Metropolitan Books.

Susskind, R., & Susskind, D. (2022). *The future of the professions: How technology will transform the work of human experts* (Updated ed.). Oxford University Press.

Talwar, R., & Koury, A. (2017). Disruptive shifts: The future of financial services in an era of global risks. *Foresight, 19*(5), 501–512. DOI: 10.1108/FS-06-2017-0021

Talwar, R., & Koury, A. (2019). Foresight and futures in the age of AI. *Futures, 105*, 10–22. DOI: 10.1016/j.futures.2018.09.004

Tegmark, M. (2017). *Life 3.0: Being human in the age of artificial intelligence.* Alfred A. Knopf.

Thomas, L. C., Crook, J. N., & Edelman, D. B. (2017). *Credit scoring and its applications* (2nd ed.). SIAM. DOI: 10.1137/1.9781611974560

van Rijmenam, M. (2020). The future of strategy is algorithmic. *Journal of Strategy and Management, 13*(4), 517–529. DOI: 10.1108/JSMA-03-2020-0074

van Rijmenam, M., & Schweitzer, J. (2021). *The organization of tomorrow: How AI, blockchain, and analytics turn your business into a data organization*. Routledge.

Walch, K. (2019). Artificial intelligence in financial services: Balancing efficiency with ethics. *Journal of Financial Transformation, 49*, 80–87.

Whittlestone, J., Nyrup, R., Alexandrova, A., Dihal, K., & Cave, S. (2019). Ethical and societal implications of algorithms, data, and artificial intelligence: A roadmap for research. *Nuffield Foundation Report.*

Wilson, H. J., & Daugherty, P. R. (2018). Collaborative intelligence: Humans and AI are joining forces. *Harvard Business Review, 96*(4), 114–123.

Zeng, Y., Lu, E., & Huangfu, C. (2019). Linking artificial intelligence principles. *Nature Machine Intelligence, 1*(8), 373–374. DOI: 10.1038/s42256-019-0088-2 PMID: 31406960

Zhang, Y., Li, J., & Song, X. (2021). Artificial intelligence and strategic foresight: Emerging approaches in finance. *Technological Forecasting and Social Change, 169*, 120822. DOI: 10.1016/j.techfore.2021.120822

Zuboff, S. (2020). *Surveillance capitalism in the financial sector*. Polity Press.

Zweig, K. A. (2021). *Awkward intelligence: Why AI needs philosophy*. MIT Press.

Chapter 8
AI in Corporate Governance:
Strengthening Oversight

Mustafa Kayyali
https://orcid.org/0000-0003-3300-262X
Maaref University of Applied Sciences, Syria

ABSTRACT

As artificial intelligence continues to reshape the fabric of modern finance, its integration into corporate governance raises urgent questions about oversight, ethics, and decision-making authority. This chapter explores how AI technologies—particularly machine learning, predictive analytics, and intelligent auditing systems—are transforming boardroom dynamics and redefining what it means to govern responsibly. Far from being a mere tool, AI is becoming a co-decision-maker, influencing everything from financial disclosures to risk mitigation strategies. Yet, alongside these efficiencies come profound challenges: algorithmic bias, opacity, and the erosion of human accountability. Through a critical lens, this chapter investigates how corporate structures can adopt AI responsibly, embedding transparency, ethical standards, and regulatory foresight into the very architecture of governance. Ultimately, it calls for a reframing of oversight itself—not as a control mechanism alone, but as a shared moral and strategic enterprise in the age of intelligent systems.

DOI: 10.4018/979-8-3373-3626-8.ch008

INTRODUCTION

Corporate governance has always carried a weight that goes beyond bylaws, financial audits, or quarterly reports. At its core, governance is a question of trust—trust in systems, in people, in accountability, and in the invisible thread of values that binds power to responsibility. But in a world where algorithms are increasingly woven into the very structure of decision-making, that trust is being renegotiated. Slowly, subtly, yet unmistakably, we are witnessing a shift. What once relied heavily on human judgment, intuition, and lived experience is now intersecting with machine logic, predictive models, and data-driven forecasts. This isn't just a technical evolution. It is a philosophical one.

Artificial intelligence, for all its promises, forces us to confront uncomfortable questions about who—or what—governs (Bremmer & Suleyman, 2023). In the sleek boardrooms of multinational firms and the fluorescent-lit offices of regulatory bodies, conversations are changing. It's no longer just about profits or compliance; it's about whether a neural network should have a say in assessing risk, flagging anomalies, or even shaping the trajectory of a company. Governance, traditionally human-centric, is being augmented, and at times challenged, by technologies that neither sleep nor forget. Algorithms don't come with conscience. They do not fear public backlash, and they do not sweat under moral ambiguity. But they do learn. They observe. They anticipate. And in doing so, they influence—sometimes invisibly—the direction of corporate choices.

The rise of AI in corporate governance is not just about automation or efficiency (Cihon et al, 2021). That's the surface layer. Dig deeper, and it becomes a reflection of our evolving relationship with authority, accountability, and truth itself. Can a system trained on past data recognize emerging ethical dilemmas? Can it weigh not just financial costs but social consequences? And if it errs—as all systems do—who takes responsibility? The board? The developer? The dataset? Or is responsibility itself becoming so diluted that no one, ultimately, is held accountable?

This chapter does not aim to either glorify AI or sound alarmist notes. Instead, it positions itself in the space between—where nuance lives. It looks at how AI is reshaping oversight structures, redefining the boundaries between human judgment and machine recommendation, and challenging governance frameworks to become not only smarter but also more ethically attuned. We'll explore both the promise and the peril: how AI can reduce fraud, increase transparency, and detect risks faster than any team of auditors ever could—but also how it can mask bias, reinforce systemic inequalities, or be weaponized in the name of "efficiency."

This is not a chapter for those looking for neat conclusions or perfect models. It is for those willing to sit with ambiguity, to ask difficult questions, and to imagine what it means to build corporate governance systems that are not only intelligent but wise. As we navigate through the landscape of algorithms and oversight, one thing becomes clear: the future of corporate governance won't be written by machines alone. It will be co-authored—messily, unpredictably—by humans and machines together, in a fragile dance that demands both technical precision and ethical depth.

RETHINKING OVERSIGHT: THE EMERGING ROLE OF AI IN CORPORATE GOVERNANCE

It starts as a whisper in boardrooms—something about automation, dashboards, smarter systems. Maybe it's an innocuous comment tucked between bullet points on an agenda: "Could we run the risk model through the new predictive engine?" And just like that, a door opens. What follows isn't a storm of disruption, but something quieter. Algorithms don't burst in the way revolutions do. They seep in. One use case at a time. One spreadsheet auto-analyzed (Bonini & Treré, 2024). One anomaly flagged by a machine instead of a manager. Before long, they're everywhere—embedded in procurement pipelines, scanning minutes of meetings, recommending compliance flags before humans even blink. But this isn't just another chapter in the evolution of technology. It's a tectonic shift in what it means to *govern*—to oversee, to weigh responsibility, to be the custodian of consequence.

The traditional architecture of corporate oversight is, at its core, deeply human. Rooted in judgment, ethics, accountability—messy things. Things that require conversation, context, a feel for the intangible. A board meeting is as much about what's said as what's not. About intuition as much as evidence. Directors pore over documents, yes, but also facial expressions, subtext, gut reactions. Oversight has always been a deeply analog endeavor (Zaman, 2024). And for good reason: people are unpredictable, power is seductive, and the most catastrophic decisions often hide in plain sight, buried not in numbers but in unspoken compromises. Enter artificial intelligence. Suddenly, oversight is no longer just retrospective—it's anticipatory. Not reactive, but predictive. The old cadence of "review and report" is being replaced by "scan, flag, simulate." With machine learning tools digesting millions of data points in minutes, the traditional role of oversight—meticulously combing through reports, double-checking ledgers, chasing accountability in the rearview mirror—starts to look painfully slow, even quaint. Why trust fallible humans when the machine never forgets, never tires, never gets distracted? And yet, that's precisely where the danger lies.

There's an illusion that clings tightly to technology—the illusion of objectivity. Algorithms, after all, don't lie (Gaudio, 2021). But that's the thing, isn't it? They don't *lie*, but they also don't *understand*. They reflect, mimic, project—based on data that's already biased, often incomplete, and always contextual. An AI might flag a financial irregularity faster than any CFO, but it won't grasp the socio-political implications of a decision to shutter a plant in a small rural town. It won't see the faces. Or hear the silence that follows. When corporate oversight starts outsourcing its discernment to systems trained on the past, what happens to foresight? To moral reflection? To those long, uncomfortable pauses in meetings when someone finally says, "This might be legal, but is it right?"

We tend to think of AI in governance as a tool—an extension of the human will (Torrance & Tomlinson, 2023). But slowly, subtly, it becomes something more structural. A board may rely on a machine to recommend executive compensation bands based on "market trends." Sounds innocuous. But what if those market trends are skewed by historical inequities? What if the data set normalizes unethical disparities? The algorithm's neutrality is a mirage—what it really reflects is our past, crystallized and amplified.

There's also the question of attention. In a digital environment saturated with signals, anomalies, and alerts, where does the human eye settle? Ironically, AI doesn't simplify governance—it complicates it. A well-designed dashboard might highlight 300 risk vectors. But a board meeting has only two hours. So, what gets discussed? What gets ignored? Oversight, then, becomes an exercise not in discovery but in triage.

I remember once sitting in on a governance review meeting for a multinational that had just integrated AI across its internal audit system. The room was dim, quiet, lit only by the glow of a massive screen. The CFO was speaking in clipped sentences. The AI had flagged a potential supply chain irregularity in Southeast Asia. But there was no fraud (Lokanan & Maddhesia, 2025). Just a deviation—barely out of range. The algorithm didn't *understand* the political volatility in that region. It just crunched probabilities. The local team, steeped in context, had already dealt with it. But now, the board was in a swirl. Was this a failure of governance? Or a failure of the machine to interpret nuance?

That story isn't exceptional—it's emblematic. And it begs a larger question: What does it mean to be a steward of oversight in a world where machines shape what we see, what we prioritize, what we believe to be *at risk*? Oversight used to be about looking at the whole chessboard. Now, increasingly, we're reacting to whichever square is blinking red.

It's tempting to imagine AI as an assistant—faithful, tireless, surgically precise. But in practice, it doesn't just assist. It reorients. It shifts the center of gravity. It tells us where to look, and in doing so, it quietly limits our field of vision. And then there's accountability. If an algorithm recommends a financial maneuver that later turns out to be catastrophic, who takes the fall? The board? The audit committee? The vendor who coded the model? There's a slipperiness here—an erosion of personal responsibility under the guise of technical delegation. The more oversight becomes digitized, the harder it becomes to trace moral ownership (Sama et al, 2022). We risk creating a culture where no one is fully to blame because everyone was just "following the data." That, to me, is the most dangerous drift of all. And yet—I'm not a cynic. I've seen the power of AI to expose what would otherwise stay hidden. To detect patterns that humans miss. To democratize oversight by making complex data intelligible. It's not the presence of AI that troubles me—it's our passivity in the face of it. It's our willingness to substitute speed for wisdom. To treat oversight as a technical challenge rather than a moral craft.

So what does rethinking oversight actually mean? Maybe it starts with a shift in posture. Away from *delegation* and toward *partnership*. Away from the idea of AI as a silent oracle, and toward a model where human insight and machine intelligence interrogate each other—where algorithms don't just recommend, but provoke debate (Vallor, 2024). Where oversight becomes not a stamp of approval, but a space of inquiry. Maybe it means rewriting boardroom rituals. Not just looking at dashboards, but asking who trained the model, what assumptions were coded in, what trade-offs were embedded in the architecture of the system. Governance, in this light, isn't about trusting the machine. It's about *questioning it better*. And maybe—just maybe—it means returning to the slow work of ethics (Davies, 2025). To reading between the lines. To inviting dissent. To letting go of the fantasy that better technology alone will make us better stewards. The emerging role of AI in corporate governance isn't about machines taking over. It's about humans deciding who we want to be in a world where machines are everywhere. It's about reclaiming the space between data and decision—not to reject automation, but to redeem it with judgment, context, and conscience. In that space—fragile, ambiguous, alive—is where real oversight still lives.

TRANSPARENCY REIMAGINED: AI AND THE EVOLUTION OF ACCOUNTABILITY STRUCTURES

Let's talk about transparency—not as a checkbox, not as a buzzword tossed into policy documents like parsley on a plate, but as something more elemental. Something lived. A quality that pulses through systems, not just as light shining on facts, but as a kind of ethical atmosphere. You can feel it—or its absence—in a room. In the silence after a question. In the nervous glance across a table. Or in the confident nod of someone who knows they'll never be asked to explain how the algorithm works.

In a world increasingly shaped by artificial intelligence, our inherited notions of transparency are undergoing an uncomfortable recalibration (Carabantes, 2023). The old metaphors—glass walls, open books, windows into operations—don't quite fit anymore. How do you peer into a neural network? How do you cross-examine a machine that can't speak in full sentences, let alone explain its reasoning in language a board can understand? What does it even mean to be "transparent" when the logic of decision-making is dispersed across millions of data points, weighted variables, and feedback loops no one fully sees?

It used to be simpler, didn't it? Transparency meant documentation, disclosure, deliberation. If a firm made a bad call, you could trace the minutes, the emails, the paper trail (Jacobs et al, 2021). You could name who sat at the table and what was known at the time. There were blind spots, of course. Deceit, sometimes. But there was a framework—human-sized, ethically legible. Now? Now we're staring into something else entirely. Systems that don't just make recommendations but shape what gets seen in the first place. Algorithms that curate dashboards, filter anomalies, flag red zones. They're not just helping with decisions; they're sculpting the very field of perception.

We tell ourselves that AI will improve transparency—and in many ways, it can (Walmsley, 2021). It can process vast amounts of data, detect financial fraud with uncanny speed, highlight irregularities invisible to the naked eye. It can catch the subtle manipulations that would otherwise go unnoticed. That part's true. But there's a paradox buried here, almost poetic in its irony: the more complex and powerful the system, the more obscure its workings often become. This is the age of algorithmic opacity. Black-box governance. Glass that looks clear until you try to see through it.

I've seen risk committees nod solemnly at AI-generated risk heatmaps, unaware that the colors on those charts were determined by models trained on historical data riddled with systemic bias. Not malicious, just... inherited. Echoes of yesterday's decisions embedded in today's tools. And when the outputs are questioned? Silence, followed by a shrug: "That's just what the model returned." As if that ends the conversation. Transparency can no longer be measured by the availability of information alone (Bhatt et al, 2021). Not when that information is shaped by models no one in the room can fully interpret. Not when accountability is diffused across layers of abstraction, from the developers who coded the system to the executives who authorized its use to the data it was trained on—collected by some intern five years ago under a different mandate. It's a web. And webs, as anyone who's tried to trace a spider in one knows, are sticky places to find clarity. So, what needs to change?

First, we have to kill the myth of neutral code. There's no such thing. Every model is a mirror of the assumptions that shaped it. Every dataset is soaked in the histories of those who generated it, labeled it, stored it (Ilyas et al, 2022). If we want transparency, we have to start asking not just what the machine *spits out*, but what it *was fed*. Who trained it? Who labeled the data? What was excluded, trimmed, re-weighted, smoothed? There's a politics in preprocessing, a bias in every filter. And pretending otherwise only deepens the illusion of objectivity.

Second, we need new rituals of disclosure. The old compliance-driven checklists are no longer enough. Transparency in the AI era means exposing the scaffolding. Showing not just the decision, but the decision process (Sasikala & Sachan, 2024). We need governance documents that explain model architecture, versioning histories, variable weightings. Not for technical audits alone, but for ethical ones. For boards. For shareholders. For the public. Because if we don't know *how* something was decided, we can't decide whether it was fair.

Third—this one's harder—we need to slow down. The logic of AI is speed. Automate. Accelerate. Optimize. But transparency takes time (Al-doseri et al, 2023). It takes the awkward pause to ask, "Wait—what does this actually mean?" It takes human beings looking at outputs and asking whether they make sense, not just whether they're statistically significant. The culture of immediacy that defines much of modern corporate life is the enemy of meaningful oversight. And AI, with its promise of real-time insight, only deepens the temptation to skip the slow, painful process of interpretation.

I once sat across from a CTO who told me, with no irony, that their new governance system "no longer requires human review for standard exceptions." The phrase haunted me. *No longer requires human review.* As if human review is some archaic ritual—like wax seals or ledgers in ink. But what is governance without interpretation? What is accountability without the uncomfortable moment of saying, "This doesn't feel right"? And that's where the emotional texture of transparency comes in. Because at its heart, transparency isn't just about data—it's about trust (Boppana, 2023). It's about people believing that those in power are acting in good faith, under watchful eyes, and with integrity. AI doesn't feel shame. It doesn't feel pride. It doesn't earn or lose trust. Humans do. And if AI is going to play a central role in governance, then the humans around it need to step up—not just to manage it, but to interrogate it, to take responsibility for it, to translate its logic into language the public can actually hold accountable.

We need roles that don't yet exist. AI translators. Ethical adjudicators. Data storytellers. People who can take a model's output and say, "Here's what this actually means in human terms. Here's what we're basing our decision on. And here's who you can talk to if it turns out we got it wrong." Because mistakes will happen. And when they do, we need to be able to say, clearly and publicly, not just *what* failed, but *why*. But let's not pretend this will be easy. There are incentives at play here—powerful ones. Transparency often makes things messier, slower, more accountable (Fox, 2022). Not everyone wants that. In fact, many would rather keep the machine running quietly in the background, using its complexity as a shield. A kind of plausible deniability disguised as technological sophistication. "We didn't choose this path," they'll say. "The data led us here." But data doesn't lead. People lead. Data suggests. People choose. Let's not forget that. Reimagining transparency in this context requires courage (Jackson, 2024). The courage to ask what's behind the curtain. The courage to admit when the tools we've built are too complex for us to govern alone. The courage to say, "We need help understanding this." And maybe most of all, the courage to hold space for the human voice—to insist that governance isn't just a technical task, but a moral one. So, where do we go from here?

Maybe we start small. Maybe it begins with questions that pierce through the fog: "Who trained this model?" "What was the goal when it was built?" "Who stands to benefit from its adoption?" "And who might be silenced by its conclusions?" Or maybe it begins with stories. Stories of where things went wrong. Where algorithms mislabeled, miscalculated, misunderstood. Not to vilify the tools, but to humanize the process (Monett & Grigorescu, 2024). To remind ourselves that in every AI-driven decision, there's still a person responsible. Someone who clicked "approve." Someone who chose not to ask a question.

Transparency, in the age of artificial intelligence, will not arrive as a single light switch (Walmsley, 2021). It will be stitched together from many small practices—acts of disclosure, moments of humility, flashes of accountability. It will be hard. It will be slow. And it will require us to resist the myth that machines can govern without us. But if we get it right—if we build systems where transparency isn't just technical but ethical, not just informational but relational—then maybe we don't just build better oversight. Maybe we build better institutions. Ones where trust isn't engineered, but earned. Where decisions don't just come faster, but come clearer. And where, in the end, we remember that the point of governance was never perfection. It was integrity.

FROM DATA TO DECISIONS: AI-POWERED INSIGHTS FOR ETHICAL GOVERNANCE

It's easy to romanticize data. We imagine it as clean, objective, humming with neutral truth—numbers that speak louder than opinion, rows and columns that transcend bias. A kind of antiseptic clarity. And in boardrooms increasingly saturated with dashboards and predictive charts, this vision is seductive. Data, in this imagined form, doesn't argue. It presents. It confirms. It feels final. But real data? The kind that flows through corporate systems, drawn from countless human inputs, institutional behaviors, and the brittle complexity of global markets—it's messier. It carries histories, blind spots, hopes, and fears. It's not neutral. It's haunted. And yet, here we are—at a moment when artificial intelligence promises to transform this messy, unruly flood into something legible. Something actionable. The holy grail of governance: insight. A pattern pulled from chaos. A signal rising through noise. Boards no longer have to wait for quarterly reports or forensic audits. AI tools can flag financial irregularities in real time, model risk scenarios across dozens of variables, and even simulate the downstream effects of policy changes before they're enacted (Kothandapani, 2022). At least, that's the promise. But the leap from data to decision—especially in matters of governance—is not merely technical. It's moral. It's interpretive. It's filled with friction.

Think about it. A machine can tell you that an executive's travel expenses fall outside the three-year norm for similar roles in similar firms. Great. But it won't know that this particular executive spent weeks flying between disaster-affected regions, rebuilding supply chains under immense pressure. A human sees intention. Context. Motivation. An AI sees variance. The math is clean, but the story is gone.

This is where ethical governance enters—less as a fixed set of policies and more as a practice. A disposition. A way of pausing in the midst of apparent clarity and asking, *What might we be missing?* Because no matter how advanced the system, no matter how deep the data lake, decisions aren't just about what's probable—they're about what's right. And what's "right" rarely comes in neat vectors or histograms. It lives in contradictions. In gut checks. In the kind of moral tension that no machine has yet learned to carry. But still, the allure of AI remains strong. And understandably so. Companies today face an overwhelming volume of information—market fluctuations, geopolitical instability, regulatory shifts, ESG expectations, stakeholder sentiment. Trying to govern without some form of intelligent assistance feels almost reckless (Gigerenzer, 2022). The problem is not whether we *should* use AI. It's whether we can learn to use it wisely.

Let's start with how decisions are shaped. AI systems, particularly those trained on massive datasets, don't just offer answers—they narrow the field of vision (Zha et al, 2025). They suggest which factors *matter*, which indicators are "significant." And this matters, because what we choose to see influences what we value. When a model prioritizes efficiency over fairness, or ROI over social impact, it does so not because it's malicious, but because someone—somewhere—encoded that preference into the architecture (Kapoor & Chatterjee, 2023). Sometimes explicitly. More often, implicitly. That's the thing about AI: it absorbs our assumptions, then reflects them back at scale. And governance, which once involved weighing conflicting values around a long table, now often begins with a screen. A report. A recommendation. There's a kind of quiet tyranny in algorithmic suggestion—polite, logical, but profoundly directive (Turnbull, 2024). Boards are told, "This is the optimal path." And unless someone asks, "Optimal for whom?"—the deeper questions remain buried.

Take predictive hiring tools, for example. They're used to screen candidates, reduce bias, increase efficiency. Except many are trained on historical hiring data—data that reflects decades of exclusionary practices. The result? Models that perpetuate the very inequities they were meant to fix. But now, with the added veneer of data-backed legitimacy.

Ethical governance, then, isn't about rejecting AI. It's about keeping our humanity intact while using it. About interrogating not just the outputs but the inputs. Who chose the variables? Who defined success? Whose data was included, and whose was left out? I once sat with a governance officer who showed me a machine-learning dashboard they were piloting. It visualized "board member effectiveness" based on speaking time, vote consistency, and alignment with key performance indicators. Clean graphs. Sharply drawn comparisons. But what it didn't show—what it couldn't show—was the quiet power of dissent. The value of the one person who consistently voted against the group. Not out of ignorance, but out of deep conviction. The AI read them as an outlier. A drag on alignment. But that person had, in the past, flagged early warnings the rest had missed.

This is the risk: that AI will flatten our understanding of value into what it can measure. That it will turn governance into a game of metrics, and reduce moral courage to statistical noise (Marwala, 2024). And yet, it doesn't have to be that way. There's something profoundly hopeful in the possibility of ethical augmentation—where AI enhances rather than diminishes human judgment. Where it prompts new questions rather than silences debate. Where it brings to light patterns we might never have seen, and in doing so, humbles us.

The key lies in design. Not just of systems, but of culture. Do organizations foster curiosity about the models they use? Do they invite cross-disciplinary critique—bringing in ethicists, sociologists, historians to sit alongside data scientists and CFOs? Do they create spaces where data-driven insights are discussed not as mandates, but as provocations? And just as importantly—do they allow room for refusal? Can a board say, "This is what the model says, but we choose otherwise"? Can they privilege principle over probability? That's the test. Not whether AI can make decisions, but whether humans can remain accountable when it does. Because governance is not just about outcomes—it's about process. About who was consulted, how risks were framed, what voices were heard. AI can assist with this, yes. It can map stakeholder networks, analyze sentiment, forecast reaction. But it cannot decide whose pain matters (Marian, 2024). Or what counts as harm. That still belongs to us. And so we return to the messy, maddening beauty of human deliberation. Slower than code. More fragile. Less scalable. But filled with nuance, empathy, memory. We remember past failures. We hold on to stories. We change our minds. We forgive.

Maybe that's what ethical governance in the age of AI looks like—not perfect alignment, but a practiced resistance to certainty. A willingness to sit with conflicting signals. To say, "Yes, the data suggests this, but the people—our people—are telling us something else." And to listen. There's a power in that. A quiet defiance. An insistence that governance is still, at its core, a human art.

NAVIGATING THE RISKS: BIAS, BLACK BOXES, AND THE MYTH OF OBJECTIVITY

Let's begin with something no one really wants to admit: we are obsessed with certainty. We crave it like oxygen. In boardrooms and governance circles, the language of risk is always framed in percentages, forecasts, simulations—quantifications that soothe our primal fear of the unknown. It's no surprise, then, that artificial intelligence fits perfectly into this psychology. A machine that takes in oceans of data and spits out elegant probabilities? That feels safe. That feels controlled. It feels, above all, objective. But here's the twist: objectivity, in the world of AI, is a mirage.

We've built machines that carry our fingerprints in every line of code, yet we pretend they float above human fallibility (Dragar, 2025). We call them "impartial," "data-driven," "rational"—as if somehow freed from the biases and blind spots of their creators. But let's be honest. AI doesn't emerge from a vacuum. It's built by people, trained on human data, shaped by institutional priorities, and constrained by the limits of what we *choose* to measure. Which means it can lie. Not overtly, not with malice—but with the quiet, insidious logic of inherited assumptions. And this is where governance gets tricky. Because once something is encoded in an algorithm, it takes on a kind of sacredness. A model recommended it. The dashboard said so. It's all too easy to hide behind the numbers. To trust the system more than the people the system affects. But let's not get ahead of ourselves. Let's break this down—bias, black boxes, and the myth we keep selling ourselves about objectivity.

Start with bias. Not the cartoonish kind where a rogue developer sneaks prejudice into a program. No, the real bias in AI is quieter, deeper, structural. It's in the data. It's in the proxies. It's in the definitions. Say you're building a model to assess "leadership potential." Seems neutral enough. But what data are you using? Past promotions? Performance reviews? Peer evaluations? All of these are soaked in cultural norms, power dynamics, and deeply gendered expectations. You're not measuring leadership. You're measuring conformity to a very specific—and historically narrow—template of what leadership has looked like.

Now multiply that across hiring decisions, investment risk models, fraud detection algorithms. You begin to see the shape of the problem. AI doesn't invent new biases. It scales existing ones. It amplifies what already was, under the banner of progress (Schwartz et al, 2022). And when the harm is done? When someone is denied a loan, passed over for promotion, flagged as high-risk because a model said so—who's accountable? The developer? The compliance officer? The board? Or no one at all? This brings us to the second danger: the black box.

In theory, AI is supposed to be explainable. Transparent. Interpretable. But in practice—especially with complex models like deep learning—we often don't fully know how a system arrived at its decision. We see the input. We see the output. What happens in between? Layers of abstraction. Mathematical weights. Statistical transformations that resist easy explanation (Devore et al, 2021). Even to experts. And yet, these models are increasingly embedded in critical decision-making processes: who gets investigated for financial irregularities, which subsidiaries are flagged for underperformance, which markets get prioritized for expansion. Decisions with real stakes, affecting real lives. But when the system's logic is a mystery—even to its creators—governance becomes a theater of control rather than the substance of it.

There's a surreal moment that plays out in more and more governance meetings. Someone asks, "Why did the model recommend this course of action?" And the answer comes back: "We're not sure. That's just what it predicts." The air shifts. People fidget. No one wants to admit that they don't really understand the engine driving the car. But the car keeps moving. And in that silence, the third danger slips in: the myth of objectivity.

This one's harder to shake because it's baked into how we talk about data and technology. Numbers don't lie. Algorithms are neutral. Insights are empirical. But objectivity isn't just about precision. It's about perspective (Dasgupta & Sen, 2022). And all perspectives are situated—anchored in worldviews, shaped by priorities, defined by what they leave out. Take risk assessment models used in global supply chains. They scan for geopolitical volatility, labor violations, environmental hazards. Sounds responsible, right? But how are these risks weighted? Whose definitions are used? A labor strike in Bangladesh might register as a disruption, but is it also seen as a sign of suppressed rights? Or is it just noise to be routed around? The model doesn't care. It reflects the priorities of those who built it. And that's the heart of the issue: AI doesn't decide what matters. We do. But once a model becomes institutionalized—once it gets blessed by process and protocol—it becomes harder to question. It calcifies. It becomes the default logic. And that logic, left unchecked, begins to shape not just decisions, but the very definitions of fairness, risk, and success. I once heard an executive say, "The algorithm is just more consistent than our people." Maybe. But consistency isn't the same as justice. A machine that replicates bias perfectly, predictably, and at scale is still wrong—just faster (Hullman et al, 2022). So, what do we do with all of this?

- First, we name it. We stop pretending that AI is apolitical or neutral. We acknowledge that every model is a mirror—of the data it was trained on, the values of its designers, the goals of its deployment. We resist the urge to treat machine outputs as gospel.
- Second, we demand explainability—not just for regulators or technical experts, but for the people affected by decisions. If a model flags an executive for compliance review, they should have the right to know why. Not a vague probability. Not a reference to "anomalous patterns." A real explanation, in human language. If we can't provide that, we shouldn't be using the model.
- Third, we diversify the design table. AI development cannot be the exclusive domain of engineers and data scientists. Governance requires interdisciplinary wisdom—ethics, law, sociology, lived experience. We need diverse minds not just reviewing outputs, but shaping inputs.

- Finally, we rebuild our tolerance for ambiguity. The rush to automate everything is, in part, a reaction to uncertainty. But governance isn't supposed to be easy. It's supposed to wrestle with complexity. To hold space for disagreement. To sit in the discomfort of moral trade-offs. Machines can't do that for us. At best, they can inform the conversation. At worst, they replace it.

So maybe the real challenge isn't AI at all. Maybe it's us—our hunger for certainty, our reluctance to slow down, our tendency to hide behind systems rather than take responsibility. Bias will always exist. Black boxes will persist, especially in the frontier models pushing the boundaries of what's possible. And the myth of objectivity? It's too convenient to vanish entirely. But governance—if it's to mean anything—must remain grounded in the messy, flawed, human work of reflection. We can build models that learn. But we must also become leaders who *unlearn*. Who challenge the systems we deploy. Who admit when they're broken. Who listen when the data doesn't tell the whole story. In that willingness to question—persistently, vulnerably, and with humility—we begin to reclaim what AI, at its worst, threatens to erase: the moral imagination at the heart of responsible governance.

TOWARD A HUMAN-AI SYNERGY: DESIGNING OVERSIGHT FRAMEWORKS FOR THE FUTURE

We don't get to rewind the clock. The age of intelligent systems is already here—quietly humming in the background of decisions that shape lives, markets, reputations. Artificial intelligence has moved from being a tool to becoming a kind of silent partner in governance (Taeihagh, 2021). It filters what we see, it anticipates what might go wrong, it recommends what we should do next. But as its role grows, so does the question we can't afford to ignore: how do we shape a future where humans and AI collaborate—not in a race for control, but in a dialogue built on mutual augmentation?

Let's begin with a truth that doesn't always make it into governance manuals: human oversight is flawed. Boards get tired. Committees miss things. Cognitive biases seep into even the most carefully prepared decisions (Berthet, 2022). We are slow, emotional, often contradictory. And yet, paradoxically, that's exactly why we matter. Because governance isn't just about catching errors or maximizing efficiency—it's about wrestling with competing values, about holding responsibility in uncertain terrain. It's about knowing when to ask more questions, and when to leave a number alone and go visit the people behind it.

Machines, for all their brilliance, can't do that. Not really. They can learn patterns, simulate options, draw inferences at mind-numbing speed—but they don't care. They don't feel the gravity of a hard choice. They don't wake up at night wondering if a decision hurt someone. What they offer is power, not wisdom. And if governance is to evolve without losing its soul, we have to design systems that recognize this difference—not to diminish AI's role, but to place it inside a framework that protects, respects, and elevates the human judgment it's meant to assist. But how do we do that—really?

Not just on paper, not in vague strategy decks or innovation whitepapers, but in the thick, messy reality of boardrooms under pressure. How do we design oversight frameworks that invite AI into the process without letting it take over? That benefit from its intelligence without ceding our responsibility? The first step might be deceptively simple: we stop pretending the machine is magic.

There's a performative awe that often surrounds AI in corporate environments (Bareis & Katzenbach, 2022). People speak of models as if they're crystal balls. Outputs become gospel. But this illusion is dangerous. It leads to blind delegation, to "AI said so" rationalizations. So the first design principle must be transparency—not just in how the system works, but in how it was built, what data it's drawing on, and what assumptions lie beneath its logic. Every recommendation from an AI system should come with a trail—explainable, accountable, human-readable (Waykar, 2023). A model's strength isn't just in what it gets right, but in how clearly we can understand *why*. But transparency alone isn't enough. We need friction—yes, friction. Points in the process where humans are required to pause, to interrogate the system's logic. The future of governance isn't seamless automation. It's mindful collaboration. An effective oversight framework should deliberately introduce checkpoints: moments where board members or compliance officers are *required* to ask, "Does this make sense in our context? Does this align with our values? Who might be harmed if we follow this blindly?"

Some of this will be cultural. The strongest frameworks won't come from engineering alone—they'll be born from values. Organizations must cultivate a culture where questioning the machine is not only permitted, but expected (Rajagopal et al, 2022). Where a junior analyst can say, "This prediction seems off," and be taken seriously. Where metrics don't silence human experience but sit alongside it, waiting to be translated into stories.

Stories—that's another overlooked component in all this. Oversight has always been part data, part narrative. And as AI grows in sophistication, the risk is that we drown in quantification. So maybe it's time to double down on storytelling—not as soft resistance, but as necessary ballast. Every decision augmented by AI should be paired with a narrative: What are we doing? Why are we doing it? Who benefits? Who risks being overlooked? And speaking of being overlooked, let's talk about inclusivity. AI systems reflect the biases of their creators unless actively countered (Zajko, 2021). That means our oversight frameworks must include diverse voices—not just in the review process, but upstream, in the design of the models themselves. Too often, corporate governance is dominated by a narrow demographic. If the data is already limited, and the perspectives at the table are homogenous, what chance do we have at building systems that serve everyone?

The answer is participatory governance. Not in the performative sense—an annual survey or a token advisory group—but in the architecture. Build in mechanisms for affected stakeholders to review, challenge, and contribute to how AI systems are used. Make room for friction from below. That's not inefficiency. That's integrity. And while we're at it, let's redefine what success looks like. The current obsession with optimization—highest return, lowest risk, fastest delivery—is inadequate for the complexity we now face. A human-AI governance framework must balance efficiency with justice, profit with principle (de Fine Licht, 2025). That means creating metrics for alignment with ethical commitments, for long-term societal impact, for trust. If we only track what's easy to measure, we'll miss what's essential.

Of course, this is all easier said than done. And I don't pretend there's a single blueprint. But maybe that's the point: oversight should be adaptive, responsive, alive. What we need is less a fixed model and more a posture—a way of thinking that stays open, that evolves as the tools do. Governance shouldn't be rigid. It should be recursive.

So, imagine this: an AI flags a financial irregularity in a regional office. The model highlights it as a high-risk anomaly based on historical fraud indicators (Munteanu et al, 2024). Under a traditional system, the alert would trigger an investigation, a report, maybe even disciplinary action. But under a human-AI synergy model, that alert doesn't just move down the pipeline—it gets paused. Reviewed. A multidisciplinary team steps in: finance, ethics, regional leadership. They don't just look at the data—they call someone on the ground. They ask questions. They contextualize.

It turns out the anomaly is due to a delayed contract renegotiation with a local supplier following a natural disaster. No fraud. Just disruption. The system wasn't wrong. But it wasn't right, either. And the decision not to act? That's where governance lives. This kind of nuance—this dance between machine insight and human wisdom—is what the future demands. It's slower. It's harder. But it's more honest. And it keeps us, somehow, anchored. Because the real danger isn't that AI will replace us. It's that we'll stop showing up. That we'll defer so completely that we forget how to reason, how to listen, how to hold uncertainty. The frameworks we build now must resist that drift. They must call us back into the room—not as passive overseers of intelligent systems, but as active participants in a shared moral experiment. So maybe the question isn't just how we design AI into oversight. Maybe it's how we design ourselves back into it—more thoughtfully, more humbly, more human. That's the future I want to bet on. Not one where machines govern us, but one where they *remind* us—constantly, imperfectly—how to govern better.

CONCLUSION

As we near the end of this exploration, it becomes clear that the question isn't whether AI will become embedded in corporate governance—it already has. The real question is how we choose to shape this integration, and whether we have the moral imagination to govern in ways that reflect more than just speed or scalability. In a time when algorithms are entrusted with decisions once reserved for seasoned professionals, when risk models are driven by data pipelines rather than deliberative boardroom dialogue, we are being called—not just as technologists or executives, but as stewards of shared institutions—to reimagine what oversight truly means.

AI, in all its complexity, has a double edge. On one hand, it offers a kind of predictive foresight that can illuminate blind spots, expose irregularities, and enhance transparency in ways traditional models cannot. Financial statements can now be cross-referenced in milliseconds against years of behavioral trends. Board performance can be modeled. Risk scenarios can be simulated. And yet, the very same systems can become black boxes, their internal logic inscrutable even to those who designed them. Errors can be masked as insights. Biases can be baked into code. And once decisions are delegated to machines, the temptation to abdicate responsibility—rather than delegate it—looms large.

There is a kind of seduction in the perceived objectivity of AI. Numbers feel neutral. Models feel fair. But fairness cannot be assumed. It must be cultivated. And governance, at its essence, is not a mathematical function—it is a moral endeavor. No algorithm can yet fully comprehend the weight of reputational harm, the nuance of a whistleblower's testimony, or the moral calculus of laying off workers to preserve shareholder value. These are deeply human judgments, often made in the messy gray zones that lie far beyond the reach of clean data and structured inputs.

So where does that leave us? Perhaps in a state of necessary tension—a kind of dynamic oversight that refuses to fall blindly into either techno-solutionism or Luddite nostalgia. A governance model that recognizes both the capabilities and the limitations of artificial intelligence. One that insists on transparency not just in financial disclosures, but in the algorithms that inform them. One that welcomes machine learning as a tool, not a replacement, and that reaffirms the role of human conscience in a world of intelligent code.

To govern well in the AI age is not simply to use better tools—it is to ask better questions. Questions about values. About justice. About who benefits, and who gets left behind. It requires boards that are not only digitally literate but ethically awake. It requires regulators willing to move at the speed of innovation without losing sight of foundational principles. And it requires a culture that understands oversight not as a bureaucratic hurdle, but as a living, breathing commitment to integrity.

Ultimately, strengthening oversight through AI is not about making corporate governance more robotic—it is about making it more human. Not in the sense of fallibility, but in the sense of humility. The humility to admit what we don't yet understand. The humility to include diverse perspectives in our data and our deliberations. The humility to question the assumptions behind the code.

This chapter ends with no grand blueprint, but rather an invitation: to co-create systems where intelligence—both human and artificial—is guided by a deeper wisdom. In that co-creation lies our greatest challenge, and perhaps our most necessary hope.

REFERENCES

Aldoseri, A., Al-Khalifa, K., & Hamouda, A. (2023). A roadmap for integrating automation with process optimization for AI-powered digital transformation. *Preprints*. DOI: 10.20944/preprints202310

Bareis, J., & Katzenbach, C. (2022). Talking AI into being: The narratives and imaginaries of national AI strategies and their performative politics. *Science, Technology & Human Values*, *47*(5), 855–881. DOI: 10.1177/01622439211030007

Berthet, V. (2022). The impact of cognitive biases on professionals' decision-making: A review of four occupational areas. *Frontiers in Psychology*, *12*, 802439. DOI: 10.3389/fpsyg.2021.802439 PMID: 35058862

Bhatt, U., Antorán, J., Zhang, Y., Liao, Q. V., Sattigeri, P., Fogliato, R., . . . Xiang, A. (2021, July). Uncertainty as a form of transparency: Measuring, communicating, and using uncertainty. In Proceedings of the 2021 AAAI/ ACM Conference on AI, Ethics, and Society (pp. 401-413).

Bonini, T., & Treré, E. (2024). *Algorithms of resistance: The everyday fight against platform power*. Mit Press. DOI: 10.7551/mitpress/14329.001.0001

Boppana, V. R. (2023). Data Ethics in CRM: Privacy and Transparency Issues. Available at *SSRN* 5005001.

Bremmer, I., & Suleyman, M. (2023). The AI power paradox: Can states learn to govern artificial intelligence-before it's too late? *Foreign Affairs*, *102*, 26.

Carabantes, M. (2023). Why artificial intelligence is not transparent: a critical analysis of its three opacity layers. In *Handbook of Critical Studies of Artificial Intelligence* (pp. 424–434). Edward Elgar Publishing. DOI: 10.4337/9781803928562.00045

Cihon, P., Schuett, J., & Baum, S. D. (2021). Corporate governance of artificial intelligence in the public interest. *Information (Basel)*, *12*(7), 275. DOI: 10.3390/info12070275

Dasgupta, D., & Sen, S. (2022). An empirical study of algorithmic bias. In *Handbook on computer learning and intelligence* (Vol. 2, pp. 895–922). Deep Learning, Intelligent Control and Evolutionary Computation.

Davies, D. (2025). *The Unaccountability Machine: Why Big Systems Make Terrible Decisions—and How the World Lost Its Mind.* University of Chicago Press.

de Fine Licht, K. (2025). Resolving value conflicts in public AI governance: A procedural justice framework. *Government Information Quarterly*, *42*(2), 102033. DOI: 10.1016/j.giq.2025.102033

Devore, J. L., Berk, K. N., & Carlton, M. A. (2021). *Modern mathematical statistics with applications.* Springer Nature. DOI: 10.1007/978-3-030-55156-8

Dragar, F. (2025). Learnable Fingerprints for Large Language Models (Master's thesis).

Fox, J. (2022). *Accountability keywords.* Accountability Research Center.

Gaudio, G. (2021). Algorithmic bosses can't lie! How to foster transparency and limit abuses of the new algorithmic managers. *Comp. Lab. L. & Pol'y J.*, *42*, 707.

Gigerenzer, G. (2022). *How to stay smart in a smart world: Why human intelligence still beats algorithms.* MIT Press.

Hullman, J., Kapoor, S., Nanayakkara, P., Gelman, A., & Narayanan, A. (2022, July). The worst of both worlds: A comparative analysis of errors in learning from data in psychology and machine learning. In Proceedings of the 2022 AAAI/ACM Conference on AI, Ethics, and Society (pp. 335-348). DOI: 10.1145/3514094.3534196

Ilyas, A., Park, S. M., Engstrom, L., Leclerc, G., & Madry, A. (2022). Datamodels: Predicting predictions from training data. arXiv preprint arXiv:2202.00622.

Jackson, G. (2024). *Courage, Clarity, and Confidence: Redefine Success and the Way You Work.* John Wiley & Sons.

Jacobs, A. M., Büthe, T., Arjona, A., Arriola, L. R., Bellin, E., Bennett, A., Björkman, L., Bleich, E., Elkins, Z., Fairfield, T., Gaikwad, N., Greitens, S. C., Hawkesworth, M., Herrera, V., Herrera, Y. M., Johnson, K. S., Karakoç, E., Koivu, K., Kreuzer, M., & Yashar, D. J. (2021). The qualitative transparency deliberations: Insights and implications. *Perspectives on Politics*, *19*(1), 171–208. DOI: 10.1017/S1537592720001164

Kapoor, A., & Chatterjee, S. (2023). *Platform and Model Design for Responsible AI: Design and build resilient, private, fair, and transparent machine learning models*. Packt Publishing Ltd.

Kothandapani, H. P. (2022). Advanced Artificial Intelligence models for Real-Time monitoring and prediction of macroprudential risks in the housing finance sector: addressing interest rate shocks and housing price volatility to support proactive Decision-Making by federal agencies. Journal of Artificial Intelligence Research. https://thesciencebrigade. com/JAIR/article/view/507

Lokanan, M. E., & Maddhesia, V. (2025). Supply chain fraud prediction with machine learning and artificial intelligence. *International Journal of Production Research*, *63*(1), 286–313. DOI: 10.1080/00207543.2024.2361434

Marian, I. C. (2024). Evaluating the impact of artificial intelligence on business through sentiment analysis. Young Economists Journal/Revista Tinerilor Economisti, 21(43).

Marwala, T. (2024). *The Balancing Problem in the Governance of Artificial Intelligence*. Springer. DOI: 10.1007/978-981-97-9251-1

Monett, D., & Grigorescu, B. (2024, October). Deconstructing the AI myth: Fallacies and harms of algorithmification. In European Conference on e-Learning (Vol. 23, pp. 242-248). Academic Conferences International Limited.

Munteanu, V., Zuca, M. R., Horaicu, A., Florea, L. A., Poenaru, C. E., & Anghel, G. (2024). Auditing the risk of financial fraud using the red flags technique. *Applied Sciences (Basel, Switzerland)*, *14*(2), 757. DOI: 10.3390/app14020757

Rajagopal, N. K., Qureshi, N. I., Durga, S., Ramirez Asis, E. H., Huerta Soto, R. M., Gupta, S. K., & Deepak, S. (2022). Future of business culture: An artificial intelligence-driven digital framework for organization decision-making process. *Complexity*, *2022*(1), 7796507. DOI: 10.1155/2022/7796507

Sama, L. M., Stefanidis, A., & Casselman, R. M. (2022). Rethinking corporate governance in the digital economy: The role of stewardship. *Business Horizons*, *65*(5), 535–546. DOI: 10.1016/j.bushor.2021.08.001

Sasikala, B., & Sachan, S. (2024). Decoding decision-making: embracing explainable AI for trust and transparency. Exploring the frontiers of artificial intelligence and machine learning technologies, 42.

Schwartz, R., Schwartz, R., Vassilev, A., Greene, K., Perine, L., Burt, A., & Hall, P. (2022). Towards a standard for identifying and managing bias in artificial intelligence (Vol. 3, p. 00). Gaithersburg, MD: US Department of Commerce, National Institute of Standards and Technology.

Taeihagh, A. (2021). Governance of artificial intelligence. *Policy and Society*, *40*(2), 137–157. DOI: 10.1080/14494035.2021.1928377

Torrance, A. W., & Tomlinson, B. (2023). Governance of the AI, by the AI, and for the AI. *Mississippi Law Journal*, *93*, 107.

Turnbull, A. (2024). Law, Language, And Authority: The Algorithmic Turn.

Vallor, S. (2024). *The AI mirror: How to reclaim our humanity in an age of machine thinking*. Oxford University Press. DOI: 10.1093/oso/9780197759066.001.0001

Walmsley, J. (2021). Artificial intelligence and the value of transparency. *AI & Society*, *36*(2), 585–595. DOI: 10.1007/s00146-020-01066-z

Waykar, Y. A. (2023). Human-AI Collaboration in Explainable Recommender Systems: An Exploration of User-Centric Explanations and Evaluation Frameworks. *International Journal of Scientific Research in Engineering and Management*, *7*(07), 2582–3930. DOI: 10.55041/IJSREM24775

Zajko, M. (2021). Conservative AI and social inequality: Conceptualizing alternatives to bias through social theory. *AI & Society*, *36*(3), 1047–1056. DOI: 10.1007/s00146-021-01153-9

Zaman, B. U. (2024, April). The weighty responsibility of creating ai navigating control and ethics.

Zha, D., Bhat, Z. P., Lai, K. H., Yang, F., Jiang, Z., Zhong, S., & Hu, X. (2025). Data-centric artificial intelligence: A survey. *ACM Computing Surveys*, *57*(5), 1–42. DOI: 10.1145/3711118

Chapter 9
Relativity of Value: Time, Space, and Context in AI-Supported Financial Decisions

Mădălina Mihăilescu
https://orcid.org/0009-0003-0736-8588
Hyperion University of Bucharest, Romania

ABSTRACT

This chapter investigates the relativity of value in financial decision-making, emphasizing the roles of time, space, and contextual framing in shaping outcomes. While classical finance often treats value as an intrinsic and static property, contemporary markets reveal its dynamic and situational character. Advances in artificial intelligence allow for real-time integration of temporal patterns, spatial heterogeneity, and contextual signals, offering a more adaptive framework for evaluating assets and risks. The chapter also addresses the epistemological challenges of embedding contextual awareness into algorithmic decision-making, including issues of bias, interpretability, and robustness. By reframing value through the lens of relativity, the authors argue for a paradigm that bridges financial theory with AI-supported practice, enabling more nuanced, flexible, and context-sensitive approaches to investment and risk management.

DOI: 10.4018/979-8-3373-3626-8.ch009

INTRODUCTION

The concept of value lies at the heart of finance, economics, and decision-making. From classical theories of intrinsic worth to modern behavioral accounts of utility, scholars and practitioners have long debated what constitutes value and how it can be determined. Yet value is not a fixed property of assets, contracts, or decisions. It is relational, contingent, and dynamic, shaped by the temporal horizon of decision-makers, the spatial configuration of markets, and the contextual framing of choices. This relativity of value has become increasingly visible in an era of artificial intelligence (AI), where decisions are supported by algorithms capable of processing vast datasets, simulating multiple scenarios, and adapting to evolving contexts in real time. The integration of AI into financial decision-making compels us to rethink value not as a static measure but as an emergent property of time, space, and context.

Historically, financial theory sought to anchor value in stable and universal metrics. Classical economists such as Adam Smith and David Ricardo distinguished between use value and exchange value, while later theorists like Marx emphasized labor as the foundation of value (Fine, 2018). The neoclassical revolution replaced these perspectives with a marginalist approach, defining value in terms of individual preferences and market equilibria. In finance, this translated into valuation models such as discounted cash flows, which treat future earnings as calculable in present terms, and capital asset pricing models, which link value to risk and return (Sharpe, 1964). These models assume rational actors, efficient markets, and predictable discounting of future outcomes. Yet crises, bubbles, and persistent anomalies challenge the idea that value can be objectively and universally determined (Shiller, 2015). Instead, value is constantly re-negotiated, contingent on shifting expectations, institutional settings, and socio-cultural contexts.

The relativity of value becomes evident when considering the temporal dimension of financial decisions. Time is not neutral in finance. Short-term traders, long-term investors, and regulators each perceive value differently depending on their temporal horizon. High-frequency trading algorithms may extract value from millisecond price discrepancies, while pension funds evaluate assets in terms of decades. The same financial instrument thus has multiple valuations depending on the timeframe under consideration. Behavioral finance further shows that human decision-makers discount the future in non-linear and inconsistent ways, often privileging immediate gains over long-term benefits (Thaler, 2016). AI complicates this picture by enabling dynamic time-sensitive valuations. Through predictive analytics, reinforcement learning, and scenario simulations, AI systems can recalibrate value in real time as new information arrives, extending or contracting temporal horizons in ways that outpace human cognition (Agrawal et al., 2018). The temporality of value is therefore not merely subjective but algorithmically mediated.

Spatiality also shapes the relativity of value. Financial globalization has created an interconnected system where assets are traded across jurisdictions, currencies, and regulatory regimes. The same asset can be valued differently depending on spatial location, not only because of exchange rates but also because of legal, institutional, and cultural environments. A sovereign bond may carry distinct value profiles in domestic markets compared to international ones, while commodities may be priced differently depending on logistical infrastructures and geopolitical risks (Strange, 2015). AI further accentuates spatial relativity by integrating geospatial data, regional market dynamics, and localized consumer behavior into valuation models. Algorithmic systems can detect spatial asymmetries invisible to traditional models, such as the influence of regional weather patterns on energy markets or the spatial clustering of default risks in mortgage portfolios. By embedding spatial data into financial decisions, AI systems redefine value as a geographically contingent construct.

Context represents a third and equally vital dimension of value relativity. Contextual framing includes cultural narratives, institutional norms, regulatory frameworks, and even technological infrastructures that shape how financial actors perceive and assign value. The same stock price movement may be interpreted as positive momentum in one context and as speculative overheating in another. Context also determines which data are considered relevant, which risks are prioritized, and which scenarios are deemed plausible. In AI-supported decision-making, context is operationalized through training data, feature selection, and interpretive frameworks embedded in algorithms (Pasquale, 2015). Yet AI systems face the challenge of contextual incompleteness: they may capture correlations without understanding the socio-political significance of events. For example, an AI system might detect correlations between social media sentiment and stock prices without recognizing the contextual importance of regulatory announcements or political instability. Future research must therefore grapple with how to integrate qualitative context into quantitative AI models, ensuring that decisions are not only efficient but also socially and ethically grounded.

AI intensifies the relativity of value because it accelerates, amplifies, and diversifies the ways in which time, space, and context interact in financial decision-making. Algorithms process information at speeds unimaginable for human agents, collapsing temporal horizons and making markets more reactive. They integrate geospatial and contextual datasets, uncovering hidden patterns but also introducing new biases depending on training inputs. They enable personalized valuation models tailored to specific investor profiles, thereby fragmenting the very notion of universal value. At the same time, AI introduces new forms of opacity, making it difficult for human actors to understand why a system assigns value in one way rather than another (Burrell, 2016). This opacity raises questions about accountability, fairness, and legitimacy in financial decisions.

The relativity of value has normative implications. If value is contingent and relational, financial regulation must acknowledge and manage this relativity rather than suppress it. Regulatory frameworks often assume stable benchmarks of value, whether in accounting standards, capital adequacy requirements, or fair value measurements. Yet crises show that benchmarks can become unstable when contexts shift dramatically. During the 2008 crisis, mortgage-backed securities were initially valued as safe investments, only to be rapidly reclassified as toxic assets once systemic fragility became evident (Gorton, 2010). Similarly, the COVID-19 pandemic altered valuations across sectors overnight, demonstrating how value can collapse or surge depending on contextual shocks. Regulators must therefore design adaptive frameworks that incorporate the temporal, spatial, and contextual variability of value. Entropy-based measures, discussed in the preceding chapter, may help by quantifying disorder and unpredictability in valuation processes.

The relativity of value also resonates with broader philosophical debates about knowledge and uncertainty. If value is not intrinsic but relational, then financial decisions are not merely technical computations but acts of interpretation situated within specific temporal and spatial contexts. AI complicates this epistemology by mediating interpretation through algorithms. This raises critical questions: whose context is embedded in the data, whose temporality shapes the forecasts, and whose space defines the boundaries of analysis? Research in science and technology studies emphasizes that AI systems are not neutral but reflect the assumptions, biases, and interests of their designers (Zuboff, 2019). In finance, this means that valuations produced by AI are always already contextualized by political, cultural, and institutional factors. Acknowledging the relativity of value is therefore not only an analytical necessity but also a democratic imperative.

This chapter seeks to explore these issues in depth. It argues that the relativity of value—across time, space, and context—is not a weakness but a defining feature of financial decision-making in the age of AI. Rather than striving for universal and objective measures of value, financial theory and practice should embrace relativity as a resource for resilience and adaptability. AI can support this shift by offering tools to model multiple scenarios, integrate diverse datasets, and reveal hidden dependencies. At the same time, reliance on AI raises risks of opacity, bias, and over-automation that must be critically examined. The goal is not to reject AI but to situate it within a broader framework that acknowledges the contingent and relational nature of value.

By developing this argument, the chapter contributes to three ongoing debates. First, it deepens the theoretical understanding of value in finance by highlighting its temporal, spatial, and contextual dimensions. Second, it assesses the role of AI in reshaping valuation practices, showing how algorithms, both enable and constrain the recognition of relativity. Third, it reflects on the normative implications of this shift, considering how regulation, governance, and ethics can adapt to a world where value is not fixed but fluid. The subsequent sections will elaborate on each of these contributions, drawing on case studies, comparative analyses, and interdisciplinary perspectives to map the contours of value in AI-supported financial decision-making.

THE TEMPORAL RELATIVITY OF VALUE: HORIZONS, DISCOUNTING, AND ALGORITHMIC TIME

The relationship between value and time has always been central to finance. From the earliest practices of lending and interest to the development of modern capital markets, the act of valuing has implied translating future outcomes into present terms. The logic of discounting, the calculation of expected returns, and the assessment of investment horizons all presuppose that value is inseparable from temporality. Yet time in finance is not neutral. The horizons of decision-makers differ radically depending on their goals, constraints, and perspectives. What appears valuable in the short term may seem negligible over decades, and what is considered safe today may appear risky in the long run. In the age of artificial intelligence (AI), this temporal relativity is magnified. Algorithms capable of processing vast datasets in real time, recalibrating valuations instantaneously, and simulating future scenarios challenge our conventional understanding of financial time.

Classical financial theory treated time as a linear and objective variable. Models such as the discounted cash flow method translate future earnings into present value by applying a discount rate that reflects opportunity cost and risk (Brealey et al., 2019). Similarly, the capital asset pricing model assumes that investors price assets based on their expected returns over a defined horizon relative to systematic risk (Sharpe, 1964). These models imply that value is stable across time once it has been properly discounted. Yet behavioral research has consistently shown that individuals do not discount the future linearly or consistently. Instead, they exhibit present bias, hyperbolic discounting, and shifting preferences depending on contextual cues (Laibson, 1997; Thaler, 2016). This makes value perception profoundly relative, varying with temporal framing. A gain that seems attractive over months may lose appeal when viewed over years, and vice versa.

AI alters this dynamic in two significant ways. First, it accelerates financial temporality. High-frequency trading algorithms extract value from millisecond discrepancies in prices, collapsing horizons into nearly instantaneous windows (Johnson et al., 2013). For these systems, value exists not in long-term fundamentals but in fleeting patterns of order flow and market microstructure. The temporality of value is redefined as ultra-short-term and machine-mediated. Second, AI expands horizons by enabling simulations of long-term scenarios that humans cannot easily imagine. Through reinforcement learning and predictive analytics, algorithms can explore thousands of possible futures, recalculating valuations as conditions evolve (Agrawal et al., 2018). This creates a paradoxical situation in which AI both compresses time to microseconds and stretches it to decades, redefining the temporal spectrum of financial value.

The relativity of value across horizons becomes evident when considering different financial actors. Day traders may interpret a stock's minute-by-minute volatility as central to its value, while pension funds focus on its decades-long dividend potential. Credit rating agencies evaluate corporate debt across years, while central banks model systemic stability over generations. The same asset can thus hold multiple simultaneous values, depending on the temporal horizon applied. AI exacerbates this plurality by enabling actors to toggle between horizons with unprecedented flexibility. An algorithm can identify short-term arbitrage opportunities while simultaneously modeling long-term climate transition risks for the same portfolio. This multiplicity of temporal frames complicates the very notion of a single, objective value.

Financial crises reveal the consequences of ignoring temporal relativity. The global financial crisis of 2008 exemplified the tension between short-term profitability and long-term sustainability. Mortgage-backed securities were highly valued in the short term due to their yield and apparent diversification, but their long-term risks were systematically underestimated. When defaults began to rise, the long horizon revealed vulnerabilities invisible to short-term valuation models (Gorton, 2010). AI systems today face similar dilemmas: should they privilege short-term returns optimized through machine learning, or account for long-term systemic risks such as climate change, cyber threats, and demographic shifts? How algorithms resolve this tension will determine whether they reinforce short-termism or foster sustainable value creation.

Discounting plays a crucial role in the temporal relativity of value. The choice of discount rate is not merely technical but profoundly normative, reflecting assumptions about opportunity costs, risk preferences, and intergenerational justice. For instance, debates about climate economics hinge on the appropriate discount rate to apply to future damages. A high discount rate minimizes the present value of future harms, justifying inaction, while a low discount rate elevates long-term risks, demanding immediate investment (Stern, 2007). AI systems can process climate data at scale, but the discount rate remains a human choice reflecting ethical judgments. The relativity of value across time is thus not only a matter of perception but also of politics.

Algorithmic time introduces new complexities. Unlike human agents, who experience time linearly, AI systems operate through asynchronous and recursive temporalities. Machine learning models are trained on historical data but update continuously as new information arrives. Reinforcement learning agents simulate millions of futures in compressed computational time. This creates a disjunction between machine temporality and human temporality. For human investors, waiting years for returns involves psychological and institutional constraints. For algorithms, simulating decades takes seconds. The relativity of value is therefore mediated not only by human horizons but also by algorithmic reconfigurations of time. Understanding financial temporality in the age of AI requires acknowledging this divergence between lived and computational time.

Another important dimension of temporal relativity concerns the speed of information diffusion. In traditional markets, information spread gradually, allowing actors to adjust valuations incrementally. Today, AI-driven trading systems react to news within milliseconds, often before human actors are even aware of the event. This acceleration means that value shifts faster than human comprehension, challenging regulators tasked with ensuring market stability. The "flash crash" of May 2010, when U.S. stock markets plunged and recovered within minutes, exemplifies how algorithmic time can generate volatility disconnected from fundamentals (Kirilenko et al., 2017). Entropy-based measures of market diversity, discussed in the previous chapter, may help monitor such phenomena by quantifying the loss of informational richness during periods of accelerated trading.

Temporal relativity also manifests in intergenerational finance. Sovereign debt, pension systems, and climate bonds extend value calculations across decades or even centuries. Here, the relativity of value is intertwined with ethical questions about obligations to future generations. AI has potential to enhance intergenerational finance by simulating demographic shifts, productivity trends, and environmental trajectories. Yet the question remains: whose horizon defines value? Future generations cannot directly input preferences into today's AI models. Their interests are mediated by current assumptions and data. This underscores the moral stakes of temporal relativity: value is always constructed from the standpoint of a temporal subject, whether individual, institutional, or algorithmic.

One might argue that AI reduces the subjectivity of temporal value by providing more accurate forecasts. Yet forecasts remain uncertain, and uncertainty grows with time. The further into the future one looks, the higher the entropy of possible outcomes. AI can expand the range of scenarios considered, but it cannot eliminate uncertainty. Indeed, by producing a multiplicity of simulated futures, AI may heighten awareness of uncertainty. In this sense, algorithmic time amplifies rather than resolves temporal relativity. It exposes decision-makers to the full range of possible futures, each with its own valuation, forcing them to confront the impossibility of a single, stable measure of value.

The relativity of value in time has profound implications for governance and regulation. Financial regulators must decide whether to emphasize short-term stability or long-term resilience. For instance, macroprudential policies may require banks to hold capital buffers to mitigate long-term systemic risks, even if this reduces short-term profitability. AI can support such policies by identifying long-horizon vulnerabilities, but regulators must still balance competing temporal perspectives. Similarly, accounting standards that require fair value measurement of assets may inadvertently encourage short-termism by focusing on current market prices rather than long-term fundamentals (Laux & Leuz, 2009). Rethinking these standards through the lens of temporal relativity could foster more sustainable financial practices.

Ultimately, the temporal relativity of value challenges the assumption that time is an objective and exogenous variable in finance. Instead, time is socially constructed, institutionally mediated, and technologically reconfigured. Human actors, institutional rules, and algorithmic systems all impose different temporalities on value. Recognizing this multiplicity does not paralyze decision-making but enriches it. It invites financial theory and practice to embrace uncertainty, diversity, and adaptability rather than seeking illusory certainty. AI can play a constructive role in this process if it is designed to acknowledge rather than suppress temporal relativity.

THE SPATIAL RELATIVITY OF VALUE: MARKETS, JURISDICTIONS, AND GEOGRAPHIES OF FINANCE

The determination of value in finance is not merely a matter of temporal horizons or abstract mathematical models; it is also profoundly shaped by space. Geography, jurisdiction, and institutional context matter in defining what assets are worth, how risks are perceived, and which opportunities are pursued. Financial markets are often presented as global and integrated, yet their functioning is always mediated by spatial configurations. The same asset can be valued differently depending on where it is traded, which legal framework governs it, and what local narratives shape investor expectations. The spatial relativity of value thus draws attention to the fact that financial decision-making cannot be abstracted from the material and institutional geographies in which it is embedded. With the growing role of artificial intelligence (AI) in financial analysis, these spatial dynamics are being both illuminated and transformed. AI systems integrate diverse datasets across geographies, uncovering patterns invisible to human actors, while also reconfiguring the spaces of value through digital platforms, cross-border flows of information, and algorithmic infrastructures.

Historically, finance has always been spatially uneven. The rise of financial centers such as Amsterdam in the seventeenth century, London in the nineteenth century, and New York in the twentieth century illustrates how geography and institutional frameworks generate comparative advantages in capital accumulation (Kindleberger, 1993). These centers concentrated expertise, liquidity, and trust, shaping global flows of capital. Yet financial globalization has not erased spatial differentiation. Instead, it has created a multilayered geography of finance where local, national, regional, and global markets interact in complex ways (Coe et al., 2014). The relativity of value across space is visible in the persistence of price differentials, arbitrage opportunities, and regional risk premiums. AI has accelerated the integration of markets by enabling high-speed cross-border transactions and the analysis of geographically dispersed data. At the same time, it has also made spatial asymmetries more visible, by detecting subtle correlations in regional consumption patterns, environmental risks, or political instabilities that influence value.

Jurisdictional diversity is one of the most salient dimensions of spatial relativity. Financial assets are embedded in legal frameworks that vary significantly across countries. A corporate bond issued under U.S. law may carry different value implications compared to an equivalent bond issued under English or Chinese law. Bankruptcy regimes, property rights, and regulatory enforcement shape the perceived security of contracts and thus their valuation (La Porta et al., 1998). For example, the same multinational firm may be valued differently by investors in New York and Shanghai because of divergent accounting standards, disclosure requirements, or investor protection rules. AI systems trained on jurisdiction-specific data can pick up these differences, but they also risk reinforcing them if algorithms are not adequately contextualized. If a model built on U.S. market data is applied without adjustment in emerging economies, it may misrepresent value by ignoring local institutional realities.

Spatial relativity also manifests in the structure of global value chains. Multinational corporations derive value from geographically distributed production, financing, and distribution networks. An AI system evaluating the value of such a corporation must take into account not only consolidated financial statements but also the geographic configuration of risks and opportunities. Supply chain disruptions during the COVID-19 pandemic demonstrated how concentrated geographies reduce resilience. Firms heavily dependent on a single region for production or logistics faced sharp declines in value when those regions went into lockdown (Baldwin & Freeman, 2020). Entropy-based measures of diversification could have highlighted the vulnerability of firms with low spatial entropy, where geographic concentration created fragility. Thus, the spatial relativity of value is not only a matter of where assets are traded but also of how underlying economic activities are geographically organized.

Geopolitical dynamics further complicate spatial valuations. Assets tied to specific regions are subject to political risks that can abruptly alter value. The annexation of Crimea in 2014, the U.S.–China trade war, and sanctions regimes against Russia and Iran have all transformed the valuation of assets linked to those regions (Farrell & Newman, 2019).

AI systems processing geopolitical datasets, news sentiment, and social media signals can detect early signs of spatial revaluation, but they also confront challenges of interpretation. Political risks are deeply contextual, and algorithmic assessments may misinterpret local developments. For instance, AI models may capture correlations between conflict events and commodity prices without understanding the strategic importance of specific geographic chokepoints such as the Strait of Hormuz. Spatial relativity thus underscores the need to complement algorithmic analysis with geopolitical expertise.

Cultural geographies also play a role in shaping value. Behavioral finance has shown that investor psychology is not uniform across space. Cultural attitudes toward risk, time, and uncertainty influence valuation. East Asian markets, for instance, often exhibit different patterns of herding, speculation, and risk aversion compared to Western markets (Chui et al., 2010). AI systems trained on global data must account for these cultural variations, or else they risk overgeneralizing. This challenge reflects a broader tension: while AI aspires to universal applicability, value remains spatially contingent. A context-aware AI must be designed to recognize that the meaning of financial signals differs across geographies, shaped by norms, expectations, and historical trajectories.

Spatial relativity is not only descriptive but normative. It raises questions about fairness, inequality, and access to financial opportunities. Financial globalization has often concentrated value in major centers, while peripheral regions struggle with capital flight, currency volatility, and underinvestment. AI could exacerbate or mitigate these inequalities. On one hand, AI-powered trading platforms may centralize decision-making in global hubs, reinforcing the dominance of established centers like New York, London, and Hong Kong. On the other hand, AI could democratize access by enabling local actors to leverage global datasets, detect opportunities, and manage risks more effectively. Future research must evaluate whether AI contributes to spatial convergence or divergence in financial value.

Spatial relativity is particularly evident in currency markets. Exchange rates encapsulate the spatial dimension of value, reflecting the relative worth of national currencies. Currencies are not valued solely by macroeconomic fundamentals but also by perceptions of political stability, institutional quality, and international credibility. The same dollar-denominated asset may have higher or lower value depending on local currency fluctuations. AI has transformed currency trading by analyzing enormous datasets in real time, identifying spatial correlations between macroeconomic indicators, capital flows, and market sentiment (King et al., 2011). Yet exchange rates remain subject to sudden revaluations driven by geopolitical shocks or speculative dynamics. Here again, entropy-based approaches may help quantify the unpredictability of currency markets, offering a richer view of spatial uncertainty.

Cross-border regulation provides another perspective on the spatial relativity of value. Financial institutions operating across multiple jurisdictions must navigate a patchwork of rules. Regulatory arbitrage—where firms exploit differences in rules across countries—creates spatial variability in value. For example, derivatives valued in one jurisdiction may be treated differently in another, affecting capital requirements and risk assessments (Tsingou, 2015). AI systems can help firms optimize across jurisdictions, but this raises ethical and systemic questions. If algorithms are used to exploit regulatory gaps, they may increase systemic fragility. Policymakers must therefore consider how AI reshapes spatial arbitrage and whether entropic indicators could be integrated into cross-border regulatory cooperation.

The materiality of financial infrastructures also shapes spatial valuations. Trading platforms, payment systems, and data centers are geographically situated. The location of servers can affect latency in high-frequency trading, creating spatial advantages for firms with physical proximity to exchanges (MacKenzie, 2019). Cloud computing and AI further complicate these dynamics by distributing computational infrastructures across regions. Value is thus partially determined by the spatial configuration of digital infrastructures. A trade executed in Chicago may have different implications than one executed in Singapore, not because of fundamentals but because of latency, regulatory oversight, and infrastructural asymmetries. Recognizing the spatial materiality of finance challenges narratives of pure virtuality and highlights how value is embedded in geographic infrastructures.

AI's role in reshaping spatial relativity is twofold. On one hand, AI provides tools to integrate diverse spatial datasets, from satellite imagery to geolocated transaction data, enabling more granular valuations. For instance, AI can assess agricultural yields by analyzing satellite images, influencing commodity valuations in global markets (Jean et al., 2016). On the other hand, AI introduces new forms of spatial opacity. Algorithms trained on global datasets may obscure local specificities, imposing homogenized valuations that fail to capture contextual nuances. The risk is that AI-driven finance creates a "view from nowhere" that overlooks the situatedness of value. Designing AI systems that are sensitive to spatial contexts requires interdisciplinary collaboration between data scientists, geographers, and financial experts.

The relativity of value across markets, jurisdictions, and geographies calls for a rethinking of regulation and governance. International organizations such as the IMF, BIS, and OECD already monitor global systemic risks, but their tools often assume universal benchmarks. Integrating entropy and AI into these frameworks could provide more nuanced assessments of spatial fragility. For example, entropy measures could quantify the diversity of cross-border capital flows, while AI could detect emerging hotspots of financial instability. Such approaches would allow regulators to move beyond aggregate indicators and address spatial differentiation directly.

Ultimately, the spatial relativity of value demonstrates that finance cannot be understood solely in abstract mathematical terms. Value is co-constructed by geography, law, culture, infrastructure, and politics. AI both amplifies and transforms these dynamics, offering new insights while also raising new risks. Recognizing the spatial relativity of value does not undermine financial analysis but enriches it, reminding us that markets are embedded in places, jurisdictions, and geographies that shape their logic. In the era of AI, financial decision-making must therefore integrate spatial awareness as a core principle. Only by acknowledging the geographic embeddedness of value can finance build resilient and equitable systems capable of navigating the complexities of the twenty-first century.

THE CONTEXTUAL RELATIVITY OF VALUE: INSTITUTIONS, CULTURE, AND ALGORITHMIC FRAMING

Institutions are the backbone of financial systems and a primary source of the contextual relativity of value. They establish the rules of calculation, the categories of legitimacy, and the standards by which assets are recognized and exchanged. Legal frameworks, accounting standards, and regulatory oversight determine not only how value is measured but also which dimensions of financial activity are visible and enforceable. Despite decades of efforts to harmonize accounting through International Financial Reporting Standards (IFRS), national interpretations and enforcement regimes continue to produce divergences in valuation practices (Carmona & Trombetta, 2021). A security issued under U.S. corporate law may be perceived as more credible than an equivalent one issued elsewhere, not because of intrinsic properties but because institutional enforcement differs. Thus, value is not universal but anchored in institutional architectures that define its meaning.

Artificial intelligence interacts with these institutional frameworks in ways that both stabilize and destabilize valuation. On the stabilizing side, AI tools can automate compliance with accounting rules, improve audit quality, and harmonize valuation practices across borders by standardizing data analysis. On the destabilizing side, AI itself becomes an object of regulation. The European Union's Artificial Intelligence Act, introduced in 2021 and expected to take effect in the coming years, explicitly designates credit scoring and algorithmic risk models as "high risk," subject to stringent requirements for transparency and human oversight (European Commission, 2021; Narayanan, 2023). In contrast, the United States maintains a fragmented regulatory regime, where financial AI is subject to sector-specific oversight but not to comprehensive federal legislation. China's approach emphasizes centralized control and the integration of AI into state planning, framing financial algorithms as instruments for macroeconomic management and social stability (Huang & Pierri, 2022). Each institutional context generates distinct conditions under which AI valuations are produced and interpreted, meaning that the same model can yield radically different legitimacy and impact depending on jurisdiction.

Culture adds another layer of relativity. Financial markets are not only shaped by institutions but also by social norms, collective imaginaries, and shared expectations. Behavioral finance has long demonstrated that attitudes toward risk and uncertainty vary across cultures. Recent research confirms that these differences extend into the age of AI. For example, Zhang and Ma (2020) found that Chinese retail investors frequently interpret algorithmic recommendations as trustworthy because they are perceived to align with state authority, while European investors often exhibit skepticism toward algorithmic mediation, reflecting traditions of individual autonomy and privacy (Zuboff, 2019). These cultural orientations affect whether algorithmic outputs are embraced, contested, or ignored, directly shaping how value is constructed in practice.

Cultural relativity is most visible during moments of crisis. In the aftermath of the COVID-19 pandemic, government interventions were interpreted differently across contexts. In the United States, aggressive fiscal and monetary stimulus was sometimes seen as distorting market fundamentals; in Europe, similar measures were interpreted as expressions of solidarity and systemic protection (Tooze, 2021). AI-supported trading systems trained on data from these regions absorbed these contextual signals, producing divergent outputs for the same types of assets. Cultural framings thereby shaped not only human perception but also algorithmic valuations. This dynamic underscores that AI does not erase cultural relativity; rather, it amplifies it by encoding differences into datasets and models.

Algorithmic framing constitutes the third dimension of contextual relativity. AI does not simply process neutral information: it frames value by prioritizing some variables over others, embedding assumptions about what matters in financial decision-making. As Crawford (2021) argues, there is no neutral AI—models reflect the socio-technical choices of their designers. In finance, this becomes particularly evident in domains like credit scoring, ESG investing, or algorithmic trading. An AI optimized for short-term arbitrage implicitly defines volatility as the primary indicator of value, while one tuned for sustainability metrics frames environmental and governance indicators as central. These framings are consequential because they shape flows of capital, direct investment priorities, and influence which risks are recognized.

Algorithmic framing is inseparable from the contexts in which models are trained. Bartlett et al. (2022) demonstrated that fintech lending algorithms in the U.S. exhibited discriminatory outcomes against minority borrowers, not because race was explicitly encoded but because proxies like ZIP codes carried historical biases. Similarly, Mehrabi et al. (2021) emphasize that fairness in AI cannot be achieved solely through technical adjustments; it requires awareness of institutional histories and cultural biases that shape datasets. Without contextual sensitivity, algorithmic valuations risk perpetuating inequality while appearing objective.

Opacity deepens the challenge. Burrell's (2016) typology of algorithmic opacity—arising from technical complexity, proprietary restrictions, and interpretive limits—remains useful, but newer studies show that opacity itself is contextual. In Europe, opacity is framed as a regulatory problem requiring explainability, while in the United States it is tolerated as a trade-off for innovation (Narayanan, 2023). In China, opacity can be instrumentalized for centralized control, where limited transparency is seen as supporting systemic stability (Huang & Pierri, 2022). The same algorithmic opacity thus carries different normative valences depending on institutional and cultural contexts, reinforcing the relativity of value.

The contextual relativity of value raises profound questions of legitimacy. If valuations depend on institutional settings, cultural orientations, and algorithmic framings, who decides which version of value is authoritative? Scholarship on algorithmic governance emphasizes the importance of participatory oversight and contestability (Cath, 2018). In finance, this translates into mechanisms that allow stakeholders to challenge credit scores, dispute ESG ratings, or interrogate algorithmic risk assessments. Without such mechanisms, algorithmic valuations risk being seen as illegitimate impositions, especially in culturally diverse or institutionally fragmented contexts.

The co-evolution of AI with institutions and culture suggests that contextual relativity is dynamic rather than static. As AI systems become embedded in financial practice, they reshape norms and expectations. The rise of algorithmic trading has normalized microsecond horizons, redefining liquidity and volatility as key dimensions of value (MacKenzie, 2019). Likewise, ESG-focused AI platforms have shifted institutional investors toward integrating sustainability metrics into mainstream valuation, altering both cultural narratives and institutional routines (Kölbel et al., 2020). AI is therefore not merely reflecting context; it is actively producing new contexts in which value is understood.

The synthesis of these dimensions points to an important conclusion: contextual relativity is not a weakness of financial systems but an unavoidable feature. Institutions, cultures, and algorithms each frame value differently, and their interplay generates plural and contested valuations. For practitioners, this pluralism demands adaptive strategies that account for multiple framings rather than assuming universal metrics. For regulators, it requires balancing cross-border comparability with sensitivity to local contexts. For scholars, it challenges universalist theories of value and calls for relational approaches that foreground context as constitutive of finance.

FUTURE RESEARCH DIRECTIONS

The analysis of the relativity of value across time, space, and context in AI-supported financial decision-making reveals not only current challenges but also the vast scope of future research. Artificial intelligence is transforming the very processes through which value is constructed, interpreted, and contested. Yet its implications remain only partially understood. The field is characterized by rapid technological change, uneven regulatory frameworks, and deep epistemological uncertainty. For scholars, regulators, and practitioners, this means that value must be investigated not as a stable metric but as a dynamic and relational phenomenon. Future research should thus advance in several interconnected directions: methodological innovation, empirical validation, cross-jurisdictional comparison, ethical and normative inquiry, and interdisciplinary integration.

A first avenue concerns the methodological development of AI-driven valuation models that explicitly incorporate temporal relativity. Current financial models often impose a single horizon through discounting techniques or capital asset pricing formulas. Yet AI enables multi-horizon analysis, where short-term volatility and long-term sustainability can be modeled simultaneously. Future research could explore how reinforcement learning and generative AI can simulate multiple temporal futures, identifying not only expected returns but also the entropic uncertainty of long-run outcomes (Agrawal et al., 2018; Chen et al., 2023). One critical challenge here is interpretability: how can AI systems communicate complex temporal dynamics to human decision-makers in ways that are actionable but not misleading? Bridging this gap requires collaboration between computer science, behavioral finance, and human-computer interaction.

Second, future work must deepen the exploration of spatial relativity in value creation and distribution. While globalization has made capital highly mobile, jurisdictional differences in law, regulation, and culture continue to shape valuation. With AI systems increasingly analyzing geospatial data—from satellite imagery of agricultural yields to transaction-level data in cross-border e-commerce—scholars must examine how spatial asymmetries are represented and potentially reinforced. Entropy-based methods may be extended to measure the geographic concentration or diversification of capital flows, offering tools for systemic risk monitoring (Zhao et al., 2018). Comparative studies of AI-supported valuations in the European Union, the United States, and China could illuminate how institutional diversity produces divergent outcomes, even when algorithms process similar datasets (Narayanan, 2023). A pressing research question is whether AI contributes to convergence in global value assessments or amplifies spatial inequality by privileging dominant centers of data and liquidity.

Contextual relativity also demands further investigation, particularly around how cultural narratives and institutional norms become encoded in AI models. Datasets are not neutral; they reflect histories of inclusion and exclusion. Future research should analyze the pathways through which institutional biases and cultural assumptions shape algorithmic outputs, particularly in areas like credit scoring, ESG ratings, and systemic risk assessment (Bartlett et al., 2022; Mehrabi et al., 2021). Beyond bias detection, scholars should explore methods for embedding contextual pluralism into AI systems, enabling models to adapt valuations across cultural and institutional settings. For example, how might an AI system account for different cultural attitudes toward risk when assessing investment opportunities? Developing context-aware AI requires not only technical innovation but also ethical frameworks sensitive to diversity and inclusion.

Another direction concerns explainability and transparency in AI-supported valuations. The opacity of AI remains a significant obstacle to trust and legitimacy in finance. Future research should examine new methods of algorithmic interpretability tailored to financial contexts, such as visualization tools that show how temporal, spatial, and contextual variables interact in valuation models. Work in explainable AI (XAI) is advancing rapidly, but much of it is not designed for the high-stakes, regulated environment of finance (Arrieta et al., 2020; Rudin, 2022). Researchers must assess how explainability tools perform under regulatory scrutiny, how they are interpreted by practitioners, and whether they genuinely increase accountability or merely provide a veneer of transparency.

The ethical and normative dimensions of value relativization in AI contexts also call for sustained inquiry. If value is contingent on time, space, and context, who gets to decide which framing is authoritative? Future research should explore mechanisms of participatory algorithmic governance, where diverse stakeholders—investors, regulators, civil society—have a voice in shaping the design and deployment of financial AI systems (Cath, 2018; Crawford, 2021). Questions of distributive justice arise: does AI-supported finance privilege certain groups or regions over others? Does it exacerbate global inequality by concentrating value recognition in data-rich environments? Scholars must also investigate the normative stakes of intergenerational value. AI systems can simulate long-term scenarios, but their outputs still reflect present-day discounting choices. Research is needed on how to embed ethical commitments to future generations into algorithmic valuation models, particularly in domains such as climate finance.

Empirical research represents another frontier. While theoretical arguments about entropy, relativity, and AI are persuasive, there is still limited large-scale empirical validation. Future studies should analyze real-world datasets to test whether entropic measures or AI-driven context-aware valuations actually improve prediction, resilience, and fairness. Longitudinal research could assess how AI adoption changes valuation practices over time across different markets and institutions. Case studies of crises—such as the Asian financial crisis, the 2008 meltdown, or the COVID-19 shock—could be revisited using entropy and AI frameworks to see whether early-warning indicators might have been constructed (Tooze,

2021). Such empirical grounding is essential for moving from conceptual promise to practical implementation.

Another promising line of inquiry is the intersection of climate finance, sustainability, and AI-driven valuation. Climate change introduces uncertainties that are temporal (long-run risks), spatial (regional vulnerabilities), and contextual (political and cultural responses). Entropy-based models combined with AI could simulate multiple climate scenarios, providing more nuanced valuations of green bonds, carbon markets, and climate-sensitive assets (Battiston et al., 2017; Kölbel et al., 2020). Future research could explore how AI systems incorporate environmental data—from satellite monitoring of deforestation to emissions reporting—and how cultural and institutional contexts influence their interpretation. Such work would contribute not only to finance but also to global sustainability efforts.

Cyber risk and digital infrastructures also present fertile ground for research. As finance becomes increasingly dependent on digital systems, from payment networks to blockchain platforms, systemic vulnerabilities proliferate. Future research should examine how entropy and AI can measure the resilience of financial infrastructures, identify weak points and assess redundancy (Kopp et al., 2017). AI may itself introduce new risks, as algorithmic trading systems create feedback loops that destabilize markets. Scholars should investigate how to design AI architectures that prioritize systemic stability, perhaps by embedding diversity and entropy principles into model training.

Finally, future research must be interdisciplinary and comparative. Finance cannot be studied in isolation. Entropy links finance to physics and information theory, AI connects it to computer science, and contextual relativity requires engagement with sociology, anthropology, and political science. Collaborative research projects could explore how lessons from ecology (biodiversity and resilience), law (comparative institutional design), and philosophy (uncertainty and ethics) enrich financial theory. Comparative perspectives across jurisdictions are also essential: the EU, the U.S., and China provide distinct models of AI regulation, each shaping the relativity of value differently (European Commission, 2021; Narayanan, 2023). Global finance requires tools that can navigate these differences without imposing a homogenized model that erases contextual diversity.

CONCLUSION

The exploration of value through the dimensions of time, space, and context demonstrates that financial decision-making in the age of artificial intelligence is not reducible to universal formulas or stable benchmarks. Instead, value emerges as a relative and relational construct, shaped by the horizons of actors, the geographies of markets, and the cultural and institutional frames within which decisions are made. Artificial intelligence does not eliminate these relativities; it intensifies them by embedding temporal, spatial, and contextual variability into algorithmic processes. The challenge for theory, practice, and regulation is to recognize this relativity and to design systems capable of navigating it rather than denying it.

Time reveals the first axis of relativity. Classical finance has long assumed that future earnings can be translated into present value through discounting, but real-world practices show that temporal horizons differ radically. Day traders, pension funds, and sovereign debt managers operate with distinct logics of time, producing multiple valuations of the same asset. Artificial intelligence accentuates these differences by collapsing time into milliseconds in high-frequency trading while simultaneously extending it into decades through climate and demographic simulations. Temporal relativity means that value cannot be pinned down to a single horizon but must be understood as a multiplicity of coexisting perspectives. AI systems that model multiple futures may help decision-makers embrace this plurality, but they also raise questions about interpretability and ethical commitments to future generations (Chen et al., 2023; Stern, 2007).

Space forms the second axis. Financial globalization has created integrated markets, yet valuation remains fragmented across jurisdictions, currencies, and geographies. Legal frameworks, regulatory enforcement, and geopolitical risks ensure that the same instrument may hold different values depending on where and under whose authority it is traded (La Porta et al., 1998). Artificial intelligence makes these spatial asymmetries more visible by analyzing geospatial datasets, detecting regional correlations, and uncovering vulnerabilities in supply chains and infrastructures (Jean et al., 2016). At the same time, AI may deepen spatial inequality by concentrating value recognition in data-rich financial centers, leaving peripheral regions underrepresented. Spatial relativity challenges the myth of a flat global market, reminding us that value is always geographically situated and politically mediated.

Context completes the triad. Institutions, cultures, and algorithmic framings shape not only how value is calculated but also what counts as valuable in the first place. Institutional frameworks such as accounting standards or AI regulations determine the legitimacy of valuations. Cultural norms influence trust in algorithms, attitudes toward risk, and interpretations of uncertainty. Algorithmic framing, in turn, operationalizes context by privileging certain variables—be it volatility, ESG metrics, or credit proxies—while marginalizing others. AI systems therefore both reflect and reconstruct contextual conditions, producing valuations that are situated, partial, and contestable (Crawford, 2021; Bartlett et al., 2022). The contextual relativity of value demonstrates that there is no neutral algorithm, only socio-technical systems embedded in histories of inequality, institutional norms, and cultural imaginaries.

The synthesis of temporal, spatial, and contextual dimensions underscores a profound epistemological shift. Traditional finance aspired to universal metrics, objective valuations, and stable risk-return equations. The relativity of value reveals instead a world of plural and contested valuations. Artificial intelligence does not resolve this plurality; it embodies it. Algorithms are trained on specific datasets, governed by particular institutions, and interpreted through cultural frames. Their outputs may appear objective but are always contingent. Recognizing this contingency is not a weakness but a strength: it allows scholars and practitioners to move beyond illusions of certainty toward strategies of resilience and adaptability.

The normative stakes of relativity are significant. If value is contingent, who decides which valuation is authoritative? The answer cannot be left solely to market dynamics or opaque algorithms. Regulators and policymakers must design frameworks that acknowledge relativity while safeguarding legitimacy and fairness. The European Union's AI Act offers one model, emphasizing transparency and accountability (European Commission, 2021). The U.S. relies on fragmented oversight, while China integrates financial AI into centralized governance (Narayanan, 2023). Each reflects contextual priorities, but all face the challenge of ensuring that algorithmic valuations are contestable and inclusive. Future regulatory innovation must therefore integrate participatory governance, algorithmic auditing, and cross-border cooperation to manage relativity responsibly.

The relativity of value also intersects with pressing global challenges. Climate change demands long-term horizons, global coordination, and contextual sensitivity to local vulnerabilities. Cyber risks highlight the fragility of digital infrastructures across geographies. Geopolitical conflicts expose the dependence of value on jurisdictional legitimacy. Artificial intelligence can support responses to these challenges by modeling diverse futures, analyzing complex interdependencies, and identifying hidden risks. Yet its use must be guided by frameworks that recognize relativity rather than impose false universals. Scholars such as Tooze (2021) and Kölbel et al. (2020) emphasize that resilience in global finance requires diversity, adaptability, and ethical orientation—principles that align closely with the recognition of relative value.

For practitioners, embracing relativity means developing strategies that are robust across horizons, geographies, and contexts. Portfolio managers must diversify not only across assets but also across timeframes and jurisdictions. Risk officers must interpret algorithmic outputs with contextual awareness, asking whose data, whose assumptions, and whose culture shape the model. Executives must balance short-term returns with long-term resilience, recognizing that AI can illuminate both but not reconcile them into a single value. Regulators must craft adaptive frameworks capable of evolving as contexts shift. And scholars must develop theories that foreground relationality, moving beyond reductionist models toward richer accounts of financial reality.

In conclusion, value in AI-supported finance is irreducibly relative. It is shaped by temporal horizons that differ across actors, by spatial geographies that reflect legal and political diversity, and by contextual framings that embed institutions, cultures, and algorithms. Artificial intelligence both reveals and intensifies this relativity, collapsing time, integrating space, and reframing context. The challenge is not to eliminate relativity but to navigate it responsibly. By acknowledging the plurality of value, designing systems that are transparent and participatory, and committing to resilience over false certainty, finance can better meet the demands of an uncertain century. The relativity of value is not a problem to be solved but a condition to be embraced—an invitation to reimagine financial decision-making as a practice that is adaptive, inclusive, and deeply attuned to time, space, and context.

REFERENCES

Agrawal, A., Gans, J., & Goldfarb, A. (2018). *Prediction machines: The simple economics of artificial intelligence*. Harvard Business Review Press.

Arrieta, A. B., Díaz-Rodríguez, N., Del Ser, J., Bennetot, A., Tabik, S., Barbado, A., & Herrera, F. (2020). Explainable Artificial Intelligence (XAI): Concepts, taxonomies, opportunities and challenges toward responsible AI. *Information Fusion, 58*, 82–115. DOI: 10.1016/j.inffus.2019.12.012

Baker, S. R., Bloom, N., Davis, S. J., Kost, K. J., Sammon, M. C., & Viratyosin, T. (2020). The unprecedented stock market reaction to COVID-19. *Review of Asset Pricing Studies, 10*(4), 742–758. DOI: 10.1093/rapstu/raaa008

Baldwin, R., & Freeman, R. (2020). Supply chain contagion waves: Thinking ahead on manufacturing 'contagion and reinfection' from the COVID concussion. *VoxEU.org*.

Bartlett, R., Morse, A., Stanton, R., & Wallace, N. (2022). Consumer-lending discrimination in the FinTech era. *Journal of Financial Economics, 146*(2), 726–765. DOI: 10.1016/j.jfineco.2021.12.011

Battiston, S., Mandel, A., Monasterolo, I., Schütze, F., & Visentin, G. (2017). A climate stress-test of the financial system. *Nature Climate Change*, *7*(4), 283–288. DOI: 10.1038/nclimate3255

Brealey, R., Myers, S., & Allen, F. (2019). *Principles of corporate finance* (13th ed.). McGraw-Hill.

Bryan, D., Rafferty, M., & Wigan, D. (2020). *Capital unchained: Finance, intangible assets and the double life of capital*. Routledge.

Burrell, J. (2016). How the machine "thinks": Understanding opacity in machine learning algorithms. *Big Data & Society*, *3*(1), 1–12. DOI: 10.1177/2053951715622512

Carmona, S., & Trombetta, M. (2021). On the global acceptance of IFRS accounting standards: The logic and implications of the institutional framework. *Accounting, Organizations and Society*, *89*, 101224. DOI: 10.1016/j.aos.2020.101224

Cath, C. (2018). Governing artificial intelligence: Ethical, legal and technical opportunities and challenges. *Philosophical Transactions. Series A, Mathematical, Physical, and Engineering Sciences*, *376*(2133), 20180080. DOI: 10.1098/rsta.2018.0080 PMID: 30322996

Chen, M., Zhang, Y., & Lee, D. (2023). Reinforcement learning in finance: Recent advances and future directions. *The Journal of Financial Data Science*, *5*(2), 1–20. DOI: 10.3905/jfds.2023.1.147

Chui, A. C., Titman, S., & Wei, K. C. (2010). Individualism and momentum around the world. *The Journal of Finance*, *65*(1), 361–392. DOI: 10.1111/j.1540-6261.2009.01532.x

Coe, N. M., Lai, K. P. Y., & Wójcik, D. (2014). *Integrating economic geography and global finance*. Routledge.

Crawford, K. (2021). *Atlas of AI: Power, politics, and the planetary costs of artificial intelligence*. Yale University Press.

European Commission. (2021). *Proposal for a Regulation laying down harmonised rules on artificial intelligence (Artificial Intelligence Act)*. COM(2021) 206 final.

Farrell, H., & Newman, A. (2019). Weaponized interdependence: How global economic networks shape state coercion. *International Security*, *44*(1), 42–79. DOI: 10.1162/isec_a_00351

Fine, B. (2018). *Value and price: An economic history of theories*. Routledge.

Gorton, G. (2010). *Slapped by the invisible hand: The panic of 2007*. Oxford University Press.

Huang, R., & Pierri, N. (2022). Fintech credit and shadow banking: Evidence from China. *Journal of Banking & Finance*, *137*, 106441. DOI: 10.1016/j.jbankfin.2022.106441

Jean, N., Burke, M., Xie, M., Davis, W. M., Lobell, D. B., & Ermon, S. (2016). Combining satellite imagery and machine learning to predict poverty. *Science, 353*(6301), 790–794. DOI: 10.1126/science.aaf7894 PMID: 27540167

Johnson, N. F., Zhao, G., Hunsader, E., Meng, J., Ravindar, A., Carran, S., & Tivnan, B. (2013). Abrupt rise of new machine ecology beyond human response time. *Scientific Reports, 3*(1), 2627. DOI: 10.1038/srep02627 PMID: 24022120

Kindleberger, C. P. (1993). *A financial history of Western Europe* (2nd ed.). Oxford University Press.

King, M. R., Osler, C. L., & Rime, D. (2011). *Foreign exchange market structure, players, and evolution. Handbook of Exchange Rates*. Wiley.

Kirilenko, A. A., Kyle, A. S., Samadi, M., & Tuzun, T. (2017). The flash crash: High-frequency trading in an electronic market. *The Journal of Finance, 72*(3), 967–998. DOI: 10.1111/jofi.12498

Kölbel, J. F., Heeb, F., Paetzold, F., & Busch, T. (2020). Can sustainable investing save the world? Reviewing the mechanisms of investor impact. *Organization & Environment, 33*(4), 554–574. DOI: 10.1177/1086026620919202

Kopp, E., Kaffenberger, L., & Wilson, C. (2017). Cyber risk, market failures, and financial stability. *IMF Working Paper WP/17/185.*

La Porta, R., Lopez-de-Silanes, F., Shleifer, A., & Vishny, R. (1998). Law and finance. *Journal of Political Economy, 106*(6), 1113–1155. DOI: 10.1086/250042

Laibson, D. (1997). Golden eggs and hyperbolic discounting. *The Quarterly Journal of Economics, 112*(2), 443–478. DOI: 10.1162/003355397555253

Laux, C., & Leuz, C. (2009). The crisis of fair-value accounting: Making sense of the recent debate. *Accounting, Organizations and Society, 34*(6–7), 826–834. DOI: 10.1016/j.aos.2009.04.003

MacKenzie, D. (2019). *Trading at the speed of light: How ultrafast algorithms are transforming financial markets*. Princeton University Press.

Mehrabi, N., Morstatter, F., Saxena, N., Lerman, K., & Galstyan, A. (2021). A survey on bias and fairness in machine learning. *ACM Computing Surveys, 54*(6), 1–35. DOI: 10.1145/3457607

Narayanan, A. (2023). Regulating AI: The EU AI Act and its implications for financial services. *AI & Society, 38*(2), 567–581. DOI: 10.1007/s00146-022-01407-5

Pasquale, F. (2015). *The black box society: The secret algorithms that control money and information*. Harvard University Press. DOI: 10.4159/harvard.9780674736061

Rudin, C., Chen, C., Chen, Z., Huang, H., Semenova, L., & Zhong, C. (2022). Interpretable machine learning: Fundamental principles and ten grand challenges. *Statistics Surveys, 16*(none), 1–85. DOI: 10.1214/21-SS133

Sharpe, W. F. (1964). Capital asset prices: A theory of market equilibrium under conditions of risk. *The Journal of Finance, 19*(3), 425–442. DOI: 10.2307/2977928

Shiller, R. J. (2015). *Irrational exuberance* (3rd ed.). Princeton University Press.

Stern, N. (2007). *The economics of climate change: The Stern review*. Cambridge University Press. DOI: 10.1017/CBO9780511817434

Strange, S. (2015). *Casino capitalism* (2nd ed.). Manchester University Press. DOI: 10.7765/9781784997212

Thaler, R. H. (2016). *Misbehaving: The making of behavioral economics*. W. W. Norton.

Tooze, A. (2021). *Shutdown: How COVID shook the world's economy*. Viking.

Tsingou, E. (2015). Club governance and the making of global financial rules. *Review of International Political Economy, 22*(2), 225–256. DOI: 10.1080/09692290.2014.890952

Zhang, W., & Ma, J. (2020). Cultural framing and algorithmic trust: Retail investor responses to AI in Chinese financial markets. *Journal of Cultural Economics, 13*(6), 651–668. DOI: 10.1080/17530350.2020.1816827

Zhao, L., Li, W., & Cai, X. (2018). Entropy-based systemic risk measure of complex financial networks. *Physica A, 503*, 318–329. DOI: 10.1016/j.physa.2018.02.156

Zuboff, S. (2019). *The age of surveillance capitalism: The fight for a human future at the new frontier of power*. PublicAffairs.

Compilation of References

Abdi M.D., & Bayu K.B. (2021). Exploring current opportunity and threats of Artificial intelligence on small and medium enterprises accounting function: Evidence from South West part of Ethiopia, Oromiya, Jimma and SNNPR, Bonga. Academy of Accounting and Financial Studies Journal, 25(2), 1-11.

Abukhader S.M. (2020). Extent of artificial intelligence into accounting and auditing work - An analytical attempt of job and duties. International Journal of Business Process Integration and Management, 10(2), 125-136. .DOI: 10.1504/IJBPIM.2020.117165

Acemoglu, D., Ozdaglar, A., & Tahbaz-Salehi, A. (2022). Systemic risk and stability in financial networks. *The American Economic Review*, *112*(3), 991–1034. DOI: 10.1257/aer.20191479

Acharya, V. V., Pedersen, L. H., Philippon, T., & Richardson, M. (2017). Measuring systemic risk. *Review of Financial Studies*, *30*(1), 2–47. DOI: 10.1093/rfs/hhw088

Achim, M. V., Borlea, S. N., & Văidean, V. L. (2021). Does technology matter for combating economic and financial crime? A panel data study. *Technological and Economic Development of Economy*, *27*(1), 223–261. DOI: 10.3846/tede.2021.13977

Adelakun, O., Akinrinola, B. T., & Islam, R. (2024). Applications of machine learning models in auditing: Opportunities and challenges. *Finance & Accounting Research Journal*.

Adeniyi, E. O. (2025). Occupational Fraud: A Quantitative Study on the Impact of Enhancing Anti-Fraud Controls With Forensic Accounting (Doctoral dissertation, South College).

Adeoye, I. O., Akintoye, R. I., Theophilus, A. A., & Olagunju, O. A. (2023). Artificial intelligence and audit quality: Implications for practicing accountants. *Asian Economic and Financial Review*, *13*(11), 756–772, 23052147. DOI: 10.55493/5002.v13i11.4861

Agrawal, A., Gans, J., & Goldfarb, A. (2018). *Prediction machines: The simple economics of artificial intelligence*. Harvard Business Review Press.

Ajiola, F. O. (2025). Urban Crime in the Lagos Traffic: An Ethnography at the Crossroads of Multiple Codes of Ethics. *Journal of African Cultural Studies*, *37*(1), 127–144. DOI: 10.1080/13696815.2024.2376544

Al Wael, H., Abdallah, W., Ghura, H., & Buallay, A. (2024). Factors influencing artificial intelligence adoption in the accounting profession: The case of public sector in Kuwait. *Competitiveness Review*, *34*(1), 3–27, 10595422. DOI: 10.1108/CR-09-2022-0137

Aldoseri, A., Al-Khalifa, K., & Hamouda, A. (2023). A roadmap for integrating automation with process optimization for AI-powered digital transformation. *Preprints*. DOI: 10.20944/preprints202310

Aldredge, M., Rogers, C., & Smith, J. (2021). The strategic transformation of accounting into a learned profession. *Industry and Higher Education*, *35*(2), 83–88, 9504222. DOI: 10.1177/0950422220954319

Ali, T. (2024). Next-generation intrusion detection systems with LLMs: real-time anomaly detection, explainable AI, and adaptive data generation (Master's thesis, T. Ali).

Ali, I., Mehreen, A., & Shah, S. (2022). The role of machine learning algorithms in fraud detection: A financial sector perspective. *International Journal of Financial Studies*, *10*(3), 45–62.

Aljaaidi K.S., Alwadani N.F., & Adow A.H. (2023). The impact of artificial intelligence applications on the performance of accountants and audit firms in Saudi Arabia. International Journal of Data and Network Science, 7(3), 1165-1178. .DOI: 10.5267/j.ijdns.2023.5.007

Alpaydin, E. (2021). *Machine learning*. MIT Press. DOI: 10.7551/mit-press/13811.001.0001

Al-Sammarraee A., & Alshareeda N. (2021). The role of artificial intelligence by using automatic accounting information system in supporting the quality of financial statement. Information Sciences Letters, 10(2), 223-254. .DOI: 10.18576/isl/100208

Amiri, Z., Heidari, A., Jafari, N., & Hosseinzadeh, M. (2024). Deep study on autonomous learning techniques for complex pattern recognition in interconnected information systems. *Computer Science Review*, *54*, 100666. DOI: 10.1016/j.cosrev.2024.100666

Appelbaum, D., Kogan, A., & Vasarhelyi, M. (2017). Big Data and analytics in the modern audit engagement: Research needs. *Auditing*, *36*(4), 1–27. DOI: 10.2308/ajpt-51684

Arrieta, A. B., Díaz-Rodríguez, N., Del Ser, J., Bennetot, A., Tabik, S., Barbado, A., & Herrera, F. (2020). Explainable Artificial Intelligence (XAI): Concepts, taxonomies, opportunities and challenges toward responsible AI. *Information Fusion*, *58*, 82–115. DOI: 10.1016/j.inffus.2019.12.012

Arthur, W. B. (2021). Foundations of complexity economics. *Nature Reviews. Physics*, *3*(2), 136–145. DOI: 10.1038/s42254-020-00273-3 PMID: 33728407

Asad, F. (2025). AI-Driven Strategies for Fraud Risk Management in Emerging Markets: Enhancing Regulatory Oversight and Digital Transparency.

Ayodeji, I. A. (2024). Fraud Detection and Prevention in the Nigerian Financial Industry (Doctoral dissertation, Walden University).

Baiod, W., & Hussain, M. M. (2024). The impact and adoption of emerging technologies on accounting: Perceptions of Canadian companies. *International Journal of Accounting and Information Management, 18347649*(4), 557–592. Advance online publication. DOI: 10.1108/IJAIM-05-2023-0123

Bakare, A. O., Odeyemi, O., & Kumar, M. (2024). Audit automation: Impact of AI platforms like Clara in Big Four firms. *Journal of Auditing Technology Research, 12*(1), 34–50.

Baker, S. R., Bloom, N., Davis, S. J., Kost, K. J., Sammon, M. C., & Viratyosin, T. (2020). The unprecedented stock market reaction to COVID-19. *Review of Asset Pricing Studies, 10*(4), 742–758. DOI: 10.1093/rapstu/raaa008

Balcıoğlu, Y. S. (2024). Revolutionizing Risk Management AI and ML Innovations in Financial Stability and Fraud Detection. In Navigating the Future of Finance in the Age of AI (pp. 109-138). IGI Global.

Baldwin, R., & Freeman, R. (2020). Supply chain contagion waves: Thinking ahead on manufacturing 'contagion and reinfection' from the COVID concussion. *VoxEU.org*.

Balogun, J., & Johnson, G. (2004). Organizational restructuring and middle manager sensemaking. *Academy of Management Journal, 47*(4), 523–549. DOI: 10.2307/20159600

Banerjee, R. (2024). *Who Cheats and How: Scams, Frauds and the Dark Side of the Corporate World*. Penguin Random House India Private Limited.

Bareis, J., & Katzenbach, C. (2022). Talking AI into being: The narratives and imaginaries of national AI strategies and their performative politics. *Science, Technology & Human Values, 47*(5), 855–881. DOI: 10.1177/01622439211030007

Barney, J. (1991). Firm resources and sustained competitive advantage. *Journal of Management, 17*(1), 99–120. DOI: 10.1177/014920639101700108

Barocas, S., Hardt, M., & Narayanan, A. (2019). *Fairness and machine learning: Limitations and opportunities*. MIT Press.

Bartlett, R., Morse, A., Stanton, R., & Wallace, N. (2022). Consumer-lending discrimination in the FinTech era. *Journal of Financial Economics, 146*(2), 726–765. DOI: 10.1016/j.jfineco.2021.12.011

Battina, D. S. (2018). The future of artificial intelligence at work: A review on effects of decision automation and augmentation on workers targeted by algorithms and third-party observers. *International Journal of Innovations in Engineering Research and Technology*, *5*(7).

Battiston, S., Mandel, A., Monasterolo, I., Schütze, F., & Visentin, G. (2017). A climate stress-test of the financial system. *Nature Climate Change*, *7*(4), 283–288. DOI: 10.1038/nclimate3255

Battiston, S., Puliga, M., Kaushik, R., Tasca, P., & Caldarelli, G. (2016). Debtrank: Too central to fail? Financial networks, the FED and systemic risk. *Scientific Reports*, *2*(1), 541–550. DOI: 10.1038/srep00541 PMID: 22870377

Bekiros, S., Nguyen, D. K., Sandoval, L., & Uddin, G. S. (2017). Information diffusion, cluster formation and entropy-based network dynamics in financial crises. *European Journal of Operational Research*, *256*(2), 473–486. DOI: 10.1016/j.ejor.2016.06.024

Berthet, V. (2022). The impact of cognitive biases on professionals' decision-making: A review of four occupational areas. *Frontiers in Psychology*, *12*, 802439. DOI: 10.3389/fpsyg.2021.802439 PMID: 35058862

Bhatt, U., Antorán, J., Zhang, Y., Liao, Q. V., Sattigeri, P., Fogliato, R., . . . Xiang, A. (2021, July). Uncertainty as a form of transparency: Measuring, communicating, and using uncertainty. In Proceedings of the 2021 AAAI/ACM Conference on AI, Ethics, and Society (pp. 401-413).

Bhattacharya, A. (2022). *Applied Machine Learning Explainability Techniques: Make ML models explainable and trustworthy for practical applications using LIME, SHAP, and more*. Packt Publishing Ltd.

Binns, R. (2018). Fairness in machine learning: Lessons from political philosophy. *Proceedings of the 2018 Conference on Fairness, Accountability, and Transparency*, 149–159. DOI: 10.1145/3287560.3287572

Birhane, A. (2024). Auditing artificial intelligence systems: Challenges and solutions. *arXiv preprint arXiv:2401.00001.*

Bisias, D., Flood, M., Lo, A. W., & Valavanis, S. (2012). A survey of systemic risk analytics. *Annual Review of Financial Economics*, *4*(1), 255–296. DOI: 10.1146/annurev-financial-110311-101754

Bogen, M., & Rieke, A. (2018). Help wanted: An examination of hiring algorithms, equity, and bias. *Upturn Report.*

Bonini, T., & Treré, E. (2024). *Algorithms of resistance: The everyday fight against platform power.* Mit Press. DOI: 10.7551/mitpress/14329.001.0001

Boppana, V. R. (2023). Data Ethics in CRM: Privacy and Transparency Issues. Available at *SSRN* 5005001.

Boritz, J. E., & Stratopoulos, T. C. (2023). AI and the Accounting Profession: Views from Industry and Academia. *Journal of Information Systems*, *37*(3), 1–9. DOI: 10.2308/ISYS-2023-054

Bose, S., Dey, S. K., & Bhattacharjee, S. (2023). Big data, data analytics and artificial intelligence in accounting: An overview. Handbook of Big Data Research Methods. DOI: 10.4337/9781800888555.00007

Brealey, R., Myers, S., & Allen, F. (2019). *Principles of corporate finance* (13th ed.). McGraw-Hill.

Bremmer, I., & Suleyman, M. (2023). The AI power paradox: Can states learn to govern artificial intelligence-before it's too late? *Foreign Affairs*, *102*, 26.

Brown, C., Davidovic, N., & Hasan, S. (2021). Enhancing audit reliability through full dataset analysis. *Accounting and Information Systems Research*, *20*(2), 85–105.

Bryan, D., Rafferty, M., & Wigan, D. (2020). *Capital unchained: Finance, intangible assets and the double life of capital.* Routledge.

Brynjolfsson, E., & McAfee, A. (2017). *Machine, platform, crowd: Harnessing our digital future.* W. W. Norton.

Bryson, J., & Winfield, A. (2017). Standardizing ethical design for artificial intelligence and autonomous systems. *Computer, 50*(5), 116–119. DOI: 10.1109/MC.2017.154

Bughin, J., Seong, J., Manyika, J., Chui, M., & Joshi, R. (2018). Notes from the AI frontier: Modeling the impact of AI on the world economy. *McKinsey Global Institute Report.*

Burrell, J. (2016). How the machine "thinks": Understanding opacity in machine learning algorithms. *Big Data & Society, 3*(1), 1–12. DOI: 10.1177/2053951715622512

Cai, S., Tian, L., & Zhou, W. (2018). Multiscale entropy analysis of stock markets: Evidence from developed and emerging economies. *Physica A, 503*, 454–463. DOI: 10.1016/j.physa.2018.02.181

Cañas, J. J. (2022). AI and ethics when human beings collaborate with AI agents. *Frontiers in Psychology, 13*, 836650. DOI: 10.3389/fpsyg.2022.836650 PMID: 35310226

Carmona, S., & Trombetta, M. (2021). On the global acceptance of IFRS accounting standards: The logic and implications of the institutional framework. *Accounting, Organizations and Society, 89*, 101224. DOI: 10.1016/j.aos.2020.101224

Cath, C. (2018). Governing artificial intelligence: Ethical, legal and technical opportunities and challenges. *Philosophical Transactions. Series A, Mathematical, Physical, and Engineering Sciences, 376*(2133), 20180080. DOI: 10.1098/rsta.2018.0080 PMID: 30322996

Challoumis, C. (2024, October). The economics of AI-How machine learning is driving value creation. In *XVI International Scientific Conference* (pp. 94-125).

Chapman, R., & Holmes, P. (2024). *Observability with Grafana: Monitor, control, and visualize your Kubernetes and cloud platforms using the LGTM stack.* Packt Publishing Ltd.

Chaquet-Ulldemolins, J., Gimeno-Blanes, F. J., Moral-Rubio, S., Muñoz-Romero, S., & Rojo-Álvarez, J. L. (2022). On the black-box challenge for fraud detection using machine learning (ii): Nonlinear analysis through interpretable autoencoders. *Applied Sciences (Basel, Switzerland)*, *12*(8), 3856. DOI: 10.3390/app12083856

Chatterjee, M., Bose, S., & Banerjee, P. (2022). Biases in natural language processing applications: Consequences for audit fairness. *ICICC Proceedings 2022*.

Cheliatsidou, A., Sariannidis, N., Garefalakis, A., Azibi, J., & Kagias, P. (2023). The international fraud triangle. *Journal of Money Laundering Control*, *26*(1), 106–132. DOI: 10.1108/JMLC-09-2021-0103

Cheng, J., Varshney, K. R., & Liu, H. (2021). Predictive analytics in financial risk assessment: A survey. *Decision Support Systems*, *146*, 113539.

Chen, M., Zhang, Y., & Lee, D. (2023). Reinforcement learning in finance: Recent advances and future directions. *The Journal of Financial Data Science*, *5*(2), 1–20. DOI: 10.3905/jfds.2023.1.147

Chivers, T. (2024). *Everything is Predictable: How Bayesian Statistics Explain Our World*. Simon and Schuster.

Choi, T. M., Wallace, S. W., & Wang, Y. (2021). Big data analytics in operations management. *Production and Operations Management*, *30*(6), 1819–1839. DOI: 10.1111/poms.13326

Cho, M. (2024). *Protecting Financial Consumers in the Era of BD• ML Innovations: What Behavioral Patterns to be Tamed?* And How.

Chowdhury, G. (2020). Natural language processing. *Annual Review of Information Science & Technology*, *54*(1), 1–42. DOI: 10.1002/aris.201900046

Chui, A. C., Titman, S., & Wei, K. C. (2010). Individualism and momentum around the world. *The Journal of Finance*, *65*(1), 361–392. DOI: 10.1111/j.1540-6261.2009.01532.x

Chun, W. H. K. (2021). *Discriminating data: Correlation, neighborhoods, and the new politics of recognition.* MIT Press. DOI: 10.7551/mitpress/14050.001.0001

Cihon, P., Schuett, J., & Baum, S. D. (2021). Corporate governance of artificial intelligence in the public interest. *Information (Basel), 12*(7), 275. DOI: 10.3390/info12070275

Cockburn, I. M., Henderson, R., & Stern, S. (2018). The impact of artificial intelligence on innovation. *NBER Working Paper No. 24449*. DOI: 10.3386/w24449

Cockfield, A. (2021). Secrets of the Panama papers: How tax havens exacerbate income inequality. Colum. *J. Tax L., 13*(1), 45–76. DOI: 10.52214/cjtl.v13i1.8979

Coe, N. M., Lai, K. P. Y., & Wójcik, D. (2014). *Integrating economic geography and global finance*. Routledge.

Cohen, A. (2025). Browser Security Posture Analysis: A Client-Side Security Assessment Framework. arXiv preprint arXiv:2505.08050.

Coman, D. M., Ionescu, C. A., Duică, A., Coman, M. D., Uzlau, M. C., Stanescu, S. G., & State, V. (2022). Digitization of Accounting: The Premise of the Paradigm Shift of Role of the Professional Accountant. *Applied Sciences (Basel, Switzerland), 12*(7), 20763417. DOI: 10.3390/app12073359

Cont, R. (2001). Empirical properties of asset returns: Stylized facts and statistical issues. *Quantitative Finance, 1*(2), 223–236. DOI: 10.1080/713665670

Costa, M., Goldberger, A. L., & Peng, C. K. (2005). Multiscale entropy analysis of complex physiologic time series. *Physical Review Letters, 95*(19), 198102. DOI: 10.1103/PhysRevLett.95.198102 PMID: 16384029

Costanza-Chock, S., Raji, I. D., & Buolamwini, J. (2022). Towards ethical algorithm auditing: Recommendations for the field. *Proceedings of the ACM Conference on Fairness, Accountability, and Transparency (FAccT)*.

Cover, T. M., & Thomas, J. A. (2006). *Elements of information theory* (2nd ed.). Wiley.

Crawford, K. (2021). *Atlas of AI: Power, politics, and the planetary costs of artificial intelligence*. Yale University Press.

Cumming, D., Hou, W., Lee, E., & Wei, J. (2024). Ethical governance frameworks for AI auditing. *Journal of Business Ethics*.

Cummings, M. L. (2017). Artificial intelligence and the future of warfare. *Chatham House Report*.

Daníelsson, J. (2022). *The illusion of control: why financial crises happen, and what we can (and can't) do about it*. Yale University Press.

Darbellay, G. A., & Wuertz, D. (2000). The entropy as a tool for analysing statistical dependences in financial time series. *Physica A, 287*(3–4), 429–439. DOI: 10.1016/S0378-4371(00)00382-4

Dasgupta, D., & Sen, S. (2022). An empirical study of algorithmic bias. In *Handbook on computer learning and intelligence* (Vol. 2, pp. 895–922). Deep Learning, Intelligent Control and Evolutionary Computation.

Davenport, T. H., & Ronanki, R. (2018). Artificial intelligence for the real world. *Harvard Business Review*, *96*(1), 108–116.

Davies, D. (2025). *The Unaccountability Machine: Why Big Systems Make Terrible Decisions—and How the World Lost Its Mind*. University of Chicago Press.

de Fine Licht, K. (2025). Resolving value conflicts in public AI governance: A procedural justice framework. *Government Information Quarterly*, *42*(2), 102033. DOI: 10.1016/j.giq.2025.102033

Devore, J. L., Berk, K. N., & Carlton, M. A. (2021). *Modern mathematical statistics with applications*. Springer Nature. DOI: 10.1007/978-3-030-55156-8

Dewi, I. (2022). Process of Vendor Bill Payment. *Lead Journal of Economy and Administration*, *1*(1), 8–13. DOI: 10.56403/lejea.v1i1.33

Dietvorst, B. J., Simmons, J. P., & Massey, C. (2015). Algorithm aversion: People erroneously avoid algorithms after seeing them err. *Journal of Experimental Psychology. General, 144*(1), 114–126. DOI: 10.1037/xge0000033 PMID: 25401381

Domingos, P. (2015). *The master algorithm: How the quest for the ultimate learning machine will remake our world.* Basic Books.

Dragar, F. (2025). Learnable Fingerprints for Large Language Models (Master's thesis).

Drucker, P. (1954). *The practice of management.* Harper & Row.

Duggineni, S. (2023). Challenges in auditing AI-driven financial environments. *Science and Technology Journal, 22*(4), 77–92.

Dyck, A., Morse, A., & Zingales, L. (2024). How pervasive is corporate fraud? *Review of Accounting Studies, 29*(1), 736–769. DOI: 10.1007/s11142-022-09738-5

Esposito, C., Landrum, G. A., Schneider, N., Stiefl, N., & Riniker, S. (2021). GHOST: Adjusting the decision threshold to handle imbalanced data in machine learning. *Journal of Chemical Information and Modeling, 61*(6), 2623–2640. DOI: 10.1021/acs.jcim.1c00160 PMID: 34100609

European Central Bank. (2021). *Financial Stability Review.* https://www.ecb.europa.eu/pub/financial-stability/fsr/html/index.en.html

European Commission. (2021). *Proposal for a Regulation laying down harmonised rules on artificial intelligence (Artificial Intelligence Act).* COM(2021) 206 final.

Fährmann, D., Martín, L., Sánchez, L., & Damer, N. (2024). Anomaly detection in smart environments: A comprehensive survey. *IEEE Access : Practical Innovations, Open Solutions, 12*, 64006–64049. DOI: 10.1109/ACCESS.2024.3395051

Fang, Y., Lai, K. K., & Wang, S. (2017). Portfolio optimization using relative entropy. *European Journal of Operational Research, 259*(1), 355–365. DOI: 10.1016/j.ejor.2016.10.039

Farrell, H., & Newman, A. (2019). Weaponized interdependence: How global economic networks shape state coercion. *International Security, 44*(1), 42–79. DOI: 10.1162/isec_a_00351

Faulconbridge, J. R., Sarwar, A., & Spring, M. (2024). Accommodating Machine Learning Algorithms in Professional Service Firms. *Organization Studies, 1708406*(7), 1009–1037. Advance online publication. DOI: 10.1177/01708406241252930

Ferrara, E. (2024). Understanding the butterfly effect in AI auditing. *Machine Learning with Applications, 10*, 100214.

Fine, B. (2018). *Value and price: An economic history of theories*. Routledge.

Firoozi, A. A., & Firoozi, A. A. (2024). Ethical Design and Development Guidelines. In *Revolutionizing Civil Engineering with Neuromorphic Computing: Pathways to Smart and Sustainable Infrastructure* (pp. 81–97). Springer Nature Switzerland. DOI: 10.1007/978-3-031-71097-1_10

Fischer, T., & Krauss, C. (2018). Deep learning with long short-term memory networks for financial market predictions. *European Journal of Operational Research, 270*(2), 654–669. DOI: 10.1016/j.ejor.2017.11.054

Floridi, L. (2023). The ethics of artificial intelligence: Principles, challenges, and opportunities.

Fotoh, L. E., & Lorentzon, J. I. (2023). The digitalization of audit: Expectations versus realities. *Accounting Horizons, 37*(1), 71–90.

Fox, J. (2022). *Accountability keywords*. Accountability Research Center.

Friedman, B., & Hendry, D. G. (2019). *Value sensitive design: Shaping technology with moral imagination*. MIT Press. DOI: 10.7551/mitpress/7585.001.0001

Fülöp, M. T., Topor, D. I., Ionescu, C. A., Cifuentes-Faura, J., & Măgda , N. (2023). Ethical concerns associated with Artificial Intelligence in the Accounting profession: A curse or a blessing? *Journal of Business Economics and Management, 24*(2), 387–404. DOI: 10.3846/jbem.2023.19251

Fulton, R., Fulton, D., Hayes, N., & Kaplan, S. (2024). The Transformation Risk-Benefit Model of Artificial Intelligence: Balancing Risks and Benefits Through Practical Solutions and Use Cases. arXiv preprint arXiv:2406.11863.

Galaz, V., Centeno, M. A., Callahan, P. W., Causevic, A., Patterson, T., Brass, I., & Levy, K. (2021). Artificial intelligence, systemic risks, and sustainability. *Technology in Society*, *67*, 101741. DOI: 10.1016/j.techsoc.2021.101741

Galdon Clavell, G. (2020). Data protection and AI in the auditing sector. *Technology and Regulation*, *10*(1), 22–31.

Gaudio, G. (2021). Algorithmic bosses can't lie! How to foster transparency and limit abuses of the new algorithmic managers. *Comp. Lab. L. & Pol'y J.*, *42*, 707.

Geiger, T. J. (2023). Enhancing audit trust through continuous monitoring and AI fairness. *Journal of Accounting and Organizational Change*, *19*(2), 289–309.

George, G., Haas, M. R., & Pentland, A. (2021). Big data and management. *Academy of Management Journal*, *64*(3), 584–590. DOI: 10.5465/amj.2021.4003

Ghosh, A., Choudhury, S. R., & Bhadury, A. (2019). Satellite data and economic forecasting: A review. *Economic Modelling*, *80*, 43–54. DOI: 10.1016/j.econmod.2019.05.002

Gigerenzer, G. (2022). *How to stay smart in a smart world: Why human intelligence still beats algorithms*. MIT Press.

Gonçalves, M. J. A., da Silva, A. C. F., & Ferreira, C. G. (2022). The Future of Accounting: How Will Digital Transformation Impact the Sector? *Informatics (MDPI)*, *9*(1), 22279709. DOI: 10.3390/informatics9010019

González-Sendino, R., Fernández-Llamas, C., & García-Díaz, V. (2023). Fairness, accountability, and bias in AI systems: Implications for auditing. *Journal of Artificial Intelligence Research*, *76*, 1–25.

Goodell, J. W., Kumar, S., & Lim, W. M. (2021). Artificial intelligence and machine learning in financial forecasting. *Journal of Behavioral and Experimental Finance*, *32*, 100574. DOI: 10.1016/j.jbef.2021.100574

Goodfellow, I., Bengio, Y., & Courville, A. (2016). *Deep learning*. MIT Press.

Gorton, G. (2010). *Slapped by the invisible hand: The panic of 2007*. Oxford University Press.

Gouldner, A. W. (1954). *Patterns of industrial bureaucracy*. Free Press.

Government of Canada. (2020). *Directive on automated decision-making*. Treasury Board Secretariat.

Grewal, D., Hulland, J., Kopalle, P. K., & Karahanna, E. (2020). The future of technology and marketing: A multidisciplinary perspective. *Journal of the Academy of Marketing Science*, *48*(1), 1–8. DOI: 10.1007/s11747-019-00711-4

Grigonytė, G. (2023). Assessing the influence of artificial intelligence on the auditor profession: a qualitative study (Doctoral dissertation, Kauno technologijos universitetas.).

Grosu, V., Cosmulese, C. G., Socoliuc, M., Ciubotariu, M. S., & Mihaila, S. (2023). Testing accountants' perceptions of the digitization of the profession and profiling the future professional. *Technological Forecasting and Social Change*, *193*, 122630. DOI: 10.1016/j.techfore.2023.122630

Gunning, D., & Aha, D. W. (2019). DARPA's explainable artificial intelligence (XAI) program. *AI Magazine*, *40*(2), 44–58. DOI: 10.1609/aimag.v40i2.2850

Hachem, K., & Song, Z. (2016). Liquidity regulation and unintended financial transformation in China. *NBER Working Paper No. 21880*. DOI: 10.3386/w21880

Haefner, N., & Sternberg, R. (2020). AI-enabled innovation management: Opportunities and challenges. *Technovation*, *98*, 102176. DOI: 10.1016/j.technovation.2020.102176

Haefner, N., Wincent, J., Parida, V., & Gassmann, O. (2021). Artificial intelligence and innovation management: A review, framework, and research agenda. *Technological Forecasting and Social Change*, *162*, 120392. DOI: 10.1016/j.techfore.2020.120392

Han, H. (2022). AI and blockchain in corporate governance: Implications for auditing. (Doctoral dissertation, Brunel University).

Handoko, B. L., Mulyawan, A. N., Samuel, J., Rianty, K. K., & Gunawa, S. (2019). Facing Industry Revolution 4.0 for Millennial Accountants. *International Journal of Innovative Technology and Exploring Engineering*, *9*(1), 1037–1042. DOI: 10.35940/ijitee.A4681.119119

Han, H., Shiwakoti, R. K., Jarvis, R., Mordi, C., & Botchie, D. (2023). Accounting and auditing blockchain review. International technology and artificial Intelligence: A literature review. *Journal of Accounting Information Systems*, *48*, 100598. DOI: 10.1016/j.accinf.2022.100598

Hartmann, F., Moers, F., & van Staden, C. (2024). Future standards for AI-enabled auditing. *International Journal of Auditing*, *28*(1), 15–30.

Hassan, M. (2024). Real-Time Risk Assessment in SaaS Payment Infrastructures: Examining Deep Learning Models and Deployment Strategies. *Transactions on Artificial Intelligence, Machine Learning, and Cognitive Systems*, *9*(3), 1–10.

Hendershott, T., Li, H., & Zhang, M. (2021). FinTech credit risk modeling using alternative data. *Journal of Financial Services Research*, *59*(2-3), 195–227. DOI: 10.1007/s10693-020-00339-w

Hezavehi, S. M., Weyns, D., Avgeriou, P., Calinescu, R., Mirandola, R., & Perez-Palacin, D. (2021). Uncertainty in self-adaptive systems: A research community perspective. [TAAS]. *ACM Transactions on Autonomous and Adaptive Systems*, *15*(4), 1–36. DOI: 10.1145/3487921

Hilal, W., Gadsden, S. A., & Yawney, J. (2022). Financial fraud: A review of anomaly detection techniques and recent advances. *Expert Systems with Applications*, *193*, 116429. DOI: 10.1016/j.eswa.2021.116429

Hildyard, N. (2023). Licensed larceny: Infrastructure, financial extraction and the Global South. In *Licensed larceny*. Manchester University Press. DOI: 10.7765/9781526169457.00009

Holmes, A. F., & Douglass, A. (2022). Artificial Intelligence: Reshaping the Accounting Profession and the Disruption to Accounting Education. *Journal of Emerging Technologies in Accounting*, *19*(1), 53–68, 15541908. DOI: 10.2308/JETA-2020-054

Horan, D. J. (2024). The Finer Points. In The Retailer's Guide to Loss Prevention and Security (pp. 145-218). Routledge. DOI: 10.4324/9781003575092-13

Huang, R., & Pierri, N. (2022). Fintech credit and shadow banking: Evidence from China. *Journal of Banking & Finance*, *137*, 106441. DOI: 10.1016/j.jbankfin.2022.106441

Huang, X., Zhou, H., & Zhu, H. (2015). A framework for assessing the systemic risk of major financial institutions. *Journal of Banking & Finance*, *79*, 283–296. DOI: 10.1016/j.jbankfin.2015.06.014

Hu, H., Shao, H., & Zhang, Y. (2021). Upskilling auditors for AI-based audit technologies: A systematic review. *Journal of Accounting Education*, *57*, 100748.

Hullman, J., Kapoor, S., Nanayakkara, P., Gelman, A., & Narayanan, A. (2022, July). The worst of both worlds: A comparative analysis of errors in learning from data in psychology and machine learning. In Proceedings of the 2022 AAAI/ACM Conference on AI, Ethics, and Society (pp. 335-348). DOI: 10.1145/3514094.3534196

Ilyas, A., Park, S. M., Engstrom, L., Leclerc, G., & Madry, A. (2022). Datamodels: Predicting predictions from training data. arXiv preprint arXiv:2202.00622.

IMF. (2016). *Macroprudential policy: Experiences and lessons for Asia and the Pacific*. International Monetary Fund.

Islam, R. (2024). Data governance strategies for AI audits. *Information Systems Management, 41*(1), 45–59.

Issar, S., & Aneesh, A. (2022). What is algorithmic governance? *Sociology Compass, 16*(1), e12955. DOI: 10.1111/soc4.12955

Ivanov, D., & Dolgui, A. (2020). Viability of intertwined supply networks: Extending the supply chain resilience angles towards survivability. *International Journal of Production Research, 58*(10), 2904–2915. DOI: 10.1080/00207543.2020.1750727

Jackson, G. (2024). *Courage, Clarity, and Confidence: Redefine Success and the Way You Work.* John Wiley & Sons.

Jacobs, A. M., Büthe, T., Arjona, A., Arriola, L. R., Bellin, E., Bennett, A., Björkman, L., Bleich, E., Elkins, Z., Fairfield, T., Gaikwad, N., Greitens, S. C., Hawkesworth, M., Herrera, V., Herrera, Y. M., Johnson, K. S., Karakoç, E., Koivu, K., Kreuzer, M., & Yashar, D. J. (2021). The qualitative transparency deliberations: Insights and implications. *Perspectives on Politics, 19*(1), 171–208. DOI: 10.1017/S1537592720001164

Jarrahi, M. H., Askay, D., Eshraghi, A., & Smith, P. (2023). Artificial intelligence and knowledge management: A partnership between human and AI. *Business Horizons, 66*(1), 87–99. DOI: 10.1016/j.bushor.2022.03.002

Jauhiainen, T., & Lehner, O. M. (2022). AI governance and the transformation of accounting practices. In *Artificial Intelligence in Accounting* (pp. 103–124). Routledge.

Jaya, I.M.L.M., & Ilahiyah, M.E. (2024). Harmonizing accounting and artificial intelligence for the sustainability of the accounting profession. Artificial Intelligence Approaches to Sustainable Accounting, 214-228. .DOI: 10.4018/979-8-3693-0847-9.ch012

Jaynes, E. T. (1957). Information theory and statistical mechanics. *Physical Review, 106*(4), 620–630. DOI: 10.1103/PhysRev.106.620

Jean, N., Burke, M., Xie, M., Davis, W. M., Lobell, D. B., & Ermon, S. (2016). Combining satellite imagery and machine learning to predict poverty. *Science*, *353*(6301), 790–794. DOI: 10.1126/science.aaf7894 PMID: 27540167

Johnson, N. F., Zhao, G., Hunsader, E., Meng, J., Ravindar, A., Carran, S., & Tivnan, B. (2013). Abrupt rise of new machine ecology beyond human response time. *Scientific Reports*, *3*(1), 2627. DOI: 10.1038/srep02627 PMID: 24022120

Johora, F. T., Hasan, R., Farabi, S. F., Alam, M. Z., Sarkar, M. I., & Al Mahmud, M. A. (2024, June). AI Advances: Enhancing Banking Security with Fraud Detection. In *2024 First International Conference on Technological Innovations and Advance Computing (TIACOMP)* (pp. 289-294). IEEE. DOI: 10.1109/TIACOMP64125.2024.00055

Jordan, M. I., & Mitchell, T. M. (2015). Machine learning: Trends, perspectives, and prospects. *Science*, *349*(6245), 255–260. DOI: 10.1126/science.aaa8415 PMID: 26185243

Jordan, M. I., & Russell, S. J. (2020). Artificial intelligence: The revolution has not happened yet. *Harvard Data Science Review*, *2*(1), 1–19. DOI: 10.1162/99608f92.f06c6e61

Jorion, P. (2007). *Value at risk: The new benchmark for managing financial risk* (3rd ed.). McGraw-Hill.

Kaakandikar, R. (2025). Ethical and Inclusive Upskilling for the AI Revolution. Available at *SSRN* 5169844. DOI: 10.2139/ssrn.5169844

Kalusivalingam, A. K., Sharma, A., Patel, N., & Singh, V. (2022). Enhancing Corporate Governance and Compliance through AI: Implementing Natural Language Processing and Machine Learning Algorithms. *International Journal of Artificial Intelligence and Machine Learning*, *3*(9).

Kamau, C. G., & Ilamoya, S. L. (2023). Accounting profession: African perspective review of steps into the future. *Multidisciplinary Journal of TUM*, *2*(1), 19–26. DOI: 10.48039/mjtum.v2i1.43

Kamuangu, P. (2024). A Review on Financial Fraud Detection using AI and Machine Learning. Journal of Economics. *Finance and Accounting Studies*, *6*(1), 67–77.

Kapoor, A., & Chatterjee, S. (2023). *Platform and Model Design for Responsible AI: Design and build resilient, private, fair, and transparent machine learning models*. Packt Publishing Ltd.

Karlsson, F., Kolkowska, E., & Petersson, J. (2022). Information security policy compliance-eliciting requirements for a computerized software to support value-based compliance analysis. *Computers & Security, 114*, 102578. DOI: 10.1016/j.cose.2021.102578

Kellogg, K. C., Valentine, M. A., & Christin, A. (2020). Algorithms at work: The new contested terrain of control. *The Academy of Management Annals*, *14*(1), 366–410. DOI: 10.5465/annals.2018.0174

Kenney, M., & Zysman, J. (2016). The rise of the platform economy. *Issues in Science and Technology*, *32*(3), 61–69.

Kenton, W., & Mulligan, C. (2021). Alternative data in finance: The rise of nontraditional sources. *Journal of Investment Management*, *19*(1), 33–48.

Kindleberger, C. P. (1993). *A financial history of Western Europe* (2nd ed.). Oxford University Press.

King, M. R., Osler, C. L., & Rime, D. (2011). *Foreign exchange market structure, players, and evolution. Handbook of Exchange Rates*. Wiley.

Kirilenko, A. A., Kyle, A. S., Samadi, M., & Tuzun, T. (2017). The flash crash: High-frequency trading in an electronic market. *The Journal of Finance*, *72*(3), 967–998. DOI: 10.1111/jofi.12498

Kirsop-Taylor, N. (2022). Leaping forwards, bouncing forwards, or just bouncing back: Resilience in environmental public agencies through after the austerity decade. *Environmental Management*, *70*(5), 697–709. DOI: 10.1007/s00267-022-01701-z PMID: 36008627

Kjoersvik, O., & Bate, A. (2022). Black swan events and intelligent automation for routine safety surveillance. *Drug Safety*, *45*(5), 419–427. DOI: 10.1007/s40264-022-01169-0 PMID: 35579807

Kleinberg, J., Ludwig, J., Mullainathan, S., & Sunstein, C. R. (2018). Discrimination in the age of algorithms. *The Journal of Legal Analysis*, *10*(2), 113–174. DOI: 10.1093/jla/laz001

Knechel, W. R., & Mintchik, N. (2022). Do personal beliefs and values affect an individual's "fraud tolerance"? Evidence from the World Values Survey. *Journal of Business Ethics*, *177*(2), 1–27. DOI: 10.1007/s10551-020-04704-0

Knight, F. H. (1921). *Risk, uncertainty, and profit*. Houghton Mifflin.

Koffman, T. (2024). *Myth of money: breaking out of the failing financial system*. John Wiley & Sons.

Kölbel, J. F., Heeb, F., Paetzold, F., & Busch, T. (2020). Can sustainable investing save the world? Reviewing the mechanisms of investor impact. *Organization & Environment*, *33*(4), 554–574. DOI: 10.1177/1086026620919202

Kopp, E., Kaffenberger, L., & Wilson, C. (2017). Cyber risk, market failures, and financial stability. *IMF Working Paper WP/17/185*.

Korhonen, T., Selos, E., Laine, T., & Suomala, P. (2021). Exploring the programmability of management accounting work for increasing automation: An interventionist case study. *Accounting, Auditing & Accountability Journal*, *34*(2), 253–280, 9513574. DOI: 10.1108/AAAJ-12-2016-2809

Korn, J. (2024). Ensemble Classification: An Analysis of the Random Forest Model.

Koshiyama, A., Kazim, E., & Preece, A. (2024). Algorithmic auditing and governance: A comprehensive framework. *Royal Society Open Science*, *11*(1), 210534.

Kothandapani, H. P. (2022). Advanced Artificial Intelligence models for Real-Time monitoring and prediction of macroprudential risks in the housing finance sector: addressing interest rate shocks and housing price volatility to support proactive Decision-Making by federal agencies. Journal of Artificial Intelligence Research. https://thesciencebrigade. com/JAIR/article/view/507

Kour, M., & Kour, R. (2024). AI and Influencer Marketing: Redefining the Future of Social Media Marketing in Industry 6.0. In Advanced Businesses in Industry 6.0 (pp. 87-103). IGI Global DOI: 10.4018/979-8-3693-3108-8.ch007

Kozlowski, A. C., Taddy, M., & Evans, J. A. (2022). The geometry of culture: Word embeddings and cultural analysis. *American Sociological Review*, *87*(5), 947–981. DOI: 10.1177/00031224221107354

Kristianto, A. H., Widya, P. R., & Nadapdap, J. P. (2021). The portrait of the underground economy and tax evasion: descriptive analysis from border region.

Kroll, J. A., Huey, J., Barocas, S., Felten, E. W., Reidenberg, J. R., Robinson, D. G., & Yu, H. (2017). Accountable algorithms. *University of Pennsylvania Law Review*, *165*(3), 633–705.

Kroon, N., & do Céu Alves, M. (2023). Examining the fit between supply and demand of the accounting professional's competencies: A systematic literature review. *International Journal of Management Education*, *21*(3), 100872. DOI: 10.1016/j.ijme.2023.100872

Kumar, M., Sharma, S., & Bakare, A. (2023). Evaluating the impact of real-time auditing platforms: The case of KPMG's Clara. *Audit Innovation Journal*, *9*(2), 64–82.

Kunkel, R. J. (2022). Artificial intelligence, automation, and proletarianization of the legal profession. *Creighton Law Review*, *56*, 69.

La Porta, R., Lopez-de-Silanes, F., Shleifer, A., & Vishny, R. (1998). Law and finance. *Journal of Political Economy*, *106*(6), 1113–1155. DOI: 10.1086/250042

Laibson, D. (1997). Golden eggs and hyperbolic discounting. *The Quarterly Journal of Economics*, *112*(2), 443–478. DOI: 10.1162/003355397555253

Laine, J., Minkkinen, M., & Mäntymäki, M. (2024). Ethics-based auditing frameworks for AI systems. *Information & Management*, *61*(2), 103624.

Lansing, A. E., Romero, N. J., Siantz, E., Silva, V., Center, K., Casteel, D., & Gilmer, T. (2023). Building trust: Leadership reflections on community empowerment and engagement in a large urban initiative. *BMC Public Health*, *23*(1), 1252. DOI: 10.1186/s12889-023-15860-z PMID: 37380973

Larioui, A., & Himran, M. (2023). Impact of Artificial Intelligence on Operational Management and Accounting. *La Revue des Sciences Commerciales*, *22*(1), 22–44.

Laux, C., & Leuz, C. (2009). The crisis of fair-value accounting: Making sense of the recent debate. *Accounting, Organizations and Society*, *34*(6–7), 826–834. DOI: 10.1016/j.aos.2009.04.003

Lee, H. (2024). Enhancing the world by mitigating fraud and emphasizing the significance of ethics.

Lee, M. K., Kusbit, D., Metsky, E., & Dabbish, L. (2015). Working with machines: The impact of algorithmic and data-driven management on human workers. *Proceedings of the 33rd Annual ACM Conference on Human Factors in Computing Systems*, 1603–1612. DOI: 10.1145/2702123.2702548

Leiponen, A. (2021). Digital platforms and management education: Rethinking curriculum design in the age of AI. *Academy of Management Learning & Education*, *20*(4), 443–456. DOI: 10.5465/amle.2020.0059

Leiser, M., & Lodder, A. R. (2024). The GDPR at a Crossroads: From Pioneering to Uncertainty.

Lepri, B., Oliver, N., Letouzé, E., Pentland, A., & Vinck, P. (2018). Fair, transparent, and accountable algorithmic decision-making processes. *Philosophy & Technology*, *31*(4), 611–627. DOI: 10.1007/s13347-017-0279-x

Levin, C., & Madsbjerg, C. (2022). *The rise of techno-strategy: Managing in an algorithmic age*. Harvard Business Press.

Liao, F.-N., Zhang, C., Zhang, J.-J., Yan, X., & Chen, T.-X. (2024). Hyperbole or reality? The effect of auditors' AI education on audit report timeliness. *International Review of Financial Analysis, 91*, 10575219. DOI: 10.1016/j.irfa.2023.103050

Lim, B., & Zohren, S. (2020). Time-series forecasting with deep learning. *Philosophical Transactions of the Royal Society A, 378*(2164), 20190147. DOI: 10.1098/rsta.2019.0147

Lin, H. (2024). Ethical and Scalable Automation: A Governance and Compliance Framework for Business Applications. arXiv preprint arXiv:2409.16872.

Liu, Y., Li, M., & Liu, B. (2020). Anomaly detection techniques for financial fraud detection: A review. *ACM Computing Surveys, 53*(4), 1–36. DOI: 10.1145/3357375

Liu, Z., & Zheng, Y. (2022). *AI ethics and governance*. Springer Singapore. DOI: 10.1007/978-981-19-2531-3

Li, Z., Liu, F., Yang, W., Peng, S., & Zhou, J. (2021). A survey of convolutional neural networks: Analysis, applications, and prospects. *IEEE Transactions on Neural Networks and Learning Systems, 33*(12), 6999–7019. DOI: 10.1109/TNNLS.2021.3084827 PMID: 34111009

Lokanan, M. E., & Maddhesia, V. (2025). Supply chain fraud prediction with machine learning and artificial intelligence. *International Journal of Production Research, 63*(1), 286–313. DOI: 10.1080/00207543.2024.2361434

Long, D., & Magerko, B. (2020). What is AI literacy? Competencies and design considerations. *Proceedings of the 2020 CHI Conference on Human Factors in Computing Systems*, 1–16. DOI: 10.1145/3313831.3376727

Longoni, C., Bonezzi, A., & Morewedge, C. K. (2019). Resistance to medical artificial intelligence. *The Journal of Consumer Research, 46*(4), 629–650. DOI: 10.1093/jcr/ucz013

Longoni, C., & Cian, L. (2022). Artificial intelligence in strategy: Implications for managers and consumers. *Journal of the Academy of Marketing Science, 50*(5), 930–950. DOI: 10.1007/s11747-021-00842-8

Lopes, C. (2024). The Disappointing Discussion About Aid Effectiveness. In *The Self-Deception Trap: Exploring the Economic Dimensions of Charity Dependency within Africa-Europe Relations* (pp. 39–57). Springer Nature Switzerland. DOI: 10.1007/978-3-031-57591-4_3

Lum, K., & Isaac, W. (2016). To predict and serve? *Significance, 13*(5), 14–19. DOI: 10.1111/j.1740-9713.2016.00960.x

Lu, N., Liu, L., Yu, D., & Fu, B. (2021). Navigating trade-offs in the social-ecological systems. *Current Opinion in Environmental Sustainability, 48*, 77–84. DOI: 10.1016/j.cosust.2020.10.014

Maasoumi, E. (1993). A compendium to information theory in economics and econometrics. *Econometric Reviews, 12*(2), 137–181. DOI: 10.1080/07474939308800260

MacKenzie, D. (2021). *Trading at the speed of light: How ultrafast algorithms are transforming financial markets*. Princeton University Press.

Magliocca, P., Canestrino, R., Carayannis, E. G., & Gagliardi, A. R. (2024). Understanding human–technology interaction: Evolving boundaries. *European Journal of Innovation Management*. Advance online publication. DOI: 10.1108/EJIM-04-2024-0341

Mahalakshmi, V., Kulkarni, N., Kumar, K. P., Kumar, K. S., Sree, D. N., & Durga, S. (2022). The role of implementing artificial intelligence and machine learning technologies in the financial services industry for creating competitive intelligence. *Materials Today: Proceedings, 56*, 2252–2255. DOI: 10.1016/j.matpr.2021.11.577

Makurumidze, S., Sifile, O., Twesige, D., Gasheja, F., Gwangwava, E., Matowanyika, K., Chinofunga, S., Mbizi, R., & Sunday, K. (2024). Leveraging on the fourth industrial revolution by African accountants in the sustenance of SDGs and AU Agenda 2063. *Sustainable Development, 9680802*. Advance online publication. DOI: 10.1002/sd.3110

Mallick, M. A. I., & Nath, R. (2024). Navigating the cyber security landscape: A comprehensive review of cyber-attacks, emerging trends, and recent developments. *World Scientific News*, *190*(1), 1–69.

Mandelbrot, B. (1963). The variation of certain speculative prices. *The Journal of Business*, *36*(4), 394–419. DOI: 10.1086/294632

Marian, I. C. (2024). Evaluating the impact of artificial intelligence on business through sentiment analysis. Young Economists Journal/Revista Tinerilor Economisti, 21(43).

Markose, S., Giansante, S., & Shaghaghi, A. R. (2012). 'Too interconnected to fail' financial network of US CDS market: Topological fragility and systemic risk. *Journal of Economic Behavior & Organization*, *83*(3), 627–646. DOI: 10.1016/j.jebo.2012.05.016

Markowitz, H. (1952). Portfolio selection. *The Journal of Finance*, *7*(1), 77–91. DOI: 10.1111/j.1540-6261.1952.tb01525.x

Martino, P. (2021). *Blockchain and banking: How technological innovations are shaping the banking industry*. Springer Nature. DOI: 10.1007/978-3-030-70970-9

Marwala, T. (2024). *The Balancing Problem in the Governance of Artificial Intelligence*. Springer. DOI: 10.1007/978-981-97-9251-1

Mateescu, A., & Nguyen, A. (2019). *Explainer: Workplace monitoring & surveillance*. Data & Society Research Institute.

Matthias, A. (2004). The responsibility gap: Ascribing responsibility for the actions of learning automata. *Ethics and Information Technology*, *6*(3), 175–183. DOI: 10.1007/s10676-004-3422-1

Mayer, C., Danelljan, M., Bhat, G., Paul, M., Paudel, D. P., Yu, F., & Van Gool, L. (2022). Transforming model prediction for tracking. In *Proceedings of the IEEE/CVF conference on computer vision and pattern recognition* (pp. 8731-8740).

McGowan, V. C., & Bell, P. (2022). "I now deeply care about the effects humans are having on the world": Cultivating ecological care and responsibility through complex systems modelling and investigations. *Educational and Developmental Psychologist*, *39*(1), 116–131. DOI: 10.1080/20590776.2022.2027212

Mehrabi, N., Morstatter, F., Saxena, N., Lerman, K., & Galstyan, A. (2021). A survey on bias and fairness in machine learning. *ACM Computing Surveys*, *54*(6), 1–35. DOI: 10.1145/3457607

Merkel, W. (2023). What Is Democratic Resilience and How Can We Strengthen It. *Policy Brief*, (169), 1–15.

Mikalef, P., Pappas, I. O., Krogstie, J., & Giannakos, M. (2020). Big data analytics capabilities: A systematic literature review. *Information Systems and e-Business Management*, *18*(3), 547–574. DOI: 10.1007/s10257-017-0362-y

Miller, H., & Raji, I. D. (2022). Out of one, many: Using AI for financial inclusion globally. *Patterns (New York, N.Y.)*, *3*(7), 100542. DOI: 10.1016/j.patter.2022.100542

Minkkinen, M., Laine, J., & Mäntymäki, M. (2022). Continuous auditing of AI systems: Toward dynamic audit processes. *Digital Society : Ethics, Socio-Legal and Governance of Digital Technology*, *1*(1), 1–17.

Mitchell, M. (2021). Why AI is harder than we think. arXiv preprint arXiv:2104.12871. DOI: 10.1145/3449639.3465421

Möhlmann, M., & Zalmanson, L. (2017). Hands on the wheel: Navigating algorithmic management and Uber drivers' autonomy. *Proceedings of the International Conference on Information Systems*.

Mökander, J. (2022). Conformity assessments and audits in European AI governance. *Minds and Machines*, *32*(1), 123–149.

Mökander, J. (2023). The interpretive turn in AI auditing: Human-machine collaboration. *AI and Ethics*, *3*(1), 79–98.

Moll J., & Yigitbasioglu O. (2019). The role of internet-related technologies in shaping the work of accountants: New directions for accounting research. The British Accounting Review, 51(6), 8908389. DOI: 10.1016/j.bar.2019.04.002

Monetary Authority of Singapore. (2018). *Principles to promote fairness, ethics, accountability and transparency in the use of AI and data analytics in financial services.*

Monett, D., & Grigorescu, B. (2024, October). Deconstructing the AI myth: Fallacies and harms of algorithmification. In European Conference on e-Learning (Vol. 23, pp. 242-248). Academic Conferences International Limited.

Moore, P. V. (2018). Tracking affective labour for agility in the quantified workplace. *Body & Society, 24*(3), 27–55. DOI: 10.1177/1357034X18775203

Moore, P. V., Upchurch, M., & Whittaker, X. (2018). *Humans and machines at work: Monitoring, surveillance and automation in contemporary capitalism*. Palgrave Macmillan. DOI: 10.1007/978-3-319-58232-0

Moore, W. B., & Felo, A. (2022). The evolution of accounting technology education: Analytics to STEM. *Journal of Education for Business, 97*(2), 105–111, 8832323. DOI: 10.1080/08832323.2021.1895045

Munoko, I., Brown-Liburd, H. L., & Vasarhelyi, M. A. (2020). The ethical implications of using artificial intelligence in auditing. *Journal of Business Ethics, 167*(2), 209–234. DOI: 10.1007/s10551-019-04407-1

Munteanu, V., Zuca, M. R., Horaicu, A., Florea, L. A., Poenaru, C. E., & Anghel, G. (2024). Auditing the risk of financial fraud using the red flags technique. *Applied Sciences (Basel, Switzerland), 14*(2), 757. DOI: 10.3390/app14020757

Murugan, M. S., & T, S. K. (2023). Large-scale data-driven financial risk management & analysis using machine learning strategies. *Measurement. Sensors, 27*, 100756. DOI: 10.1016/j.measen.2023.100756

Musa, A.M.H., & Lefkir, H. (2024). The role of artificial intelligence in achieving auditing quality for small and medium enterprises in the Kingdom of Saudi Arabia. International Journal of Data and Network Science, 8(2), 835-844. .DOI: 10.5267/j.ijdns.2023.12.021

Mutemi, A., & Bacao, F. (2023). A numeric-based machine learning design for detecting organized retail fraud in digital marketplaces. *Scientific Reports*, *13*(1), 12499. DOI: 10.1038/s41598-023-38304-5 PMID: 37532696

Narayanan, A. (2023). Regulating AI: The EU AI Act and its implications for financial services. *AI & Society*, *38*(2), 567–581. DOI: 10.1007/s00146-022-01407-5

Nash, J., Smith, C., & Zhao, Y. (2022). Alternative data in financial decision-making: The role of artificial intelligence. *The Journal of Financial Data Science*, *4*(3), 12–29. DOI: 10.3905/jfds.2022.1.089

Nguyen, T., Yoon, J., & Lee, J. (2021). AI-based scenario simulation for strategic decision-making. *Technological Forecasting and Social Change*, *171*, 120963. DOI: 10.1016/j.techfore.2021.120963

Njoku, D. O., Iwuchukwu, V. C., Jibiri, J. E., Ikwuazom, C. T., Ofoegbu, C. I., & Nwokoma, F. O. (2024). Machine learning approach for fraud detection system in financial institution: A web base application. Machine Learning, 20(4), 1-12.

O'Neil, C. (2016). *Weapons of math destruction: How big data increases inequality and threatens democracy*. Crown.

O'Reilly, C. A.III, & Tushman, M. L. (2013). Organizational ambidexterity: Past, present, and future. *The Academy of Management Perspectives*, *27*(4), 324–338. DOI: 10.5465/amp.2013.0025

Odeyemi, O., Bakare, A., & Kumar, M. (2024). Blockchain-based assurance in EY's auditing practices. *Accounting and Blockchain Review*, *5*(1), 12–33.

OECD. (2021). *AI in society: Implications for finance and governance*. OECD Publishing.

OECD. (2021). Artificial Intelligence, Machine Learning and Big Data in Finance: Opportunities, Challenges, and Implications for Policy Makers. https://www.oecd.org/finance/financial-markets/Artificial-intelligence -machine-learning-big- data-in-finance.pdf

Olushola, A., & Mart, J. (2024). Fraud Detection using Machine Learning. ScienceOpen *Preprints*.

Omoruyi, N. (2025). Advanced Computational Methods for Financial Planning and Analysis Risk Assessment using Data Science-Driven Model Validation Techniques. International Journal of Research Publication and Reviews. doi: https://www. semanticscholar. org/paper/4d27d96c40e-20c0bd7df2d9220bd4b355a381c82

Osei-Assibey Bonsu, M., Wang, Y., & Guo, Y. (2023). Does fintech lead to better accounting practices? Empirical evidence. *Accounting Research Journal*, *36*(2/3), 129–147, 10309616. DOI: 10.1108/ARJ-07-2022-0178

Owolabi, I. (2024). Regulation and assurance of AI in financial auditing: A global perspective. *International Journal of Accounting Information Systems*, *44*, 100614.

Parent-Rocheleau, X., & Parker, S. K. (2021). Algorithms as work designers: How algorithmic management influences job design. *Human Resource Management Review*, *31*(4), 100763. DOI: 10.1016/j.hrmr.2020.100763

Paschen, J., Pitt, C., & Kietzmann, J. (2020). Artificial intelligence in business-to-business marketing. *Journal of Business Research*, *116*, 209–220. DOI: 10.1016/j.jbusres.2020.05.001

Paschen, J., Wilson, M., & Ferreira, J. J. (2020). Collaborative intelligence: How human and artificial intelligence create value along the B2B sales funnel. *Business Horizons*, *63*(3), 403–414. DOI: 10.1016/j. bushor.2020.01.003

Pasquale, F. (2015). *The black box society: The secret algorithms that control money and information*. Harvard University Press. DOI: 10.4159/ harvard.9780674736061

Patel, P., & Uddin, M. N. (2022). Ethical AI auditing tools for big data systems. *International Journal of Stochastic Analysis*, *4*(1), 1–16.

Pauceanu, A. M., Rabie, N., & Moustafa, A. (2020). Employability under the Fourth Industrial Revolution. *Economics & Sociology (Ternopil)*, *13*(3), 269–283. DOI: 10.14254/2071-789X.2020/13-3/17

Petrini, L. (2023). Breaking the Curse of Dimensionality in Deep Neural Networks by Learning Invariant Representations. arXiv preprint arXiv:2310.16154.

Philippatos, G. C., & Wilson, C. J. (1972). Entropy, market risk, and the selection of efficient portfolios. *Applied Economics*, *4*(3), 209–220. DOI: 10.1080/00036847200000017

Pillai, V. (2022). *Anomaly Detection for Innovators: Transforming Data into Breakthroughs*. Libertatem Media Private Limited.

Pincus, S. M. (1991). Approximate entropy as a measure of system complexity. *Proceedings of the National Academy of Sciences of the United States of America*, *88*(6), 2297–2301. DOI: 10.1073/pnas.88.6.2297 PMID: 11607165

Praveen, R. V. S. (2024). *Data Engineering Concepts: From Basics To Advance Techniques*. Addition Publishing House.

Prianthara, I. B. T., Darmawan, N., Adriati, I. G. A. W., & Munidewi, I. A. B. (2021). Emotional Intelligence, Intellectual Intelligence, And Spiritual Intelligence Towards Professional Quality Of Accountant Development Artificial Intelligence As A Moderating Variable In The Era Of Industrial Revolution 4.0. *Academy of Strategic Management Journal*, *20*, 1–15.

Prokopenko, M., Boschetti, F., & Ryan, A. J. (2009). An information-theoretic primer on complexity, self-organization, and emergence. *Complexity*, *15*(1), 11–28. DOI: 10.1002/cplx.20249

Raghavan, M., Barocas, S., Kleinberg, J., & Levy, K. (2020). Mitigating bias in algorithmic hiring: Evaluating claims and practices. *Proceedings of the 2020 Conference on Fairness, Accountability, and Transparency*, 469–481. DOI: 10.1145/3351095.3372828

Rahwan, I., Cebrian, M., Obradovich, N., Bongard, J., Bonnefon, J.-F., Breazeal, C., Crandall, J. W., Christakis, N. A., Couzin, I. D., Jackson, M. O., Jennings, N. R., Kamar, E., Kloumann, I. M., Larochelle, H., Lazer, D., McElreath, R., Mislove, A., Parkes, D. C., Pentland, A. S., & Wellman, M. (2019). Machine behaviour. *Nature*, *568*(7753), 477–486. DOI: 10.1038/s41586-019-1138-y PMID: 31019318

Raisch, S., & Krakowski, S. (2021). Artificial intelligence and management: The automation–augmentation paradox. *Academy of Management Review*, *46*(1), 192–210. DOI: 10.5465/amr.2018.0072

Rajagopal, N. K., Qureshi, N. I., Durga, S., Ramirez Asis, E. H., Huerta Soto, R. M., Gupta, S. K., & Deepak, S. (2022). Future of business culture: An artificial intelligence-driven digital framework for organization decision-making process. *Complexity*, *2022*(1), 7796507. DOI: 10.1155/2022/7796507

Rajkomar, A., Dean, J., & Kohane, I. (2019). Machine learning in medicine. *The New England Journal of Medicine*, *380*(14), 1347–1358. DOI: 10.1056/NEJMra1814259 PMID: 30943338

Rane, N., Choudhary, S. P., & Rane, J. (2024). Ensemble deep learning and machine learning: Applications, opportunities, challenges, and future directions. *Studies in Medical and Health Sciences*, *1*(2), 18–41. DOI: 10.48185/smhs.v1i2.1225

Ransbotham, S., Kiron, D., & Prentice, P. (2017). Cognitive technologies in auditing: Early lessons. *MIT Sloan Management Review*, *58*(4), 1–12.

Rautiainen, A., Scapens, R. W., Järvenpää, M., Auvinen, T., & Sajasalo, P. (2024). Towards fluid role identity of management accountants: A case study of a Finnish bank. *The British Accounting Review*, *56*(4), 8908389. DOI: 10.1016/j.bar.2024.101341

Ravn, I. (2022). Beyond chaos and rigidity, flexstability. *New Ideas in Psychology*, *66*, 100948. DOI: 10.1016/j.newideapsych.2022.100948

Rawashdeh A. (2023). The consequences of artificial intelligence: an investigation into the impact of AI on job displacement in accounting. Journal of Science and Technology Policy Management. DOI: 10.1108/JSTPM-02-2023-0030

Rényi, A. (1961). On measures of entropy and information. *Proceedings of the Fourth Berkeley Symposium on Mathematics, Statistics and Probability, 1*, 547–561.

Richman, J. S., & Moorman, J. R. (2000). Physiological time-series analysis using approximate entropy and sample entropy. *American Journal of Physiology. Heart and Circulatory Physiology*, *278*(6), H2039–H2049. DOI: 10.1152/ajpheart.2000.278.6.H2039 PMID: 10843903

Ridwan, I. B. (2025). Dynamic strategic foresight using predictive business analytics: Strategic modeling of competitive advantage in unstable market and innovation ecosystems.

Rockström, J., Gupta, J., Lenton, T. M., Qin, D., Lade, S. J., Abrams, J. F., … Xu, J. (2021). Identifying a safe and just corridor for people and the planet. *Earth's Future, 9*(4), e2020EF001866. DOI: 10.1029/2020EF001866

Rolnick, D., Donti, P. L., Kaack, L. H., Kochanski, K., Lacoste, A., Sankaran, K., Ross, A. S., Milojevic-Dupont, N., Jaques, N., Waldman-Brown, A., Luccioni, A. S., Maharaj, T., Sherwin, E. D., Mukkavilli, S. K., Kording, K. P., Gomes, C. P., Ng, A. Y., Hassabis, D., Platt, J. C., & Bengio, Y. (2022). Tackling climate change with machine learning. *ACM Computing Surveys*, *55*(2), 1–96. DOI: 10.1145/3485128

Rosenblat, A. (2018). *Uberland: How algorithms are rewriting the rules of work.* University of California Press. DOI: 10.1525/9780520970632

Rudin, C., Chen, C., Chen, Z., Huang, H., Semenova, L., & Zhong, C. (2022). Interpretable machine learning: Fundamental principles and ten grand challenges. *Statistics Surveys*, *16*(none), 1–85. DOI: 10.1214/21-SS133

Rufo, D. D., Debelee, T. G., Ibenthal, A., & Negera, W. G. (2021). Diagnosis of diabetes mellitus using gradient boosting machine (LightGBM). *Diagnostics (Basel), 11*(9), 1714. DOI: 10.3390/diagnostics11091714 PMID: 34574055

Russell, S., & Norvig, P. (2021). *Artificial intelligence: A modern approach* (4th ed.). Pearson.

Salazar-Rebaza C., Chujutalli J.F., Ríos-Sánchez N., Salazar-Quispe A., & Cordova-Buiza F. (2024). Artificial intelligence in accounting as seen by accountants. RISTI - Revista Iberica de Sistemas e Tecnologias de Informacao, E69, 676-686.

Sama, L. M., Stefanidis, A., & Casselman, R. M. (2022). Rethinking corporate governance in the digital economy: The role of stewardship. *Business Horizons, 65*(5), 535–546. DOI: 10.1016/j.bushor.2021.08.001

Samanthi D., & Gooneratne T. (2023). Bean counter to value-adding business partner: the changing role of the accountant and situated rationality in a multinational firm. Journal of Accounting and Organizational Change, 19(3), 513-535. .DOI: 10.1108/JAOC-04-2022-0063

Sánchez-Zas, C., Villagrá, V. A., Vega-Barbas, M., Larriva-Novo, X., Moreno, J. I., & Berrocal, J. (2023). Ontology-based approach to real-time risk management and cyber-situational awareness. *Future Generation Computer Systems, 141*, 462–472. DOI: 10.1016/j.future.2022.12.006

Sandoval, L., & Franca, I. D. P. (2012). Correlation of financial markets in times of crisis. *Physica A, 391*(1–2), 187–208. DOI: 10.1016/j.physa.2011.07.023

Sarker, I. H. (2021). Machine learning: Algorithms, real-world applications and research directions. *SN Computer Science, 2*(3), 160. DOI: 10.1007/s42979-021-00592-x PMID: 33778771

Sasikala, B., & Sachan, S. (2024). Decoding decision-making: embracing explainable AI for trust and transparency. Exploring the frontiers of artificial intelligence and machine learning technologies, 42.

Sawyer, K. R. (2024). Scams: Blaming the Victims.

Schiff, D. S., Kelley, S., & Camacho Ibáñez, J. (2024). The emergence of artificial intelligence ethics auditing. *Big Data & Society*, *11*(4), 20539517241299732. DOI: 10.1177/20539517241299732

Schoemaker, P. J. H., Day, G. S., & Snyder, S. A. (2013). Integrating organizational networks, weak signals, strategic radars, and scenario planning. *Technological Forecasting and Social Change*, *80*(4), 815–824. DOI: 10.1016/j.techfore.2012.10.020

Schoemaker, P. J., & Tetlock, P. E. (2017). Building a more robust forecasting system: Lessons from the Good Judgment Project. *Harvard Business Review*, *95*(3), 72–77.

Schreiber, T. (2000). Measuring information transfer. *Physical Review Letters*, *85*(2), 461–464. DOI: 10.1103/PhysRevLett.85.461 PMID: 10991308

Schwartz, R., Schwartz, R., Vassilev, A., Greene, K., Perine, L., Burt, A., & Hall, P. (2022). Towards a standard for identifying and managing bias in artificial intelligence (Vol. 3, p. 00). Gaithersburg, MD: US Department of Commerce, National Institute of Standards and Technology.

Seligson, A., & Lehner, O. M. (2022). AI's role in fraud detection and risk management: Challenges and opportunities. *Journal of Financial Crime*, *29*(3), 745–761.

Shan, W. (2025). AI-powered fraud detection in banking: innovations, challenges and preventive strategies (Doctoral dissertation).

Shannon, C. E. (1948). A mathematical theory of communication. *The Bell System Technical Journal*, *27*(3), 379–423. DOI: 10.1002/j.1538-7305.1948.tb01338.x

Sharma, M., Paliwal, T., & Baniwal, P. (2024). Challenges in Digital Transformation and Automation for Industry 4.0. In AI-Driven IoT Systems for Industry 4.0 (pp. 143-163). CRC Press.

Sharpe, W. F. (1964). Capital asset prices: A theory of market equilibrium under conditions of risk. *The Journal of Finance*, *19*(3), 425–442. DOI: 10.2307/2977928

Sherif, K., & Mohsin, H. (2021). The effect of emergent technologies on accountant's ethical blindness. *The International Journal of Digital Accounting Research*, *21*, 61–94, 15778517. DOI: 10.4192/1577-8517-v21_3

Shevlane, T., Farquhar, S., Garfinkel, B., Phuong, M., Whittlestone, J., Leung, J., . . . Dafoe, A. (2023). Model evaluation for extreme risks. arXiv preprint arXiv:2305.15324.

Shiller, R. J. (2015). *Irrational exuberance* (3rd ed.). Princeton University Press.

Shmueli, G., & Koppius, O. R. (2011). Predictive analytics in information systems research. *Management Information Systems Quarterly*, *35*(3), 553–572. DOI: 10.2307/23042796

Shneiderman, B. (2020). Human-centered artificial intelligence: Reliable, safe & trustworthy. *International Journal of Human-Computer Interaction*, *36*(6), 495–504. DOI: 10.1080/10447318.2020.1741118

Shrestha, Y. R., Ben-Menahem, S. M., & von Krogh, G. (2019). Organizational decision-making structures in the age of artificial intelligence. *California Management Review*, *61*(4), 66–83. DOI: 10.1177/0008125619862257

Silver, D., Schrittwieser, J., Simonyan, K., Antonoglou, I., Huang, A., Guez, A., Hubert, T., Baker, L., Lai, M., Bolton, A., Chen, Y., Lillicrap, T., Hui, F., Sifre, L., van den Driessche, G., Graepel, T., & Hassabis, D. (2017). Mastering the game of Go without human knowledge. *Nature*, *550*(7676), 354–359. DOI: 10.1038/nature24270 PMID: 29052630

Simon, H. A. (1947). *Administrative behavior*. Free Press.

Sinnreich, A., & Gilbert, J. (2024). *The secret life of data: Navigating hype and uncertainty in the age of algorithmic surveillance*. MIT Press. DOI: 10.7551/mitpress/14040.001.0001

Sjödin, D., Parida, V., Leksell, M., & Petrovic, A. (2021). Smart factory implementation and process innovation: A study of AI-enabled manufacturing. *Technovation, 102*, 102222. DOI: 10.1016/j.technovation.2020.102222

Skitka, L. J., Mosier, K., & Burdick, M. (2000). Accountability and automation bias. *International Journal of Human-Computer Studies, 52*(4), 701–717. DOI: 10.1006/ijhc.1999.0349

Slota, S. C., Fleischmann, K. R., Greenberg, S., Verma, N., Cummings, B., Li, L., & Shenefiel, C. (2023). Many hands make many fingers to point: Challenges in creating accountable AI. *AI & Society, 38*(4), 1–13. DOI: 10.1007/s00146-021-01302-0

Sriram, H. K. (2024). Leveraging AI and Machine Learning for Enhancing Secure Payment Processing: A Study on Generative AI Applications in Real-Time Fraud Detection and Prevention. Available at *SSRN* 5203586.

Stefanija, A. P. (2023). Power asymmetries, epistemic imbalances and barriers to knowledge: the (im) possibility of knowing algorithms. In *Handbook of Critical Studies of Artificial Intelligence* (pp. 563–572). Edward Elgar Publishing. DOI: 10.4337/9781803928562.00058

Stern, N. (2007). *The economics of climate change: The Stern review.* Cambridge University Press. DOI: 10.1017/CBO9780511817434

Strange, S. (2015). *Casino capitalism* (2nd ed.). Manchester University Press. DOI: 10.7765/9781784997212

Suri, T., Aker, J., Batista, C., Callen, M., Ghani, T., Jack, W., & Sukhtankar, S. (2023). Mobile money. *VoxDevLit, 2*(2), 3.

Susskind, R., & Susskind, D. (2022). *The future of the professions: How technology will transform the work of human experts* (Updated ed.). Oxford University Press.

Susskind, D. (2022). *A world without work: Technology, automation, and how we should respond.* Metropolitan Books.

Taeihagh, A. (2021). Governance of artificial intelligence. *Policy and Society, 40*(2), 137–157. DOI: 10.1080/14494035.2021.1928377

Taleb, N. N. (2010). *The black swan: The impact of the highly improbable* (2nd ed.). Random House.

Talwar, R., & Koury, A. (2017). Disruptive shifts: The future of financial services in an era of global risks. *Foresight, 19*(5), 501–512. DOI: 10.1108/FS-06-2017-0021

Talwar, R., & Koury, A. (2019). Foresight and futures in the age of AI. *Futures, 105*, 10–22. DOI: 10.1016/j.futures.2018.09.004

Tan, J. (2021). *Survival Kit for Stressful Times*. Jackie Tan.

Tarashev, N., Borio, C., & Tsatsaronis, K. (2016). Risk attribution using the Shapley value: Methodology and policy applications. *Review of Finance, 20*(3), 1189–1213. DOI: 10.1093/rof/rfv028

Tariq, M. U., Babar, M., Poulin, M., Khattak, A. S., Alshehri, M. D., & Kaleem, S. (2021). Human behavior analysis using intelligent big data analytics. *Frontiers in Psychology, 12*, 686610. DOI: 10.3389/fpsyg.2021.686610 PMID: 34295289

Taylor, F. W. (1911). *The principles of scientific management*. Harper & Brothers.

Tegmark, M. (2017). *Life 3.0: Being human in the age of artificial intelligence*. Alfred A. Knopf.

Thaler, R. H. (2016). *Misbehaving: The making of behavioral economics*. W. W. Norton.

Thomas, L. C., Crook, J. N., & Edelman, D. B. (2017). *Credit scoring and its applications* (2nd ed.). SIAM. DOI: 10.1137/1.9781611974560

Thottoli, M. M. (2024). Leveraging information communication technology (ICT) and artificial intelligence (AI) to enhance auditing practices. *Accounting Research Journal, 37*(2), 134–150, 10309616. DOI: 10.1108/ARJ-09-2023-0269

Tiron-Tudor, A., Rodgers, W., & Deliu, D. (2024). The accounting profession in the Twilight Zone: Navigating digitalisation's sided challenges through ethical pathways for decision-making. *Accounting, Auditing & Accountability Journal, 9513574*. Advance online publication. DOI: 10.1108/AAAJ-12-2022-6173

Tooze, A. (2021). *Shutdown: How COVID shook the world's economy*. Viking.

Topol, E. (2019). *Deep medicine: How artificial intelligence can make healthcare human again*. Basic Books.

Torrance, A. W., & Tomlinson, B. (2023). Governance of the AI, by the AI, and for the AI. *Mississippi Law Journal*, *93*, 107.

Tsantekidis, A., Passalis, N., & Tefas, A. (2022). Recurrent neural networks. In *Deep learning for robot perception and cognition* (pp. 101–115). Academic Press. DOI: 10.1016/B978-0-32-385787-1.00010-5

Tsingou, E. (2015). Club governance and the making of global financial rules. *Review of International Political Economy*, *22*(2), 225–256. DOI: 10.1080/09692290.2014.890952

Turnbull, A. (2024). Law, Language, And Authority: The Algorithmic Turn.

Ustaoglu, M. (2018). Entropy as a measure of credit risk: An application to credit default swaps. *Physica A*, *503*, 380–388. DOI: 10.1016/j.physa.2018.02.163

Valavanidis, A. (2023). Artificial intelligence (ai) applications. Department of Chemistry, National and Kapodistrian University of Athens, University Campus Zografou, 15784.

Vallor, S. (2024). *The AI mirror: How to reclaim our humanity in an age of machine thinking*. Oxford University Press. DOI: 10.1093/oso/9780197759066.001.0001

Valov, D. (2025). The fracture that learns: Belief as a recursive system.

van Rijmenam, M. (2020). The future of strategy is algorithmic. *Journal of Strategy and Management, 13*(4), 517–529. DOI: 10.1108/JSMA-03-2020-0074

van Rijmenam, M., & Schweitzer, J. (2021). *The organization of tomorrow: How AI, blockchain, and analytics turn your business into a data organization*. Routledge.

Varona, J., & Suárez, J. P. (2022). Transparency in AI decision-making: An imperative for auditors. *Information Systems Frontiers, 24*(2), 425–439.

Vărzaru, A. A. (2022). Assessing Digital Transformation of Cost Accounting Tools in Healthcare. *International Journal of Environmental Research and Public Health, 19*(23), 16617827. DOI: 10.3390/ijerph192315572 PMID: 36497649

Verma, A., & Singhal, N. (2023, September). Integrating Artificial Intelligence for Adaptive Decision-Making in Complex System. In International Conference on Advances in Data-driven Computing and Intelligent Systems (pp. 95-105). Singapore: Springer Nature Singapore.

Wagner, B. (2018). Ethics as an escape from regulation: From ethics-washing to ethics-shopping? In Bayamlıoğlu, E., Baraliuc, I., Janssens, L., & Hildebrandt, M. (Eds.), *Being profiled: Cogitas ergo sum* (pp. 84–89). Amsterdam University Press. DOI: 10.2307/j.ctvhrd092.18

Walch, K. (2019). Artificial intelligence in financial services: Balancing efficiency with ethics. *Journal of Financial Transformation, 49*, 80–87.

Walker, S. (2023). *Design for resilience: Making the future we leave behind*. MIT Press. DOI: 10.7551/mitpress/14924.001.0001

Walmsley, J. (2021). Artificial intelligence and the value of transparency. *AI & Society, 36*(2), 585–595. DOI: 10.1007/s00146-020-01066-z

Warren, J. D.Jr, Moffitt, K. C., & Byrnes, P. (2015). How Big Data will change accounting. *Accounting Horizons, 29*(2), 397–407. DOI: 10.2308/acch-51069

Wasserman-Rozen, H., Gilad-Bachrach, R., & Elkin-Koren, N. (2024). Lost in translation: The limits of explainability in AI. *Cardozo Arts & Ent. LJ*, *42*, 391.

Waykar, Y. A. (2023). Human-AI Collaboration in Explainable Recommender Systems: An Exploration of User-Centric Explanations and Evaluation Frameworks. *International Journal of Scientific Research in Engineering and Management*, *7*(07), 2582–3930. DOI: 10.55041/IJSREM24775

Weber, M. (1947). *The theory of social and economic organization*. Oxford University Press.

Weber, M. (1978). *Economy and society: An outline of interpretive sociology*. University of California Press.

Whittlestone, J., Nyrup, R., Alexandrova, A., Dihal, K., & Cave, S. (2019). Ethical and societal implications of algorithms, data, and artificial intelligence: A roadmap for research. *Nuffield Foundation Report*.

Wilson, C., Denton, E., & Williams, M. (2023). Domain-specific fairness auditing for automated candidate screening systems. *Proceedings of the ACM FAccT Conference*.

Wilson, H. J., & Daugherty, P. R. (2018). Collaborative intelligence: Humans and AI are joining forces. *Harvard Business Review*, *96*(4), 114–123.

Wilson, H. J., & Daugherty, P. R. (2018). *Human + machine: Reimagining work in the age of AI*. Harvard Business Review Press.

Womack, J. P., & Jones, D. T. (2003). *Lean thinking: Banish waste and create wealth in your corporation* (2nd ed.). Free Press.

Wood, A. J., Graham, M., Lehdonvirta, V., & Hjorth, I. (2019). Good gig, bad gig: Autonomy and algorithmic control in the global gig economy. *Work, Employment and Society*, *33*(1), 56–75. DOI: 10.1177/0950017018785616 PMID: 30886460

Xu, T., & Liang, F. (2021). Machine learning for hydrologic sciences: An introductory overview. *WIREs. Water*, *8*(5), e1533. DOI: 10.1002/wat2.1533

Yarovenko, H. (2024). Digital transformation: economy development and fighting against illegal practices. Publishing House "Baltija Publishing".

Youvan, D. C. (2024). Anatomy of a Financial Collapse: The Role of Technical Glitches in Modern Financial Systems.

Zajko, M. (2021). Conservative AI and social inequality: Conceptualizing alternatives to bias through social theory. *AI & Society*, *36*(3), 1047–1056. DOI: 10.1007/s00146-021-01153-9

Zakaria, I. (2021). The impact of artificial intelligence on auditing practices: An ethical perspective. *Journal of Accounting and Organizational Change*, *17*(2), 254–274.

Zaman, B. U. (2024, April). The weighty responsibility of creating ai navigating control and ethics.

Zeng, Y., Lu, E., & Huangfu, C. (2019). Linking artificial intelligence principles. *Nature Machine Intelligence*, *1*(8), 373–374. DOI: 10.1038/s42256-019-0088-2 PMID: 31406960

Zha, D., Bhat, Z. P., Lai, K. H., Yang, F., Jiang, Z., Zhong, S., & Hu, X. (2025). Data-centric artificial intelligence: A survey. *ACM Computing Surveys*, *57*(5), 1–42. DOI: 10.1145/3711118

Zhang C., Zhu W., Dai J., Wu Y., & Chen X. (2023). Ethical impact of artificial intelligence in managerial accounting. International Journal of Accounting Information Systems, 49, 100619. DOI: 10.1016/j.accinf.2023.100619

Zhang, C., Xie, Y., Bai, H., Yu, B., Li, W., & Gao, Y. (2021). A survey on federated learning. *Knowledge-Based Systems*, *216*, 106775. DOI: 10.1016/j.knosys.2021.106775 PMID: 34909232

Zhang, W., & Ma, J. (2020). Cultural framing and algorithmic trust: Retail investor responses to AI in Chinese financial markets. *Journal of Cultural Economics, 13*(6), 651–668. DOI: 10.1080/17530350.2020.1816827

Zhang, Y., Li, J., & Song, X. (2021). Artificial intelligence and strategic foresight: Emerging approaches in finance. *Technological Forecasting and Social Change, 169*, 120822. DOI: 10.1016/j.techfore.2021.120822

Zhao, L., Li, W., & Cai, X. (2018). Entropy-based systemic risk measure of complex financial networks. *Physica A, 503*, 318–329. DOI: 10.1016/j.physa.2018.02.156

Zhou, R., Cai, R., Tong, G., & Wang, Y. (2013). Portfolio selection model based on entropy. *Entropy (Basel, Switzerland), 15*(12), 5338–5351. DOI: 10.3390/e15125338

Zuboff, S. (2015). Big other: Surveillance capitalism and the prospects of an information civilization. *Journal of Information Technology, 30*(1), 75–89. DOI: 10.1057/jit.2015.5

Zuboff, S. (2019). *The age of surveillance capitalism: The fight for a human future at the new frontier of power*. PublicAffairs.

Zuboff, S. (2020). *Surveillance capitalism in the financial sector*. Polity Press.

Zunino, L., Tabak, B. M., Figliola, A., Pérez, D. G., Garavaglia, M., & Rosso, O. A. (2007). A multifractal approach for stock market inefficiency. *Physica A, 376*(1–2), 429–438. DOI: 10.1016/j.physa.2006.10.034

Zweig, K. A. (2021). *Awkward intelligence: Why AI needs philosophy*. MIT Press.

About the Contributors

Ionica Oncioiu's research interests include security risk management, fiscal judgment and statistical sampling in accounting, the development of SMEs innovation, project management, big data and E-commerce marketing. She has previously published three book: in 2013 called "Business Innovation, Development, and Advancement in the Digital Economy" (IGI Global Book), in 2016 called "Driving Innovation and Business Success in the Digital Economy", in 2017 called "Ethics and Decision-Making for Sustainable Business Practices", in 2018 called "Network Security and Its Impact on Business Strategy ", in 2019 called "Throughput Accounting in a Hyperconnected World", in 2020 called "Improving Business Performance Through Innovation in the Digital Economy" and is interested in continuing writing in the accounting, finance, big data and robotics area.

* * *

Manjit Kour is working as Professor at University Business School at Chandigarh University. She holds a PhD in Business Management from IK Gujral Punjab Technical University, India. She has a good research record with several research papers published in reputed journals. She is an editorial board member and reviewer of many reputed journals including Scopus and ABDC-indexed journals. Her areas of interest include sustainability, green practices, Fintech, online marketing trends and business ethics.

Diana Mândricel, Lecturer at the Faculty of Economic Sciences within Titu Maiorescu University in Bucharest, specializes in the field of economic sciences, with a focus on business relationships and ethical conduct in organizations. With a strong academic background, she teaches the following subjects: Customer and Supplier Relationship Management; Business Ethics; Microeconomics. Her main areas of interest include: Optimizing supply chain relationships; Corporate Social Responsibility (CSR); Consumer behavior analysis; Decision-making foundations in economic environments. Lecturer Mândricel is actively involved in research activities, participating in academic conferences and publishing scientific articles in the fields of management and business ethics. Additionally, she collaborates with the business environment on educational projects and applied consulting.

Mădălina Mihăilescu is a PhD university lecturer and dean of the Faculty of Exact Sciences and Engineering at Hyperion University in Bucharest. Her academic activity focuses on areas such as automation, applied computer science and new digital technologies. She coordinates bachelor's and master's programs, actively contributing to the modernization of the curriculum and the promotion of interdisciplinary research. She has participated in numerous scientific conferences and published papers in specialized journals. Through her involvement, she supports the connection between the university environment, industry and technological innovation, strengthening the prestige of the institution at national and international levels.

Tarun Sai Raavi is currently an Assistant Professor at Vishwa Vishwani Institute of Systems and Management and is pursuing his Ph.D. from Aurora University, focusing on designing AI and machine learning tools for individual investor decision-making. He holds double MBA degrees in Finance (GITAM University) and Analytics (Osmania University). He has industry experience as a Research Analyst at Buzz Board and as a Data Analyst at Cognizant for Google. He specializes in R, Python, Tableau, Hadoop, IBM SPSS, and MS Excel, and specializes in data modeling, statistical analysis, and algorithmic development. His research areas include Fintech, data mining, deep learning, and IoT, with several publications in high-impact journals and active participation in national and international conferences, seminars, and management development programs.

Raavi Radhika is a Professor in the Department of Accounting and Finance at GITAM University, with an outstanding record of research and academic contributions. She has published several high-impact research papers indexed in Scopus, Elsevier, ABDC, and ABC, and has presented at premier institutions like AIMS International, IIMs, and IITs. Her case studies have been published by Harvard Business Review, Emerald, and The Case Centre, and she has delivered lectures internationally. Dr. Radhika has successfully guided four Ph.D. scholars at HBS and won Second Prize at the ISB-Ivey League Global Case Competition for her co-authored case study. She completed a UGC-sponsored Minor Research Project and received the Macro Research Fellowship from the Indian Institute of Banking and Finance, earning multiple awards including GITAM's Best Researcher Award in 2018 for her excellence in research.

Shefali is an accomplished researcher in quantitative and AI application in finance with over 4 years of experience. She holds a M.com from MDU University and has published extensively in leading journals. Her research focuses on investment practices in emerging markets and AI application in finance. Ms. Shefali is also a dedicated educator, known for her engaging teaching methods and commitment to student success.

Index

A

B

C

D

E

F

G

U

www.ingramcontent.com/pod-product-compliance
Lightning Source LLC
LaVergne TN
LVHW081528300926
849161LV00006B/1337
* 9 7 9 8 3 3 7 3 3 6 2 6 8 *